LIFESTYLE IN THE EIGHTIES

CONTEMPORARY ISSUES IN SOCIAL ETHICS
Ronald J. Sider, General Editor

Lifestyle in the Eighties: An Evangelical Commitment
to Simple Lifestyle, *ed. Ronald J. Sider*
Evangelicals and Development: Toward a Theology
of Social Change, *ed. Ronald J. Sider*

General Preface

An historic transformation is in process. In all parts of the world, evangelical Christians in growing numbers are rediscovering the biblical summons to serve the poor, minister to the needy, correct injustice and seek societal shalom. The Chicago Declaration of Evangelical Social Concern (1973), the Lausanne Covenant's section on social responsibility (1974), the Evangelical Fellowship of India's Madras Declaration on Evangelical Social Action (1979) and the Evangelical Commitment to Simple Lifestyle (1980) are symptomatic of far-reaching change. A fundamentally new worldwide movement is emerging. It seeks justice and peace in the power of the Spirit. It consists of biblical Christians passionately committed to a new search for social justice that is thoroughly biblical, deeply immersed in prayer, and totally dependent on the presence of the Holy Spirit.

Substantive theological and ethical reflection is imperative if the growing movement of evangelical social concern is to be biblical and effective. The Unit on Ethics and Society of the Theological Commission of the World Evangelical Fellowship hopes this new series of books, *Contemporary Issues in Social Ethics*, will contribute to that goal. We hope and believe that evangelicals will have something significant and different to add to current debates on urgent social questions. But we dare never forget that other Christians have long been discussing these problems. Hoping to avoid reinventing the wheel, we intend to profit from what others have written and done. We also acknowledge in painful repentance that we have too long neglected what we ought to have done.

The Unit on Ethics and Society of the World Evangelical Fellowship believes that the content of the volumes in the forthcoming series merits the careful attention of all Christians although the Unit does not necessarily endorse every viewpoint expressed.

Ronald J. Sider, Convenor
Unit on Ethics & Society
Theological Commission
World Evangelical Fellowship

LIFESTYLE IN THE EIGHTIES

An Evangelical Commitment to Simple Lifestyle

Edited by
RONALD J. SIDER

THE WESTMINSTER PRESS
Philadelphia

Published by The Westminster Press℠
Philadelphia, Pennsylvania

PRINTED IN THE UNITED STATES OF AMERICA
9 8 7 6 5 4 3 2 1

Library of Congress Cataloging in Publication Data

Main entry under title:

Lifestyle in the eighties.

(Contemporary issues in social ethics : v. 1)
Papers from the International Consultation on
Simple Lifestyle, Mar. 17-21, 1980, at High Leigh
Conference Centre sponsored by the Theology and Education
Group of the Lausanne Committee for World Evangeliza-
tion and the Unit on Ethics and Society of the World
Evangelical Fellowship's Theological Commission.
   Includes index.
   1. Simplicity—Religious aspects—Christianity—
Congresses. I. Sider, Ronald J. II. International
Consultation on Simple Lifestyle (1980 : High Leigh Con-
ference Centre) III. Lausanne Committee for World
Evangelization. Theology and Education Group. IV. World
Evangelical Fellowship. Unit on Ethics and Society.
V. Series.
BV4647.S48L53   248.4   82-7067
ISBN 0-664-24437-8   AACR2

DEDICATION
For Mark Cerbone,
whose sacrificial work made possible
the Consultation, the Commitment
and this book

Participants at I.C.O.S.L.

Tokunboh Adeyemo
John Alexander
Pedro Arana
Ramez Atallah
Jorge Atiencia
Kwame Bediako
Ulrich Betz
Wayne Bragg
Donald Cameron
John Capon
Robinson Cavalcanti
Mark Cerbone
Harvie Conn
Donald Dayton
Robert DeMoss
Oeistein de Presno
Linda Doll
Ron Elsdon
Leif Engedal
Rob von Essen
Richard Foster
Buzz Frum
John Gladwin
Jorgen Glenthoj
J. van der Graff
Paul Hampsch
Donald Hay

Horst-Klaus Hofmann
Robert Hughes
Simon Ibrahim
Neuza Itioka
Pippa Julings
Arthur Johnston
L. de Jong
Sione Kami
Israel Katoke
Graham Kerr
Andrew Kirk
Alan Kreider
Dan Lam
Fritz Lampartner
Gregorio Landero
Daryl LaRusso
Kan-chun Barnabas Lee
Magnus Malm
Vishal Mangalwadi
Ted Martin, Jr.
Tad Maruyama
Charles Massey
Bruce McConchie
Peter Meadows
Karl-Heinz Michel
John Mitchell
Nobumasa Mitsuhashi

George Monsma, Jr.
B. Howard Mudditt
Jeremy Mudditt
Alan Nichols
Lennart Nordin
Gottfried Osei-Mensah
René Padilla
Clark Pinnock
Tacito Pinto
M. G. Reuben
D. John Richard
Bong Rin Ro
Colleen Samuel
Vinay Samuel
Waldron Scott
Ronald J. Sider
Kevin Smith
John Stott
Gordon Strachan
Morris Stuart
Chris Sugden
Dich Van Halsema
J. A. Emerson Vermaat
Jim Wardwell
David Watson
Dolphus Weary
Waldo Werning

Contents

Preface

"Life" and "lifestyle" obviously belong together and cannot be separated. All Christians claim to have received a new life from Jesus Christ; what lifestyle, then, is appropriate for them? If the life is new, the lifestyle should be new also. But what are to be its characteristics? In particular, how is it to be distinguished from the lifestyle of those who make no Christian profession? And how should it reflect the challenges of the contemporary world — its alienation both from God and from the earth's resources which he created for the enjoyment of all?

It was such questions as these which led the participants in the Lausanne Congress on World Evangelization (1974) to include in paragraph 9 of their Covenant the following sentences:

All of us are shocked by the poverty of millions and disturbed by the injustices which cause it. Those of us who live in affluent circumstances accept our duty to develop a simple lifestyle in order to contribute more generously to both relief and evangelism.

After the congress these expressions were much debated, and it became clear that their implications needed to be carefully examined.

So the Theology and Education Group of the Lausanne Committee for World Evangelization and the Unit on Ethics and Society of the World Evangelical Fellowship's Theological Commission agreed to co-sponsor a two-year process of study, culminating in an international gathering. Local groups met in 15 countries. Regional conferences were arranged in India, Ireland and the United States. Then from March 17 to 21, 1980, at High Leigh Conference Centre (about 17 miles north of London, England) an International Consultation on Simple Lifestyle was convened. It brought together 85 evangelical leaders from 27 countries.

Our purpose was to study simple living in relation to evangelism, relief and justice, since all three were mentioned in the Lausanne Covenant's sentences on simple lifestyle. Our perspective was on the one hand the teaching of the Bible and on the other the suffering world, that is, the billions of men, women and children who, though made in God's image and the objects of his love, are either unevangelized or oppressed or both, being destitute of the gospel of salvation and of the basic necessities of human life.

During the four days of our Consultation we lived, worshipped and prayed together; we studied the Scriptures together; we listened to the background papers and heard the moving testimonies included in this book; we struggled to relate the theological and economic issues to one another; we debated in both plenary sessions and small groups; we laughed and cried and repented and made resolutions. Although at the beginning we sensed some tension between representatives of the First and Third Worlds, yet by the end the Holy Spirit of unity had brought us into a new solidarity of mutual respect and love.

Above all, we tried to expose ourselves with honesty to the challenges of both the Word of God and the world of need, in order to discern God's will and seek his grace to do it. In this process our minds have been stretched, our consciences pricked, our hearts stirred and our wills strengthened.

The original text of the "Evangelical Commitment to Simple Lifestyle", drafted out of the papers and the discussion, was carefully studied during three exacting hours of plenary debate, and numerous alterations were agreed. The revised text was resubmitted at a final plenary session and, with a few further and minor amendments, was approved. None of the Participants was asked to subscribe to it by personal signature, but it carries the substantial endorsement of the Consultation. As individuals too we have all made our own private commitment, in response to its call.

We recognize that others have been discussing these issues for several years, and we are ashamed that we have lagged behind them. We have no wish, therefore, to claim too much for our consultation or its findings. Nor have we any grounds for boasting. Yet for us the week was historical and transforming. So we publish this Commitment in order to encourage individuals, groups and churches to study it. We hope and pray that many will be moved, as we have been, to resolve, commitment and action.

John Stott
Chairman
Lausanne Theology and
Education Group
Lausanne Committee for
World Evangelization

Ronald J. Sider
Convenor
Unit on Ethics & Society
Theological Commission of
the World Evangelical
Fellowship

Section One
The Commitment

The Commitment

Preamble

For four days we have been together, eighty-five Christians from twenty-seven countries, to consider the resolve expressed in the Lausanne Covenant (1974) to "develop a simple lifestyle". We have tried to listen to the voice of God, through the pages of the Bible, through the cries of the hungry poor, and through each other. And we believe that God has spoken to us.

We thank God for his great salvation through Jesus Christ, for his revelation in Scripture which is a light for our path, and for the Holy Spirit's power to make us witnesses and servants in the world.

We are disturbed by the injustice of the world, concerned for its victims, and moved to repentance for our complicity in it. We have also been stirred to fresh resolves, which we express in this Commitment.

1. Creation

We worship God as the Creator of all things, and we celebrate the goodness of his creation. In his generosity he has given us everything to enjoy, and we receive it from his hands with humble thanksgiving (1 Timothy 4:4, 6:17). God's creation is marked by rich abundance and diversity, and he intends its resources to be husbanded and shared for the benefit of all.

We therefore denounce environmental destruction, wastefulness and hoarding. We deplore the misery of the poor who suffer as a result of these evils. We also disagree with the drabness of the ascetic. For all these deny the Creator's goodness and reflect the tragedy of the fall. We recognize our own involvement in them, and we repent.

2. Stewardship

When God made man, male and female, in his own image, he gave them dominion over the earth (Genesis 1:26-28). He made them stewards of its resources, and they became responsible to him as Creator, to the earth which they were to develop, and to their fellow human beings with whom they were to share its riches. So fundamental are these truths that authentic human fulfilment depends on a right relationship to God, neighbour and the earth with all its resources. People's humanity is diminished if they have no just share in those resources.

By unfaithful stewardship, in which we fail to conserve the earth's finite resources, to develop them fully, or to distribute them justly, we both disobey God and alienate people from his purpose for them. We are determined, therefore, to honour God as the owner of all things, to remember that we are stewards and not proprietors of any land or property that we may have, to use them in the service of others, and to seek justice with the poor who are exploited and powerless to defend themselves.

We look forward to "the restoration of all things" at Christ's return (Acts 3:21). At that time our full humanness will be restored; so we must promote human dignity today.

3. Poverty and Wealth

We affirm that involuntary poverty is an offense against the goodness of God. It is related in the Bible to powerlessness, for the poor cannot protect themselves. God's call to rulers is to use their power to defend the poor, not to exploit them. The church must stand with God and the poor against injustice, suffer with them and call on rulers to fulfil their God-appointed role.

We have struggled to open our minds and hearts to the uncomfortable words of Jesus about wealth. "Beware of covetousness" he said, and "a person's life does not consist in the abundance of his possessions" (Luke 12:15). We have listened to his warnings about the danger of riches. For wealth brings worry, vanity and false security, the oppression of the weak and indifference to the sufferings of the needy. So it is hard for a rich person to enter the kingdom of heaven (Matthew 19:23), and the greedy will be excluded from it. The kingdom is a free gift offered to all, but it is especially good news for the poor because they benefit most from the changes it brings.

We believe that Jesus still calls some people (perhaps even us) to follow him in a lifestyle of total, voluntary poverty. He calls all his followers to an inner freedom from the seduction of riches (for it is impossible to serve God and money) and to sacrificial generosity ("to be rich in good works, to be generous and ready to share" — 1 Timothy 6:18). Indeed, the motivation and model for Christian generosity are nothing less than the example of Jesus Christ himself, who, though rich, became poor that through his poverty we might become rich (2 Corinthians 8:9). It was a costly, purposeful self-sacrifice; we mean to seek his grace to follow him. We resolve to get to know poor and oppressed people, to learn issues of injustice from them, to seek to relieve their suffering, and to include them regularly in our prayers.

4. The New Community

We rejoice that the church is the new community of the new age, whose members enjoy a new life and a new lifestyle. The earliest Christian church, constituted in Jerusalem on the Day of Pentecost, was characterized by a quality of fellowship unknown before. Those Spirit-filled believers loved one another to such an extent that they sold and shared their possessions. Although their selling and giving were voluntary, and some private property was retained (Acts 5:4), it was made subservient to the needs of the community. "None of them said that anything he had was his own" (Acts 4:32). That is, they were free from the selfish assertion of proprietary rights. And as a result of their transformed economic relationships, "there was not a needy person among them" (Acts 4:34).

This principle of generous and sacrificial sharing, expressed in holding ourselves and our goods available for people in need, is an indispensable characteristic of every Spirit-filled church. So those of us who are affluent in any part of the world are determined to do more to relieve the needs of less privileged believers. Otherwise, we shall be like those rich Christians in Corinth who ate and drank too much while their poor brothers and sisters were left hungry, and we shall deserve the stinging rebuke Paul gave them for despising God's church and desecrating Christ's body (1 Corinthians 11:20-24). Instead, we determine to resemble them at a later stage when Paul urged them out of their abundance to give to the impoverished Christians of Judea "that there may be equality" (2 Corinthians 8:10-15). It was a beautiful demonstration of caring love and of Gentile-Jewish solidarity in Christ.

In this same spirit, we must seek ways to transact the church's corporate business together with minimum expenditure on travel, food and accommodation. We call on churches and para-church agencies in their planning to be acutely aware of the need for integrity in corporate lifestyle and witness.

Christ calls us to be the world's salt and light, in order to hinder its social decay and illumine its darkness. But our light must shine and our salt must retain its saltness. It is when the new community is most obviously distinct from the world — in its values, standards and lifestyle — that it presents the world with a radically attractive alternative and so exercizes its greatest influence for Christ. We commit ourselves to pray and work for the renewal of our churches.

5. Personal Lifestyle

Jesus our Lord summons us to holiness, humility, simplicity and contentment. He also promises us his rest. We confess, how-ever, that we have often allowed unholy desires to disturb our inner tranquility. So without the constant renewal of Christ's peace in our hearts, our emphasis on simple living will be one-sided.

Our Christian obedience demands a simple lifestyle, irrespec-tive of the needs of others. Nevertheless, the facts that 800 million people are destitute and that about 10,000 die of star-vation every day make any other lifestyle indefensible.

While some of us have been called to live among the poor, and others to open our homes to the needy, all of us are deter-mined to develop a simpler lifestyle. We intend to re-examine our income and expenditure, in order to manage on less and give away more. We lay down no rules or regulations, for either ourselves or others. Yet we resolve to renounce waste and oppose extravagance in personal living, clothing and housing, travel and church buildings. We also accept the distinction between necessities and luxuries, creative hobbies and empty status symbols, modesty and vanity, occasional celebrations and normal routine, and between the service of God and slavery to fashion. Where to draw the line requires conscientious thought and decision by us, together with members of our family. Those of us who belong to the West need the help of our Third World brothers and sisters in evaluating our standards of spending. Those of us who live in the Third World acknowledge that we too are exposed to the temptation to covetousness. So we need each other's understanding, encouragement and prayers.

6. International Development

We echo the words of the Lausanne Covenant: "We are shocked by the poverty of millions, and disturbed by the injustices which cause it." One quarter of the world's population enjoys unparalleled prosperity, while another quarter endures grinding poverty. This gross disparity is an intolerable injustice; we refuse to acquiesce in it. The call for a New International Economic Order expresses the justified frustration of the Third World.

We have come to understand more clearly the connection between resources, income and consumption: people often starve because they cannot afford to buy food, because they have no income, because they have no opportunity to produce, and because they have no access to power. We therefore applaud the growing emphasis of Christian agencies on development rather than aid. For the transfer of personnel and appropriate technology can enable people to make good use of their own resources, while at the same time respecting their dignity. We resolve to contribute more generously to human development projects. Where people's lives are at stake, there should never be a shortage of funds.

But the action of governments is essential. Those of us who live in the affluent nations are ashamed that our governments have mostly failed to meet their targets for official development assistance, to maintain emergency food stocks or to liberalize their trade policy.

We have come to believe that in many cases multi-national corporations reduce local initiative in the countries where they work, and tend to oppose any fundamental change in government. We are convinced that they should become more subject to controls and more accountable.

7. Justice and Politics

We are also convinced that the present situation of social injustice is so abhorrent to God that a large measure of change is necessary. Not that we believe in an earthly utopia. But neither are we pessimists. Change can come, although not through commitment to simple lifestyle or human development projects alone.

Poverty and excessive wealth, militarism and the arms industry, and the unjust distribution of capital, land and resources are issues of power and powerlessness. Without a shift of power through structural change these problems cannot be solved.

The Christian church, along with the rest of society, is inevitably involved in politics which is "the art of living in community". Servants of Christ must express his lordship in their political, social and economic commitments and their love for their neighbours by taking part in the political process. How, then, can we contribute to change?

First, we will pray for peace and justice, as God commands. Secondly, we will seek to educate Christian people in the moral and political issues involved, and so clarify their vision and raise their expectations. Thirdly, we will take action. Some Christians are called to special tasks in government, economics or development. All Christians must participate in the active struggle to create a just and responsible society. In some situations obedience to God demands resistance to an unjust established order. Fourthly, we must be ready to suffer. As followers of Jesus, the Suffering Servant, we know that service always involves suffering.

While personal commitment to change our lifestyle without political action to change systems of injustice lacks effectiveness, political action without personal commitment lacks integrity.

8. Evangelism

We are deeply concerned for the vast millions of unevangelized people in the world. Nothing that has been said about lifestyle or justice diminishes the urgency of developing evangelistic strategies appropriate to different cultural environments. We must not cease to proclaim Christ as Saviour and Lord throughout the world. The church is not yet taking seriously its commission to be his witnesses "to the ends of the earth" (Acts 1:8).

So the call to a responsible lifestyle must not be divorced from the call to responsible witness. For the credibility of our message is seriously diminished whenever we contradict it by our lives. It is impossible with integrity to proclaim Christ's salvation if he has evidently not saved us from greed, or his lordship if we are not good stewards of our possessions, or his love if we close our hearts against the needy. When Christians care for each other and for the deprived, Jesus Christ becomes more visibly attractive.

In contrast to this, the affluent lifestyle of some Western evangelists when they visit the Third World is understandably offensive to many.

We believe that simple living by Christians generally would

release considerable resources of finance and personnel for evangelism as well as development. So by our commitment to a simple lifestyle we recommit ourselves wholeheartedly to world evangelization.

9. The Lord's Return

The Old Testament prophets both denounced the idolatries and injustices of God's people and warned of his coming judgement. Similar denunciations and warnings are found in the New Testament. The Lord Jesus is coming back soon to judge, to save and to reign. His judgement will fall upon the greedy (who are idolaters) and upon all oppressors. For on that day the King will sit upon his throne and separate the saved from the lost. Those who have ministered to him by ministering to one of the least of his needy brothers and sisters will be saved, for the reality of saving faith is exhibited in serving love. But those who are persistently indifferent to the plight of the needy, and so to Christ in them, will be irretrievably lost (Matthew 25:31-46). All of us need to hear again this solemn warning of Jesus, and resolve afresh to serve him in the deprived. We therefore call on our fellow Christians everywhere to do the same.

Our Resolve

So then, having been freed by the sacrifice of our Lord Jesus Christ, in obedience to his call, in heartfelt compassion for the poor, in concern for evangelism, development and justice, and in solemn anticipation of the Day of Judgement, we humbly commit ourselves to develop a just and simple lifestyle, to support one another in it and to encourage others to join us in this commitment.

We know that we shall need time to work out its implications and that the task will not be easy. May Almighty God give us his grace to be faithful! Amen.

Section Two
Background Papers

1

Living More Simply for Evangelism and Justice

RONALD J. SIDER

Why have eighty-five of the world's busiest Christians from all parts of the globe spent tens of thousands of dollars to consult together for five days in England? The answer, I believe, is that the affluent Christians of the world face an urgent crisis of conscience. One quarter of the world's people enjoy material prosperity unheard of in human history. But they partake of this unprecedented affluence in a global village where another quarter of God's children face grinding poverty and three-fifths have never heard of Jesus Christ.

The rich of the earth — and I include not only the majority in industrialized nations but also the small affluent élite in developing nations — need help. That help, I believe, can come only from the worldwide body of believers, especially the poor members of Christ's body. So-called "necessities of life" and "ordinary enjoyments" look dramatically different when viewed in a global context where 750 million people have incomes of less than $75 per year. Lest the rich of the world slip slowly into a numbing indifference that destroys the soul, the worldwide body of Christ must issue an urgent summons to sacrificial sharing of ourselves and our abundance with the poor and oppressed, and with the unevangelized billions. We are here then as representatives of the one global body of Christ to pray together, to search the scriptures together, to analyze the world's unbelief and anguish together in the hope and confidence that, as we listen diligently to each other, the Holy Spirit will speak a word to the church about the nature of faithful lifestyles in the 1980's.

Before continuing, I feel compelled to insert two provisos. First of all I cannot stand here and talk about simple lifestyle in an international consultation without deep uneasiness. I am painfully aware of the fact that in spite of honest efforts to live more simply, my family still enjoys a standard of living that would appear astonishingly affluent to the vast majority of the world's people. My prayer is that honest awareness of that reality will produce humility and an open eagerness to listen and change.

Second, I do not want to concoct some new variety of Western imperialism that would try to impose simple lifestyles on developing nations in order to preserve the world's limited natural resources for the industrialized world. Those of you who come from developing nations must bear the responsibility of thinking through what faithful lifestyles are for the small body of educated Christian leaders in your nations. My primary responsibility is to call brothers and sisters in developed nations to more simple lifestyles.

But what is a simple lifestyle? Perhaps $8,000 a year for a North American family might qualify. (But we had better not ask the 750 million who live on annual incomes of $75.) Would $13,000 per year be simple living? $35,000 if one were a wealthy businessman whose peers normally spent $100,000 on themselves?

Obviously poverty is a relative concept. An annual income that would constitute grinding poverty in inner-city Philadelphia would seem like abundance to a peasant in Brazil or India. It is essential to remember that concepts like "poverty" and "simple lifestyle" are relative concepts — relative to an astonishingly large number of diverse circumstances. Therefore, any legalistic attempt to prescribe some precise definition of a simple lifestyle would be as absurd as it would be fruitless.

At the same time, we dare never forget that something approaching absolute poverty exists. According to the report just released by the Brandt Commission on International Development Issues, 30 million children under five years of age die of starvation each year (*Newsweek*, Feb. 18, 1980, p.63). The 750 million people with annual incomes of less than $75 per year have absolutely no access to health care, cannot read or write, and lack a minimally adequate supply of calories and/or protein. Certainly poverty is relative to one's context. But let the rich of the world never engage in the self-indulgent rationalization that permits us to obscure the vast, growing gulf between ourselves and the millions of desperately poor of the world. In a world where hundreds of millions confront absolute poverty, those of us who enjoy relative abundance must learn to live more simply.

I am convinced that the affluent, comfortably satisfied church in the northern hemisphere will not be able to learn how to do that without the help of brothers and sisters from poor nations. In ourselves, we are already too blinded by our material comforts. If we are to escape our blindness, Christians from contexts of poverty must help us think more clearly about three things: the purpose for a simple lifestyle; the biblical/theological foundations for a simple lifestyle; and a process for discernment of the shape of a simple lifestyle.

In each case, the help of our brothers and sisters from developing nations is absolutely crucial. If anything can help us see that we need to live more simply in order to share more, it will be the awareness that some brothers and sisters in Christ lack health care, cannot even read the scriptures and have to watch their children suffer permanent brain damage because of malnutrition. If anything can help affluent Christians discover how they have neglected vast sections of biblical teaching about the poor and God's desire for justice, if anything can challenge the heretical Gospel of prosperity so popular in affluent nations, it will be careful study of the Word with Christians who are poor and oppressed. And, if there is any process that can help affluent Christians more honestly to assess their desire for more clothes, bigger houses and grander churches, it will be a process that involves creative new ways to enable rich Christians to evaluate their lifestyles in dialogue with poor Christians.

Theologically, of course, that is as it should be. It corresponds perfectly to the fantastic Pauline vision of one body of mutually interdependent believers who share each other's joys and sorrows, bear responsibility for each other's growth in obedience and carry one another's economic burdens — "that there may be equality" (2 Cor. 8:13-15). "For by one Spirit we were all baptized into one body — Jews or Greeks, slaves or free" (1 Cor. 12:13). Certainly it would be less upsetting if Northern Christians did not need to discuss their affluent lifestyles with poor fellow believers. But our doctrine of the church precludes that kind of isolation. We dare not say to any other part of the body, "I have no need of you."

How then can mutual dialogue in the one universal body of Christ help us all think more carefully about the three areas of purpose, biblical/theological foundations, and a process of discernment for a simple lifestyle?

The Purpose of a Simple Lifestyle

Christians are not called to a simple lifestyle because poverty is good or because asceticism is a biblical ideal. The earth is a fantastically beautiful gift from the hand of the Creator who wants us to enjoy its glory and splendour.

It is the need of the world at this point in time that summons Christians in the 1980's to live a simple lifestyle. Paragraph 9 of the Lausanne Covenant, which has drawn us together for this consultation, underlines this point: "All of us are shocked by the poverty of millions and disturbed by the injustices which cause it. Those of us who live in affluent circumstances accept our duty to develop a simple lifestyle in order to contribute more generously to both relief and evangelism." This statement recognizes two basic reasons for a simple lifestyle: the desperate poverty of hundreds of millions and the existence of billions who need to hear the Gospel.

Let's look briefly at both of those reasons.*

First, the need for evangelism and the way that a simple lifestyle would make a difference. Almost all (five out of six) of the more than 2.7 billion persons who have never heard the Gospel live in social groupings and sub-nations where the church has not yet effectively taken root. Cross-cultural missionaries are needed. Gottfried Osei-Mensah has recently challenged every 1,000 evangelicals to send two missionaries to these unreached people.

There are abundant economic resources to do that if even a significant minority of Christians would live more simply. Ralph Winter presents some startling statistics in his excellent proposal that those who believe in missionary work live as simple a lifestyle as do missionaries. He points out that the Christians in the U.S. give $700 million per year to mission agencies — a figure equal to what Americans spend on chewing gum! Americans spend as much money on pet food every 52 days as U.S. Christians spend on missions every 365 days. If just the few million American Presbyterians were willing to live on the salary of the average Presbyterian minister in the U.S. (hardly an austere poverty-level existence!), two billion dollars (almost three times the total U.S. expenditure on missions) would become available. (Ralph D. Winter, *Penetrating the Last Frontiers* (Pasadena: William Carey Library, 1978), pp.50-52.)

*This is not to say that these are the only reasons for living more simply. Much of the affluent world has been caught in a secularizing materialism. Instead of following the biblical mandate to seek first the kingdom of God and exhibit a careful indifference to other things, many Christians are trapped in a materialistic rat-race. For all of us who are more or less infected by surrounding materialism, living more simply can be liberating and spiritually beneficial for us quite apart from its positive impact on others.

To our shame, Christians who are far poorer are vastly more generous. The Friends Missionary Prayer Band of South India has 8,000 people in their prayer bands, but they support 80 full-time missionaries in North India. "If my denomination," Winter comments, "(with its unbelievably greater wealth per person) were to do that well, we would not be sending 500 missionaries but 26,000" (*Ibid., p.50*).

The evangelistic mandate then is one central reason for living a simple lifestyle in our time.

The other fundamental reason is the existence of desperate poverty among one quarter of the world's people. Evangelical Christians have responded to this need through relief and development agencies like Tear Fund, World Relief Commission, World Vision and Mennonite Central Committee.

But the response has been only a tiny fraction of what is possible. A couple of years ago, I calculated what the average U.S. family could give to combat world hunger if they would be willing to live just $2,500 below the U.S. median income — surely a comfortable lifestyle by global standards. I discovered that every group of 50,000 U.S. Christians who would live $2,500 below the median U.S. income and donated the rest of their income to relief and development, could by themselves start a new World Vision. (I am using 1974 figures, but the ratios would be approximately the same today.) By itself, the United Methodist Church in the U.S. could start 200 new World Visions. If Christians in affluent nations were willing to live even moderately simple lifestyles, they could make a truly enormous contribution to the reduction of hunger and starvation in the world.

But we dare not think simply of relief and development. The Lausanne Covenant rightly refers to the *"injustices which cause"* the poverty of millions. One of the most urgent agenda items for the church in the industrialized nations of the northern hemisphere is to help our people begin honestly to explore to what extent our abundance depends on international economic structures that are unjust. To what extent do current patterns of international trade and the operations of the International Monetary Fund, for instance, contribute to affluence in some nations and poverty in others? Fortunately, we have an Oxford economist to help us with questions of that sort on Wednesday, so I need not try to comment here. But, unless we grapple with that systemic question, our discussion of simple lifestyle has not gone beyond Christmas baskets and superficial charity which at times can even be, consciously or unconsciously, a philanthropic smokescreen diverting the oppressed from the structural causes of their poverty and our affluence.

Nor is the question of simple lifestyle irrelevant to the struggle to overcome the systemic causes of poverty. First of all, it frees up resources which enable Christians to model an alternative model of global sharing. Alternative models can have a powerful impact on the larger society. Second, it provides integrity to our call for significant structural change in secular society. It is simply a farce to ask Washington, Whitehall, or New Delhi to legislate what Christians refuse to live. Third, beginning to live more simply frees one from the seductive materialism that prevents the masses of folk in industrialized nations from any serious exploration of genuinely costly proposals for changes in the current international economic order. If we cannot discover a significant minority of Christians who care enough about justice to start now to live a lifestyle consistent with a new kind of global community, then there is no hope whatsoever to develop peacefully the political will in industrialized nations to effect a fundamental systemic change.

Newsweek (Feb. 18, 1980, p.63) summarizes The Brandt Commission on International Development as follows: "If mankind is to survive, say Brandt and his colleagues, the gap between the rich and the poor must be closed — quickly." If a few million Christians in rich nations are willing to adopt simple lifestyles as part of their commitment to that struggle for peace through justice, they will profoundly influence the course of world history in the next decade.

Unevangelized billions wait for Good News they have never heard. 30 million starving children and a billion hopelessly poor folk wait painfully for an end to unnecessary poverty. In response to our world's desperate need for evangelism and justice, Christians today will begin to live more simply.

But our concern for simple lifestyle does not simply grow out of our analysis of the world. It comes finally from an analysis of the world that is guided and shaped by the scriptures.

Biblical Foundations for a Simple Lifestyle

Again the global perspective of the worldwide body of Christ is crucial. Millions of Christians in industrialized nations have adopted a distorted Gospel of Wealth. Their preachers reassure uneasy consciences (even the least informed Western Christian has heard enough about starving millions to feel a glimmer of guilt in the face of massive affluence) with the comfortable message that Northern nations have become wealthy solely by hard work and daily diligence. God has rewarded our Christian faith and hard work with material abundance that we have every right to enjoy. The Christians in the industrialized nations urgently need the assistance of brothers and sisters in Christ living in contexts of poverty and oppression to help them read the scriptures more faithfully.

As we do that, the following biblical themes will be especially important as a foundation for a simple lifestyle.

First, God is on the side of the poor and oppressed. Now please do not misunderstand me. I do not mean that poverty is the biblical ideal. I do not mean that the poor are Christians just because they are poor. Nor do I mean that God cares more about the salvation of the poor than the salvation of the rich.

But the Bible does teach three very surprising things (largely ignored by rich Christians) that are helpfully summarized by the statement that God is on the side of the poor:

1) At the central moments of revelation history (e.g., the Exodus, the destruction of Israel and Judah, and the Incarnation), the Bible repeatedly says that God acted not only to call out a chosen people and reveal his will (although he certainly did that!); he also acted to liberate poor, oppressed folk (Ex. 3:7-8; 6:5-7; Deut. 26:5-8; Amos 6:1-7; Is. 10:1-4; Jer. 5:26-29; Lk. 4:16-20).

2) God actually acts in history to pull down the unjust rich and to exalt the poor (Lk. 1:46-53; 6:20-25; James 5:1). And God does this both when the rich get rich by oppression (James 5:3-5; Ps. 10; Jer. 5:26-29; 22:13-19; Is. 3:14-25) and also when they are rich and fail to share (Ezek. 16:49-50).

3) The people of God, if they are really the people of God, are also on the side of the poor (Matt. 25:31-46; Lk. 14:12-14; 1 Jn. 3:16-18; Is. 1:10-15; 58:3-7).

If we want to worship, we must also imitate, the God who, scripture says, is on the side of the poor.

Second, the uniform teaching of scripture in both Old and New Testaments is that God wills transformed economic relationships among his people. God desires major movement toward economic equality in the new society of the church. Paul's advice to Greek-speaking, European Christians collecting an offering for Aramaic-speaking Asian Christians puts it bluntly:

I do not mean that others should be eased and you burdened, but that as a matter of equality your abundance at the present time should supply their want so that their abundance (later) should supply your want, that there may be equality (2 Cor. 8:13-14).

If we had time to examine what the Bible says about economic relationships among the people of God, we would discover that over and over again God specifically commanded his people to live together in community in such a way that they would avoid extremes of wealth and poverty. That is the point of Old Testament legislation on the Jubilee (Lev. 25), the sabbatical release of debts (Deut. 15), on tithing (Deut. 14:28-29), gleaning (Deut. 24:19-22) and loans (Ex. 22:25).

Jesus shared a common purse with the new community of his disciples (Jn. 12:6). The first church in Jerusalem (Acts 2:43-47; 4:32-37) and Paul in his collection (2 Cor. 8-9) were implementing what the Old Testament and Jesus had commanded.

Compare that with the contemporary church. Present economic relationships in the worldwide body of Christ are unbiblical, sinful, a hindrance to evangelism and a desecration of the body and blood of Jesus Christ. The dollar value of the food North Americans throw in the garbage each year equals about one-fifth of the total annual income of Africa's 120 million Christians. It is a sinful abomination for a small fraction of the world's Christians living in the Northern hemisphere to grow richer year by year while our brothers and sisters in Christ in the Third World ache and suffer for lack of minimal health care, minimal education, and even — in thousands and thousands of cases — just enough food to escape starvation.

We are like the rich Corinthian Christians who feasted without sharing their food with the poor members of the church (1 Cor. 11:20-29). Like them, we fail today to discern the reality of the one worldwide body of Christ (v.29).

Third — and this is the point I want to stress most — the Incarnation presents an example of radical, costly identification with those one serves.

When God became flesh, he did not come as a wealthy Roman imperialist or a comfortable Hellenistic intellectual. He was born in an insignificant, oppressed province controlled by imperialist Rome. Too poor to bring a lamb, the normal offering of purification, his parents brought two pigeons to the temple. Carpenters were, presumably, not the poorest folk in Galilean society, but they were hardly wealthy either. And when he entered his public ministry, he gave up even a carpenter's comforts. "Foxes have holes, and birds of the air have nests; but the Son of Man has nowhere to lay his head" (Mt. 8:20).

His identification with the poor and the weak was, he said, a sign that he was the Messiah. When John the Baptist asked if he was the expected Messiah, Jesus simply pointed to what he was doing. "Go and tell John what you have seen and heard: the blind receive their sight, the lame walk, lepers are cleansed, and the deaf hear, the dead are raised up and the poor have good news preached to them" (Lk. 7:22). Certainly he preached to the rich. But it was his preaching to the poor that validated his Messiahship. Indeed his identification with the poor went so far that he said his followers would meet him in the lives of the poor. "I was hungry and you gave me food, I was thirsty and you gave me drink . . . Truly I say to you, as you did it to one of the least of these my brethren, you did it to me" (Mt. 25:35-40). We begin to fathom that teaching only when we see that it was spoken by the Almighty One who had become flesh in the person of a homeless Galilean evangelist.

It is God Incarnate, God become flesh in a homeless teacher, that the scriptures repeatedly invite Christians to imitate. When Paul wanted to encourage Greek-speaking Christians in Europe to share economically with the even poorer Aramaic-speaking believers in Asia, he reminded them of the Incarnation: "For you know the grace of our Lord Jesus Christ, that though he was rich, yet for your sake he became poor, so that by his poverty you might become rich" (2 Cor. 8:9). Certainly Paul's words refer to more than economics. But Paul cites the total identification of God Incarnate with those he came to serve to urge the Corinthians to reduce their lifestyles so they could share with the poor.

The Incarnate One as the model for radical, costly, self-giving appears again in Philippians 2:

Let each of you look not only to his own interests but also to the interests of others. Have this mind among yourselves which you have in Christ Jesus, who, though he was in the form of God, did not count equality with God a thing to be grasped, but emptied himself, taking the form of a slave, being born in the likeness of men. And being found in human form, he humbled himself and became obedient unto death, even death on a cross (Phil. 2:4-7).

Imagine what would happen if one-tenth of the Christians in the world would really start to follow the model of the Incarnation. They would cast aside self-centred concern for their own affluent way of life and instead focus on the needs of the poor and unevangelized. They would identify as fully with those who need the Gospel and those who need food and justice as did Jesus who took the form of a slave. Hundreds of thousands would move physically to contexts of oppression or unevangelized cultures and sub-cultures. Millions more would support those who move by identifying through radically transformed lifestyles that enabled them to share sacrificially in the work of evangelism and justice.

Looking not only to our own interests, but also to the needs of others in our kind of world will mean a costly imitation of the God of the poor who cared so much for us that he became flesh as a homeless Galilean to die for our sins and gave us a perfect model of incarnational identification with those who yearn for food, justice and reconciliation with God.

A Process for Discernment of a Simple Lifestyle

Let me start with a simple proposal. In light of biblical revelation and the needs of the world, every congregation in affluent circumstances (and that includes the overwhelming majority of congregations in the Northern hemisphere) that dares to call itself biblical should place the following question high on its agenda for mutual prayer and discernment:

What is a faithful economic lifestyle for the people of this congregation at this point in history?

And it ought to have a clear process that includes careful study of scripture, sophisticated analysis of the world, mutual discernment and prayer in the congregation, and dialogue with the wider body of Christ throughout the world.

The last point is essential. Affluent Christians are in desperate need of gentle, courageous assistance and admonition from Christians in contexts of poverty. I want to propose that the worldwide body of Christ develop creative new ways to help affluent Christians. In fact, I want to go further and suggest that the universal body of Christ should at this focal point in world history attempt to formulate general criteria and general guidelines for a simple lifestyle.

Now I know some will instantly raise the spectre of legalism and regimentation and that is appropriate. These must be avoided. There is no one lifestyle that is right for all Christians in one country or even for all Christians in one congregation. There must be room for the variety and diversity so gorgeously displayed in the creation.

But surely that does not mean that we should fall back into typical Western individualism where each person or family does what is good in their own eyes. We all need the insight of the other members of Christ's body. We need the help of other Christians in our congregation, city, country, and finally in the whole worldwide body of Christ to help us decide what a faithful lifestyle would mean for us.

Legalism and individualism are equally pernicious dangers. We must avoid both if Christians today are to develop joyful, diverse, truly self-sacrificing lifestyles that promote evangelism and justice. Self-righteous legalism is a danger. We dare not prescribe specific models for others. I suspect, however, that individualism is the greater danger for most affluent Christians. We want to decide by ourselves about how to spend our money. We are not eager to have the Holy Spirit use other Christians, especially poor Christians, to help us decide what a faithful lifestyle for us might be. Hopefully this proposal for mutual discernment in the universal body of Christ can avoid both legalism and individualism.

How could the worldwide body of Christ develop processes of discernment? I think the process should start in each local congregation.

My assumption is that the Holy Spirit wants to guide individual Christians as they prayerfully seek his will by studying both the Bible and the newspaper in the context of Christian community. A congregation could decide, say at an annual business meeting, that in the course of the next two years it would try to help all members of the congregation discover what lifestyle God wills for them. An extended process of Bible study on topics like the biblical perspective on the poor, justice, evangelism, etc. would be initiated. So would in-depth analysis of the facts of evangelistic opportunity and world poverty (and the underlying systematic causes of poverty). Such study could be done in sermons, Sunday school classes, and ongoing study/fellowship/action groups.

Ideally everybody would be in a weekly fellowship group where each person's or family's expenditures on clothes, housing, transportation, etc. could be examined with gentle thoughtfulness and with the goal of developing a specific budget that each would consider faithful in today's world. Larger expenditures for housing, cars and long vacations could be discussed and prayed about in the group. After the initial period during which every member arrived at a specific budget, family budgets could be discussed in the small group at least once a year.

Please note carefully that I am *not* suggesting that the group dictate what any individual person or family should spend on anything. I assume that *each person or family* should prayerfully decide for *themselves*. But surely the wisdom and loving insight of other sisters and brothers should provide helpful assistance to uncover blind spots, selfishness and neglected alternatives.

A supportive context for living this kind of lifestyle is indispensable. Sociologists have discovered that people tend to accept the beliefs and values of the people with whom they live. Significant others, persons that they particularly respect and look up to, are especially important in shaping values. That is why Amish children frequently remain with the values and beliefs under which they were raised whereas Amish and Mennonite children raised on television become typical American materialistic consumers. Consequently decisions about where we choose to live and who we choose to associate with are among the most free and most important decisions to make.

It is virtually impossible for a single person or a single family to live a biblically faithful simple lifestyle in a typical affluent materialistic community. And that includes typical affluent materialistic Christian churches in the North Atlantic.

One excellent solution is to live among the poor — the rural or urban poor in either the developed nations or the Third World. Literally hundreds of thousands of Christians ought to move (in groups) to the poor sections of large cities. Housing costs less. More important, as we live among people who are poor, our own and our children's desires for more and more toys, gadgets and clothes tend to decrease. In the face of such immediate need, sharing becomes easier. One's values begin to change.

Of course not all Christians (I'd settle for a tenth!) ought to move to the inner city. Many ought to live in suburban areas. But it will be possible to sustain a simple lifestyle there only if communities of Christians committed to a simple lifestyle for the sake of evangelism and justice can be created. One solution would be for a dozen singles and couples from a particular congregation to decide to buy housing close together in a particular suburban neighbourhood. They could then share cars, tools, garden space, playground equipment, etc. They could be a house church within a large congregation and their weekly meetings would constitute a support group for nurturing their holistic biblical commitment including their concern for a simple lifestyle.

Thus far I have suggested that each congregation ought to make the question of a faithful lifestyle an important one for congregational life, that there should be a process for sharing the mutual wisdom of all members of the congregation, and that supportive contexts of genuine *koinonia* are essential.

How can we extend the dialogue to the universal body of believers? If the insight of brothers and sisters in the local congregation is crucial for overcoming individualism, so is the counsel of other parts of the worldwide body of Christ. Think of how the discussion would change if your family's discussion of a new car or a summer vacation took place in the presence of a Christian family from rural Brazil surrounded by poverty, malnutrition and starvation. We need processes in the worldwide body of Christ by which poor Christians in the inner city and the Third World can help affluent Christians discuss the question of faithful lifestyles.

Perhaps denominational or interdenominational agencies could develop structures to enable an individual congregation in an affluent context to become a sister congregation to a local church in a developing country. They could then ask the sister congregation in the Third World to discuss the specific family budgets they had developed (with their rationale) and invite a response. The sister congregation would also be invited to share some of its typical family budgets.

I also think it would be helpful if the worldwide body of Christ would develop some general criteria for simple lifestyle and some general guidelines in many areas including clothing, housing, transportation and church construction.

A. General Criteria

First, some general criteria. I offer the following not as a final product (and certainly not as revealed norms!) but rather as an initial attempt to illustrate my proposal and initiate discussion.

1. We ought to move toward a personal lifestyle that could be sustained over a long period of time if it were shared by everyone in the world. In its controversial *Limits to Growth,* the Club of Rome suggested the figure of $1,800 per year per person. In spite of the many weaknesses of that study, the Club of Rome's estimate may be the best available. Hopefully Christians will be involved in the extensive, sophisticated study required for a more precise estimate of what could be sustained long term. In the meantime, we can all safely assume that it will be below the average annual per capita expenditure in North America and Western Europe today!

2. We need to distinguish between necessities and luxuries and normally reject both our desire for the latter and our inclination to blur the distinction.

   But what are necessities and what are luxuries? It is not too difficult to define a minimal level of *physical* needs —

adequate food and medical care for a healthy body and mind; appropriate clothes and housing for one's environment; the education needed for one's vocation. But what cultural things are necessities? Art and music in some form are a necessary expression of our humanity. Does that justify Gothic (or glass) cathedrals or the purchase of $10,000 paintings when millions of people are malnourished? Does the need for "privacy" and "space" make it right for one family to occupy a house that (as Christian communities have demonstrated) could easily meet the needs of ten or fifteen people?

3. Expenditure for the purpose of status, pride, staying in fashion, and "keeping up with the Joneses" is wrong.

   Here, too, of course, ambiguities arise. Is there a difference between buying things for the sake of status and — until we can persuade the other members of our church and community to live more simply — purchasing things so that one's children (even oneself!) have a healthy sense of self-worth rather than an inferiority complex? (People like myself need to ask if a large personal library feeds one's ego any less than an up-to-date wardrobe!)

4. We need to distinguish between expenditures to develop one's particular creative gifts and legitimate hobbies and a general demand for all the cultural items, recreational equipment and current hobbies that the "successful" of our class or nation enjoy. Each person has unique interests and gifts. Within limits, we should be able to express our creativity in those areas. But if we discover that we are justifying lots of things in many different areas, we should become suspicious.

5. We need to distinguish between occasional celebration and normal day-to-day routine. A turkey feast with all the trimmings at Thanksgiving to celebrate the good gift of creation is biblical (Deut. 14:22-27). Unfortunately, most of us overeat every day, and that is sin.

6. There is no necessary connection between what we earn and what we spend on ourselves. We should not buy things just because we can afford them.

B. *General Guidelines*

This area in particular requires extremely sensitive treatment. The goal is to enable the larger body of Christ to offer its collective wisdom to individual persons and families in a way that preserves their freedom, individuality and uniqueness. Perhaps the suggestion of general guidelines is not a helpful way to proceed. But, if it is not, then we need alternate proposals for concrete ways to enable all parts of the body of Christ to assist affluent Christians in developing more faithful lifestyles.

The general guidelines would *not* be laws that everyone followed on pain of excommunication! Rather they would be lists of issues, questions, suggestions, and especially processes for decision-making relevant to a given area available for the prayerful consideration of persons and churches as they allow the Holy Spirit to lead them to a faithful decision for their unique situation. General guidelines could be shared through publications and denominational and interdenominational agencies and tested in congregations around the country and around the world. Especially important would be a process for input of poor Christians in the inner city and the Third World.

The following suggestions on jet travel, housing, clothing, and church construction are offered as a possible beginning.

C. Guidelines for Evangelical Leaders

1. *Salary:* Is my salary consistent with biblical teaching, the needs of the world, and the sacrifices of those who give to and work in this agency?
2. *Personal Lifestyle:* Do my clothes, car, house, etc. offer a model of a simple lifestyle for the larger evangelical world?
3. *Travel:* Do I keep my expenditures on travel to a minimum or have I allowed the style and values of secular peers to shape what I do?
4. *Offices:* Do my office and my organization's offices reflect the urgency of the world's need for the Gospel, food and justice or have secular patterns shaped decisions in this area?

D. Guidelines on Jet Travel*

Unless we are to call into question our whole way of life (perhaps we should), no one is going to say that all jet travel is wrong. Yet many Christians would question whether it is right to spend $1500 to fly somewhere for a week's vacation. So the question becomes: what factors weigh against travel and what factors weigh for it?

1. *Purpose:* One key question is: why are you going? Do you hope to do something worthwhile whether it is to relax, visit relatives, or give a lecture? Is the purpose enough to justify the use of money and resources?

2. *Irreplaceability:* Are you the closest person who can do what you are going for, or is it the nearest place you can get what you are after? We are, of course, very likely to "cheat" and consider ourselves more irreplaceable than we are, or our destination more irreplaceable than it is.
3. *Length of stay:* The longer you stay, the less your travel costs per day away; on the other hand, your being needed somewhere else (e.g., at home) is also important.
4. *Value of time:* We go by jet rather than bus or on foot mostly because jets take less time. So part of the question is whether we will use the time saved in going by jet well enough to justify the cost in money and resources.

   Roughly speaking, the faster we travel, the more resources and money we use. We go by jet because "time is money". So perhaps the basic question is how long the earth can support the West's tendency to busy-ness and our frantic pace. Nature may need us to slow down.
5. *How money is used otherwise:* Of some relevance is how the money would be used otherwise. If a conference is going to fly a speaker in anyway, why not you? Of course, similar reasoning has been used to justify every known crime.
6. *Role:* Some persons need to travel more than others. Some worthwhile jobs/roles include a lot of travel and others do not.

E. Guidelines on Housing

1. *Purpose:* Why do I want different (larger, newer, renovated etc.) housing? Do I need it because of marriage, a larger family, greater convenience, social status? How many of the conveniences planned for the new (or renovated) housing are truly necessary and how many are planned because "that's the way they are doing things these days"?
2. *Alternative ways to meet the same need:* Could I go on using what I have? Could I find something less expensive which would satisfy my legitimate needs?
3. *Location:* Will I be living among the poor or the affluent? Will the new setting help make my thinking and living more biblical? Will it enable me to engage in my Servant King's mission more effectively?
4. *Value of investment:* Will the advantages of the new (or renovated) housing outweigh the costs?
5. *Inner attitudes:* How can I avoid pride and self-righteousness in this decision?

6. *Global perspective:* Do I think I could convince a Third World Christian that my answers to the above were valid?

F. Guidelines on Clothing

1. *Need:* Why do I think I need it? For business, to keep up with fashion? To bolster a weak self-image? To celebrate an important occasion? To celebrate the gorgeous beauty and variety that God has scattered everywhere throughout his good creation?
2. *Alternative ways to meet the same need:* Could I make it (or is my time worth more than that?) or buy it at a thrift shop instead of an expensive store? Could I get discarded second-hand clothes from a friend or borrow for the occasion?
3. *Cost and size of wardrobe:* How many outfits do I need at one time (and by whose standards)? Extra outfits in the closet that are not needed are tying up money that could be used to meet human need. Have I worn out what I have? Is there any reason why *I* should not wear out no-longer fashionable clothing rather than the poor person to whom I could give part of my present wardrobe? Can I buy clothes that will be suitable for a wide variety of occasions and thereby require fewer outfits?
4. *Witness:* Will this purchase encourage other Christians to live the kind of lifestyle God is calling them to live? Will it provide a model for secular society?
5. *Inner attitudes:* How can I avoid pride and self-righteousness in this decision?
6. *Global perspective:* Do I think I could convince an inner-city person or a Third World peasant that my answers to the above questions are valid?

G. Guidelines on Church Construction*

1. *Relevant biblical teaching:* The congregation could spend a couple of months studying how the Bible's teaching on the evangelistic mandate, God's special concern for the poor, and redeemed economic relationships among the worldwide body of Christ, relate to the proposed plans. Sermons, Sunday school sessions, prayer meetings, and fellowship evenings would all be appropriate opportunities.
2. *The world scene today:* How would the building programme

---

*These guidelines were drawn up in my church, Jubilee Fellowship of Germantown, Pennsylvania (after considerable discussion!).

relate to current needs for world evangelism, relief, development and justice programmes among the poor here and
abroad?

3. *Motives:* Motives should be examined with ruthless honesty.
Do we want a new (or larger or renovated) building because it
is necessary to carry on the biblically-defined mission of the
church, or because other Christian congregations have similar facilities? How many of the items (rugs, organ, etc.) are
truly necessary and how many are planned ''because that's
the way they're doing things these days''?

4. *Alternative ways to meet the same need:* Could other facilities
in the community be used? Could the presen church facility
be used on Saturday evening or Sunday afternoon by a
second congregation? Would we be willing to make modest
changes in our traditional time of worship in order to free significant resources (money saved by sharing facilities) for
worldwide evangelism? If not, what does that say about our
priorities?

5. *How will new facilities affect the thinking and activity of
church members?* Will the new building (or organ) help the
members of the congregation identify more easily with the
poor? If building a new structure requires a new location, will
that location make it easier to engage in Jesus' special concern to preach to the poor?

6. *Extended dialogue with other members of the worldwide
body of Christ:* Nearby congregations could be asked if they
had any suggestions on how to meet the growing demands for
additional space. The board of elders could spend a weekend
visiting an inner-city congregation (or a congregation
composed of another ethnic group) to review the building
plans, to pray together about them and to seek their honest
reactions. The denomination's cross-cultural missionary
agency and a relief, development and justice agency could be
invited to respond to the proposals in light of evangelistic
opportunities and justice programmes. A few key members
of the congregation could visit a Third World country to discuss the building plans with Christian leaders there.

7. *Matching funds:* Equal matching funds for Third World (or
inner-city) evangelism and long-term development ought to
be included in every fund-raising proposal for church construction in affluent circumstances. If we decide we need a
$500,000 educational facility, then we should raise $1,000,000
and give one half of it for evangelism and justice around the
world.

If groups of Christians were to set to work formulating general criteria and general guidelines of this sort and sharing them with other Christians, it would produce creative ferment in our churches. There would be vigorous debate! Such criteria and guidelines would at least provide a concrete way for us to live out our confession that all Christians in the world are our brothers and sisters.

Undoubtedly better proposals could be made. I beg others to make them. Somehow we must help each other learn how to live more simply for the sake of evangelism and justice.

A Just and Responsible Lifestyle — An Old Testament Perspective

VINAY SAMUEL and CHRIS SUGDEN

Introduction and Thesis

From what perspective did Old Testament writers view the life-style of God's people? They did not base their perspective on a pragmatic or compassionate reaction to endemic poverty. Apart from emergencies in times of famine and war, grinding poverty did not disfigure their society in the way it plagues our world today. Our thesis is that they viewed the lifestyle of God's people from the perspective that their true human fulfilment is inextricably bound to their relationship with the land (resources) that God gifts to them and for which he holds them account-able. This relationship should be ordered by the moral principles of justice, equality and equity. In stating this we do not mean in any way to reduce human fulfilment only to man's relationship to resources. The right relationship of man with God through Christ is central to human fulfilment. Rather we wish to draw attention to an important aspect of human fulfilment which must not be omitted from a true biblical understanding.

The Old Testament records the life and practice of God's people in widely differing social conditions: in nomadic tribes, in settled urban life, under an increasingly oppressive mon-archy, and in exile. In all these conditions we perceive some fun-damental units for developing a world view which demands a righteous lifestyle. We seek to root simple lifestyle today in the Old Testament basis for a just and responsible lifestyle.

Methodology

First our approach will be primarily descriptive. The Old Testa-ment is a history of the obedience and disobedience of God's people over many centuries and in different cultural settings.

We will be analytical at crucial points of this history to show the relationship between the people of God, their land and God's demands.

Secondly we will focus on the experience of the people of God. The overarching theme of the Old Testament is the people of God in their obedience and disobedience to God and their responsibility over the land gifted to them by him. We will focus therefore on the social and economic aspects of the lifestyle of the people of God rather than on the religious aspect.

Thirdly we will not isolate the so-called creation-ordinances or any other legislative material on the basis of their relevance to our society. For all these ordinances take their meaning from their relationship to the people of God and their history.

We will try to discover what kind of lifestyle the people of God were called to model in their use of the land, their legal systems, their social relationships and political institutions. We shall also discover what lifestyle they did model. Our hermeneutical bridge to the obedience of God's people today is that the people of the Old Covenant were to be a light to the nations of the pattern of humanity God willed for all his creation. God's people today are called to the same task.

Humanity and the Land

Man's true humanity is closely bound to his relationship with the resources God has given him. The Old Testament lays great stress on man's relationship to the land. This stress is not merely the reflection of a religion of a primitive agricultural society. It is a theological principle about the context in which man discovers his true humanity. In the story of creation man was made out of the dust of the earth. Man's vocation is to till the earth and bring it to its full flowering. Man's worship from the first offerings of Cain and Abel to the fully developed Israelite cult includes thanksgiving and offering to God of the fruit of the land. God's blessings and curses on his people were to be experienced in relation to the land (Dt. 28). True humanity does not consist in a balanced psyche or a right relationship with God apart from the concrete context of man's relationship to, responsibility for and offering of the land God has given him.

We will examine the concrete instances of this theological principle in the four periods of Israel's life we have described. E. Von Waldow describes the nomadic period of the patriarchs and the wilderness wanderings in these words:

There is no social differentiation in this kind of community. Either the whole clan or tribe is rich or all together are poor, depending primarily on the yields of the pasture land . . . In such a society private property is never used to oppress the neighbour, or as in the case in a capitalist society, as a means to come to more property. Instead it is used generously to entertain guests and to help the poor. Due to this attitude and this use of property, wealth can never create social classes, because according to the way of life in the desert a tent community can be wealthy (e.g. by a successful raid against the neighbouring tribe) today, and tomorrow lose everything to plundering enemies.[1]

For all the equality of the nomadic society, God's intended goal for Israel was the *settled community* in her own permanent land. Israel was conscious in her desert march, the settlement period and the exile that her existence as God's people could be affirmed only when she was in possession of the land. But the laws preserved the same principles of equality which were evident in the nomadic society for the organization of the settled community.

First the land was distributed on the basis of the size and need of each tribe not on the basis of power, achievement or reward. It was divided into equal portions according to the number of families and distributed by lot (Numbers 33:54). The division was decided by representatives from each tribe, not by the strongest tribe (Numbers 34:16-29).

Secondly adequate provision was to be made even for the landless. The Levites could hold no land as personal property. They were allotted cities and pasture land according to the size of the territory of the tribe to which they belonged.

Once this division was made so that each family had its own inheritance, other laws were designed to prevent dispossession. The land really belonged to Jahweh and so could never be alienated from those families he gave it to and their descendants.

The law of levirate marriage and the institution of the *go'el* redeemer, who as the next of kin had to buy the land which his relative had to abandon, was designed to prevent the alienation of family property. The Sabbath principle governed debts and land use. If money was borrowed and repaid, the debt was cancelled in the seventh year, so that the land pledged as collateral had to be redeemed (Dt. 15:1-2). Land could not be cultivated in the seventh year but its produce was available for all. And in the sabbath of sabbath years, the forty-ninth year, jubilee was to be proclaimed and all property restored to its original owners (Lev. 25).

The settlement was of course a gradual process under the judges. There is not much evidence as to how far these provisions for land tenure were put into practice. However, when the settlement was complete we do have evidence of an equality in Israelite life that was never paralleled in her later history. Roland De Vaux writes:

All Israelites enjoyed more or less the same standard of living. Wealth came from the land and the land had been shared out between the families, each of whom guarded its property jealously (cf. the story of Naboth in 1 Kings 21:1-3). Commerce, and the buying and selling of real estate for profit, were as yet unimportant factors in economic life ... Excavations in Israelite towns bear witness to this equality in the standard of living. At Tirzah ... the houses of the tenth century B.C. are all of the same size and arrangement. Each represents the dwelling of a family which lived in the same way as its neighbours. The contrast is striking when we pass to the eighth century houses on the same site. The rich houses are bigger and better built and in a different quarter from that where the poor houses are huddled together. Between these two centuries, a social revolution had taken place.[2]

The Canaanite Model

A striking change comes over Israelite society in the two centuries from the institution of the monarchy. Two factors influenced this: contact with Canaanite culture and the institution of the monarchy. The people of Israel lived in the hilly areas, the Canaanites in the coastal plain and fortified cities. During David's reign these cities were taken into the state. The major significance of this was contact with the Canaanite social organization and understanding of the land which underlay it. The Israelites were taught to understand the land as a gift for whose use they were responsible and whose distribution was ordered by moral principles. The Canaanites in their fertility religions were much more interested in the land as an asset whose fruits were to be maximized by religious ritual. Land was a marketable commodity and economic growth was the goal. The Mosaic code had no religious ritual to coax the fruits of the land: Israel had to borrow any such rites from others. For the Mosaic code, God's blessings on the land depended on covenant faithfulness to God and justice among the people of God (Dt. 28). Justice and humanity in responsible use of their land came before techniques to ensure maximum profit.

Gunther Wittenberg writes:

(Among the Canaanites) landed property was treated as a saleable commodity and could be freely disposed of. The inclusion of Canaanite property into the Israelite state therefore meant that now two types of property ownership existed side by side. More enterprizing families could now increase their estates and this tended to undermine the old principle of equality. Wealthy land owners lived in the cities and had their 'latifundia' worked by slaves or paid farm labourers. Commerce in the cities again led to increased wealth which provided the means to buy more real estate on the countryside. This tended to increase class divisions.[3]

The Monarchy

The second factor was the institution of the monarchy. The Old Testament is essentially ambiguous about monarchy. The warnings of the lifestyle of kings in 1 Sa. 8:10-18 reflect contemporary Canaanite models. We increasingly find that the goal of the kings in Israelite society was to maximize the economic affluence of their court and the society. This was probably in response to the Canaanite models of kingship and to the need to compete favourably with other kings and so prove their credentials. They put their responsibility to preserve people from exploitation a long second. The trade off for economic affluence was inequality and injustice. We cite the following evidences:

a. To maintain his soldiers and court the king needed crown lands. Family possessions which fell vacant did not revert to the clan for re-allotment but to the crown.[4] Royal domains were handed out to royal officials in return for service.[5]
b. Free Israelite peasants were conscripted for labour. This was one of the causes of Jeroboam's revolt (1 Kings 12).
c. The incident of Naboth's vineyard shows the power of the king to subvert justice to dispossess people.
d. To maintain the social control required to develop this economic growth from which they benefited, Rehoboam's youthful advisers urged him to take even harsher measures than Solomon.

Henry writes:

A movement of dispossession, of slow impoverishment of former free land owners started on the one hand, together on the other hand with the rise of a new rich land owning class created by the king's grace and favour and built up on the fief system.[6]

It is no wonder that there is no *evidence* in the Old Testament that Israel ever practised the jubilee legislation. It would be entirely against the king's interest to allow it. Even Josiah's reforms when the law book was discovered affected matters of ownership only. It was only a spiritual and cultic reformation. The lack of evidence is no argument that God is not concerned that the principle which the jubilee legislation enshrines should be practised. The prophetic writings give abundant evidence that this was his concern.

The Prophets

Prophecy found its essential role in relation to the kingship. The prophets did not provide economic solutions. They made value judgements on the economic arrangements under monarchic oppression. We strongly suspect that a major concern of the prophets was that any true national reformation required a return to the right social relationships between the people and the land and one another. They called the ruling groups to return the nation to the lifestyle that God intended for his people in their land. They warned that if they refused to institute such a reform God would judge them by removing them from the land. The fact that the prophets concentrate on the injustice of landowners, money-lenders, luxurious women, corrupt judges, and the resulting oppression of the poor shows the central place a proper social relationship between the people and their land had in their concept of righteousness, true humanity and a just lifestyle. Wittenberg concludes a study of the prophets:

The prophets are concerned with affluence and poverty, because they realize that God's saving acts in history, the liberation from Egypt and the giving of the promised land, imply that God wants free men on free soil who can serve him and their fellow men intentionally and joyfully. This basic relationship is seriously disrupted if landed property is used as a basis for an unscrupulous exploitation of the neighbour, depriving him of freedom and of all means of existence.[7]

Christopher Wright describes the ideal Israelite society as "a society in which families would enjoy a degree of economic independence based upon an equitable share in the nation's wealth; in which a family could feel some social relevance and significance in its community — in which every family had the opportunity of learning the message of divine redemption in a culturally relevant and meaningful way and the freedom to respond to it."[8]

The Exile and After

In the *exile* we find that Israel experiences the judgement of God for her injustice by expulsion from the land. She experiences a crisis of faith and identity. "How can we sing a song to the Lord in a foreign land?'' (Ps. 137:4). The king, the source of so much oppression, is removed.

In the restoration to the land we find little evidence of attempts to order the land on the basis of the economic laws in the Mosaic code. This is probably because at least five hundred years now separated the restoration from the situation when landholding was according to those laws. So the people would find it very hard to see the importance of those arrangements for the well-being of the nation. The freedom of the land from foreign nations became the dominant concern from the early restoration until the time of Jesus. Apart from the Maccabaean rule this period saw Israel's holy land defiled by the Gentile boot. The question of the economic and social relationships of the land dropped from the agenda altogether. By the time of Jesus, dispossession and oppression were on a massive scale. Small peasants were impoverished by the following means: (1) the numerous contributions paid to the temple which enriched the priestly caste; (2) the Roman taxes which transferred the agricultural surplus to Rome. There was high unemployment and many were in debt. Armed brigands appeared in the rural areas. Jerusalem in A.D. 60 had about 18,000 landless labourers alone. Meanwhile large land holdings were owned by absentee landlords whose interests coincided with that of Rome. The president of the Sanhedrin was selected from the four most wealthy families by the Roman Procurator.[9]

In contrast to the Zealots Jesus identified the key issue as just relationships within the land rather than the freedom of the land. He challenged the ideology of the rulers who sanctioned social oppression in the name of religion. He attacked their greed, oppression and love of power. His kingdom was good news to the poor and encouraged just economic and social relationships in the new people of God. Luke clearly portrays Jesus as the true king of righteousness and peace who takes the side of the poor and oppressed in Israelite society to establish true humanity: the news of his birth is first announced to outcast shepherds; in his ministry he brings release to the demon-possessed and diseased who were often beggars, he gives new status to women and children, he attacks wealthy people who ignore the rights of the poor, calls on his followers to share resources with the poor and make economic amends, crosses divisive social barriers of wealth, race and class, and describes forgiveness as the remission of debts. John Howard Yoder[10] and Robert Sloan[11] have argued persuasively that within the context of his time Jesus was seeking to apply the jubilee principle of restoring to people their economic inheritance as members of the people of God.

In surveying the Old Testament we note the following important points:

a) The nomadic period of equality always exercized an influence in Israelite life. The Rechabites sought to continue the lifestyle of the nomadic period in the settled community. They modelled a simple lifestyle. But it was a simple lifestyle at the expense of the context that God intended for them. It was opting out. God expected his people to live a just and responsible lifestyle surrounded by all the pressures of Canaanite market economies. So the Rechabites cannot be a model for our obedience.

b) Closely associated with the land is man's vocation to work, and the use of his skills to draw out the land's bounty. The land would respond to man's work, not to fertility rituals. The tithes were an offering of the fruits of man's work on the land not part of a fertility cult. No one was exempt from the vocation. In Proverbs the wise warn the wealthy young nobles of the power one man's laziness has to destroy a vineyard. Amos condemns the idle rich. Man's stewardship was to exercize his work and skills on the land.

c) Economic goals exercized a great influence on political structures. Solomon's goals of economic affluence determined a highly centralized political system. The amphictyonic structure and tribal leaders disappeared. Economic growth was felt to be incompatible with the decentralized power structure of the early settlement. Economic goals set the agenda for political structures. Central power and wide class divisions resulted.

d) Israel's call to a just and responsible lifestyle was not so that she could enjoy true humanity herself alone. Her lifestyle was to be a light to the Gentiles through the use of the land, her work, her legal, political and economic institutions. Her lifestyle was to be a witness of God's power at work in her society. Jerusalem was to be a model and a teacher of God's ways to men. In her failure to model this lifestyle Israel witnessed to God's judgement on injustice among the nations. Even in this judgement God never deserted his people or abandoned his project of perfecting them. Hope arose that God would finally establish a just society under a righteous king which would draw all the nations to him. This hope was developed in apocalyptic and is concretely foreshadowed in the people of God of the New Dispensation. The Holy Spirit gives an earnest of the fulfilment of God's purposes in the presence of the kingdom among his people.

e) The historical record of and the prophetic emphasis on the crucial relationship between the people, their land and justice show that in those situations where a just and responsible lifestyle calls for a comparative simplicity of lifestyle, the following objections cannot be sustained: i) that since the Old Testament records men of great wealth such as Abraham and Solomon as God's servants, the issue of level of lifestyle is irrelevant to Christian obedience. This argument treats Abraham and Solomon as isolated individuals and neglects the overall thrust of equality, justice and responsibility in the biblical evaluation of the socio-economic context. Abraham had wealth in which all his tribe shared equally. Solomon was wealthy but oppressive. ii) that since a massive redistribution of personal incomes by Christians to poor nations will at best delay poverty by only a matter of months, the issue of simple lifestyle can be only a futile gesture. The consequentialist argument focuses on the economic fruits of a lifestyle rather than on the inherent quality of justice in a lifestyle. It is the Canaanite reply.

Interpretation for Today

How shall we interpret this biblical material today? We understand the land God gives to be all the material resources God gives to man. These will yield their true bounty in response to man's work and skill and will provide the context for true humanity if administered justly.

The issue of lifestyle is not to be an emergency procedure in the face of grinding poverty. In the end such a reaction is either emotional or pragmatic. It is as likely to promote lifeboat ethics as an ethic of sharing. For every family who shares in response to emotional appeals about poverty, how many concentrate further on ensuring their own security as they see a crisis drawing nearer and resources running out? The issue of a just and responsible lifestyle is the issue of the nature of man-in-society-in-the-land. A just and responsible lifestyle will include working for those social arrangements which encourage men to discover true humanity.

In many periods of Israel's life we see that God is more concerned for a just and responsible use of these resources for the benefit of all than with maximizing these resources, a process which seems to benefit only some. Lifestyle is to be set in the context of the resources God gives a people for which they are accountable. A lifestyle in which a man does not have integral relationship with and responsibility for physical resources to shape his environment and use it for service will dehumanize him. Dispossession of control over resources through unjust distribution of wealth or through exclusion from decision-making procedures in a common undertaking leads to false dependence, lack of responsibility and powerlessness. Since excess possession causes dispossession it is as wrong for some to possess too much as for others to possess nothing.

There are many current examples of dispossession. State ownership denies the individual any responsibility for his physical resources. What everybody owns nobody cares about. Global corporations tend to concentrate power in the hands of a few executives accountable only to the profit level of their few shareholders' investments. Highly sophisticated technology either removes men from responsibility for their environment by employment and gives other excess power (micro chips) or purchases economic benefits at an appallingly high social cost (the social control needed to run nuclear power). None of these provides the conditions for responsible mastery of the earth.

We suggest that the biblical criteria of equality, justice and responsibility can help us evaluate social arrangements. They would affirm the emphasis on personal responsibility for use of resources in capitalism but raise serious questions about the adequacy of pure capitalism to allot resources with equity or justice. The same criteria would affirm the concern of socialism for just and equitable distribution of goods in the community, but find that its concern to abolish forms of personal ownership diminishes meaningful responsibility for the use of resources. In political systems those criteria would question even the most benevolent autocracy on the basis of removal of responsibility and some democracies, which are in fact representative oligarchies, on the basis of equality.

The Bottom Line

Our task has been to set the call for a just and responsible lifestyle in a wider context. The call in the Old Testament is neither for a pragmatic response to endemic poverty (which did not exist) nor for individual rectitude. The people of God are called to witness a just lifestyle through their use of the land, their work, their legal systems, social relationships and political institutions. These arrangements were to make possible a true and dignified humanity not only for individuals but for society to encourage a lifestyle that brings human life for all.

The call for a just and responsible lifestyle must be directed essentially and primarily to communities of God's people. God's people are no people unless they demonstrate their peoplehood in economic, social and political relationships and not in religious and liturgical relationships alone. Jeremiah insisted it would be of no avail for Israel to plead that in her midst stood the Temple of the Lord unless in her society she demonstrated his presence. This means that Christian communities must develop models of just patterns of employment, pay, sharing, division of labour, leadership, participation in decision-making and use of resources, marketing and trade. Only if Christian communities develop these just relationships can they provide the models and support necessary for individual Christians to exercize an incisive presence in the other world communities of office, factory, community and school. It is unfair and unbiblical to call on individual Christians to exercize an individual Christian presence in these situations without the model or support of a Christian community.

We therefore seriously question the tradition of biblical interpretation which sets aside the pattern of the lifestyle of the community of God's Old Covenant. We do not believe that this community pattern and its concern for economic, social and political relationships was set aside by the New Covenant. Jesus was, we believe, very concerned for justice in these relationships.

Individuals may in their own lifestyle have a prophetic role to their communities. The goal of a just and responsible lifestyle is not the isolation of the Rechabite, seeking to live at the lowest possible level compatible with human survival or at the level of street beggars of Calcutta. The goal is for the life of God's people set within the settled urban community with all its attendant dangers.

The call for a just and responsible lifestyle is not only to make me more human by freeing me from greed or need: it is to make others human too. So the Christian community must by its example and questions challenge contemporary power structures as to the degree to which they encourage and enable people to live a fully human life in the social, economic, legal and political spheres.

For minority Christian communities living in predominantly non-Christian cultures the call for a just and responsible lifestyle means that they should not apologize for being a distinct community with different social and economic relationships by which they seek to model God's laws. Such communities can be tempted to sink all possible differences with the predominant culture in order to prove their commitment to the good of the nation, or for a quiet life in order to preach the gospel unhindered. They must resist this temptation, for they are bearers of priceless human values in a largely apostate society. They are not only beacons to guide and warn, and refuges to receive the broken, frustrated and hopeful. They are the very leaven which can change the whole society.

3

New Testament Perspectives on Simple Lifestyle

C. RENÉ PADILLA

A paper on any topic related to lifestyle is likely to show more about the writer than about the subject matter. One's lifestyle cannot be separated from one's person; in writing about lifestyle, therefore, one can hardly avoid exposing oneself, with one's values and ambitions.

That being the case, it is legitimate to ask whether an authoritative word on the question of lifestyle can ever be given. Show me a person's lifestyle and I will tell you what he is likely to say on the question of lifestyle.

The problem is not readily solved when the question of lifestyle is viewed as a topic of Bible study. Does Jesus' poverty, for instance, have any relevance to Christian discipleship today, or should it be regarded as totally incidental to his ministry? Should "blessed are the poor in spirit" be interpreted in the light of "blessed are the poor" or vice versa? What did Jesus mean when he introduced himself as one coming to preach good news to the poor? Does the "love communism" of the primitive church have meaning for people living in "the Age of Plenty" in their relationship to people living in "the Age of Hunger", or should it be cast aside as no more than an interesting experiment inspired by the idealism of people living in "the Age of the Spirit"? All these, and many other, questions bearing on lifestyle will find different answers from different interpreters. But are all the answers equally valid? Is there not a way to let the Bible speak without imposing on it our own ideology?

For the Christian, to raise questions concerning lifestyle is to raise questions concerning the kingdom of heaven. It is to ask, not speculative questions, but questions about what kind of life corresponds to the fact that the New Age has already come in Jesus Christ. And here too, it is "those who know they are spiritually poor" who will see the kingdom of heaven.

I approach my subject as one who recognizes the ease with which the gospel can be spiritualized in order to avoid its demands in relation to lifestyle. I do not share the optimism of those who believe that if we Christians only understood what the Bible says on this question, we would readily submit to its demands in order to put our lives in line with them. At the same time, I recognize the possibility of reading the Bible in order to find support for a lifestyle conformed to a leftist ideology. My honest desire is to hear and to help others hear what the Spirit of God is saying to the church today on the question of simple lifestyle, for the sake of obedience. In the first part of this paper I will briefly examine the meaning of Jesus' poverty in relation to Christian discipleship; in the second part I will take a look at the way in which Jesus' teaching and example was reproduced in the early church; finally, in the third part I will explore the teaching of the apostles bearing on the question of riches.

I. Jesus and Poverty

1. Jesus' poverty

The picture of Jesus which emerges out of the Gospels is that of a person who knew economic poverty throughout his entire life. His birth took place without the normal comforts, in a feeding trough for animals (Lk. 2:7). The offering that Joseph and Mary brought on the occasion of his presentation in the Temple was the one that the Old Testament stipulated for poor people, namely two doves or pigeons (Lk. 2:23). Quite early in his life he was a refugee (Mt. 2:14). He grew up in Galilee, an underdeveloped region of Palestine (Mt. 2:22-23), in the home of a carpenter, and this placed him in a position of disadvantage in the eyes of many of his contemporaries (cf. Jn. 1:46; Mt. 13:55; Mk. 6:3). During his ministry, he had no home he could call his (Lk. 58) and he depended on the generosity of a group of women for the provision of his needs (Lk. 8:2).

Jesus' poverty is a hard historical fact unanimously portrayed in all four Gospels. In order to understand its significance, it must be viewed in the light of Jewish piety in Jesus' day, according to which poverty was usually regarded as a curse and wealth was praised as evidence of God's favour.[1] At the same time, however, it must also be viewed in its relation to what Martin Hengel has rightly called "Jesus' free attitude to property",[2] evidenced in Jesus' contact with well-to-do women (Lk. 8:2-3; cf. Lk. 10:38f.) and his willingness to attend banquets organized by the rich (Lk. 7:36ff; 11:37; 14:1, 12; Mk. 14:3ff.) and to incur the label of "a glutton and a drunkard" (Lk. 7:34). Obviously, Jesus was not a propounder of rigorous asceticism. With this qualification in mind, we still have to ask whether his willingness to defy Jewish piety by identifying himself with the poor, while at the same time maintaining a free attitude to riches, throws any light on the question of the kind of lifestyle which corresponds to the kingdom of God, or is Jesus' example at this point totally irrelevant to Christian discipleship?

The answer to that question should also take into account Jesus' special concern for the poor, which we intend to discuss further on. Suffice it for now to say that if Jesus was poor and at the same time regarded himself as sinless, he could not have thought of poverty as a direct result of personal sin. The possibility would seem to be open that to him poverty was something desirable for his disciples throughout the ages, perhaps as a virtue or as a means to improve their relationship to God. Such an idealization of poverty, however, can hardly be maintained in view of Jesus' "free attitude to property". Whatever the motivation for his own poverty might have been, it is quite obvious that he did not intend to depict it as a positive value. As Julio de Santa Ana[3] has insisted, all through the Bible poverty is not a virtue but an evil which must be eliminated and with regard to which God is specially concerned. All the evidence suggests that Jesus shared the same attitude.

2. Jesus' Concern for the Poor

As we have seen, the Gospel records clearly show that Jesus was materially poor. Equally, they show that he was especially concerned for the poor, the needy, the oppressed. *Prima facie*, it is most unlikely that at a time when people were subjected to hard taxation linked to both their temple obligations and the Roman government Jesus could go about cities and villages without taking notice of the poverty that afflicted the masses. The diseases and infirmities of which he healed many could only be an aspect of the destitute condition of those crowds which inspired his compassion because "they were harassed and helpless, like sheep without a shepherd" (Mt. 9:36).

Jesus' attitude to the poor is clearly stated in Luke's version of one of the Beatitudes: "Blessed are you poor, for yours is the Kingdom of heaven" (Lk. 6:20). To be sure, the reference to material poverty can be and has in fact been denied by appealing to Matthew's modification, according to which the poor who are blessed are the "poor in spirit" (Mt. 5:3). The disagreement calls for the following observations.

First, it is true that poverty in the Bible cannot be reduced to absence of material resources and that it is safe to assume that behind the use of the term "poor" in the New Testament oftentimes lies an earlier Jewish tradition in which "poor" is almost synonymous with "pious" and "righteous".[4] In Luke 6:20, however, the poor stand in contrast with the rich, concerning whom Jesus pronounces a woe because they have already received this consolation, that is, the comforts provided by wealth (6:24). No one would claim that the riches of the rich to whom Jesus refers are spiritual riches; why should the poverty of the poor be regarded as spiritual poverty (i.e. poverty in spirit)?

Second, if the Beatitude in Luke 6:20 is prematurely spiritualized, the very basis for interpreting the Matthean version of Jesus' saying is removed. For what does it mean to be "poor in spirit" if it is not primarily to share the outlook of the materially poor? If every time that the term "poor" is used in the Gospels it is taken to mean "poor in spirit", then the beatitude in its Matthean form has no reference to concrete reality. To be poor in spirit is to be like those who being materially poor acknowledge their needs and are willing to receive help.

Third, the Beatitude is pronounced from the perspective of a poor man and addressed to the poor; its spiritualization, by contrast, usually reflects a way of thinking characteristic of people who have all their material needs met and are therefore unable to claim for themselves the blessedness of the materially poor. Unless one is willing to become literally poor, the literal interpretation of Jesus' saying is too threatening for one to prefer it over against the spiritualistic reading of it.

If the literal interpretation is accepted, however, how are we to understand that Jesus should describe as "blessed" those who are so poor as to have to beg (which is the meaning of *hoi ptochoi*)? What kind of link does Jesus see between the Kingdom of God and the poor?

Latin American theologian Enrique Dussel has claimed that since the Kingdom of God stands in contrast to the prevailing system, and since the poor are not constituent parts of the system, they are the people of God and therefore "the active subjects and carriers of the Kingdom of God". Quoting the Beatitude in Luke 6:20 he writes:

For inasmuch as the poor are not subjects of the system, owners of capital and holders of power, they are both a negative factor (the pure

negativity of the oppressed) and at the same time, positively (the posi-
tivity of the *exteriority*), they are the subject-carriers of the Kingdom
who co-labour to build it. By being oppressed (and by that non-
sinners, thus righteous) and active liberators (as members of the
people), the poor are the subjects of the Kingdom.[5]

If being materially poor is equivalent to being righteous, one
is tempted to ask, Why should anyone fight poverty? Let
poverty abound so that righteousness may also abound!

The poor are blessed, not because they are poor and as such
righteous, but because the Kingdom of God is *already (estin)*
theirs. They are not the subjects of the Kingdom, for God himself is the King; but he has given them a share in his Kingdom
through Jesus Christ. Already the Kingdom of God belongs to
the poor, because Christ is in their midst, as one of them and
bestowing on them the blessings of the Kingdom. The New Age
announced by the prophets has arrived and is being manifest
among the poor. Neither their material condition nor their own
merits, but Jesus' concern for them is the source of their
blessedness.

That particular concern for the poor on Jesus' part is well
supported by the evidence. Right at the beginning of his ministry, in his manifesto on his mission in the synagogue of Nazareth, he read the prophetic pronouncement in Isaiah 61:1-2 and
went on to claim that the fulfilment of it had arrived. The application of that passage to himself makes it obvious that Jesus
understood his mission in terms of the inauguration of a new era
— "the day of the Lord's favour", "the day of vengeance of
our Lord" — marked by the proclamation of good news to the
poor, release for the captives, sight for the blind, and liberty for
the oppressed. Seen in the light of the Old Testament background, Jesus' view of his mission implies that he, as the Messiah, is bringing in "the acceptable year of the Lord", that is,
the year of jubilee and consequently of the structuring of society
according to the demands of justice and love.[6] He is the bearer
of the blessings of the Kingdom and these blessings will be released among people living in a condition of deprivation and
oppression, poverty and exploitation.

This interpretation of Jesus' mission should not be taken to
mean that he was exclusively or even primarily concerned with
material prosperity and physical or economic oppression. What
it does mean is that Jesus understood his mission in terms of the
fulfilment of Old Testament promises with a concrete historical
content, related to the re-establishment of justice in the messi-
anic age, and consequently the poverty and oppression referred

to in the definition of his mission cannot be limited to a spiritual condition with which he is to deal. The blessings of the Kingdom ushered in by Jesus relate to the totality of human existence. Because this is so, when John the Baptist, having heard about the deeds of Christ, sent his disciples to ask him, "Are you he who is to come, or shall we look for another?", he replied, "Go and tell John what you hear and see: the blind receive their sight and the lame walk, lepers are cleansed and the deaf hear, and the dead are raised up, and the poor have good news preached to them" (Mt. 11:1). The listing of the "poor" among the blind, the lame, the lepers, the deaf and the dead makes it clear that this poverty is just as literal as the condition of all the others. And just as for all the others Jesus' ministry means the end of suffering, thus also for the poor his proclamation is good news because it means the end of poverty through the establishment of a new order, characterized by justice and love.

Does that mean that anyone who is literally poor automatically shares in the blessings of the Kingdom by virtue of his poverty? Are the poor "the active subjects and carriers of the Kingdom of God"? The answer is that the good news of the Kingdom should not be objectivized but kept in strict relation to Jesus' call to discipleship. Neither the poor nor the rich have a part in the Kingdom unless, regardless of their deprivation or material possessions, they are "poor in spirit" and as such totally dependent on God's grace.

According to Jesus' answer to John the Baptist, Jesus' concern for the poor, expressed in word and deed, is a sign that he is the Messiah. In order to meet John's doubts regarding his messiahship, Jesus acts on behalf of the poor, the sick, the oppressed. The clear implication is that his mission is related to those people in a very special way. He is not a conquering Messiah who establishes his rule by means of violence. He is, rather, the Messiah-Servant who comes as a poor man among the poor and the needy and announces to them the end of their suffering. According to the expectations expressed in the Magnificat, he comes to put down the mighty from their thrones and to exalt those of low degree; to fill the hungry with good things and to send the rich empty away (Lk. 1:52-53). But he does that in the role of "the servant of Yahweh" who takes the side of the poor for the sake of bringing in the Kingdom.

Is salvation then restricted to the poor? Is there hope for the rich? It is quite clear that no one is saved or condemned because of what he has or does not have in terms of material possessions. Jesus' special concern for the poor does not mean that he does not care for the rich; Jesus came to proclaim good news to the poor, but the rich are not excluded. Jesus' identification with and special concern for the poor does not limit salvation to a social class. The fact remains, however, that the good news is addressed to "the poor", that is, "to those who are literally poor, or who share the outlook of the poor."[7] Consequently, it can be a word of salvation to the rich only when they set aside their riches as a means to find their identity and adopt instead the attitude of the poor.

A more extended discussion of the topic under consideration would have to deal carefully with the meaning of Jesus' solidarity with the poor — the hungry, the thirsty, the stranger, the naked, the sick, and the prisoner — according to Matthew 25:31-46. In all probability this passage should be interpreted in the light of the biblical concept of "corporate personality", taking "the least of these my brethren" to mean Jesus' disciples (cf. Mt. 10:42; Mk. 9:41).[8] Even so, it clearly shows: (1) Jesus' special concern for the poor and needy with whom he identifies himself in such a way that he claims that what is done to them is in fact done to him; (2) the very close connection between salvation and concern for the poor and needy in such a way that the saved ("the righteous", the truly "poor in spirit") are identified with those who feed the hungry, give a drink to the thirsty, welcome the stranger, clothe the naked and visit the sick and the prisoner.

Interpreters may differ as to the way they understand Jesus' solidarity with the poor and the oppressed. But no one can deny without setting aside the evidence, that Jesus conceived his ministry as the ushering in of a new era in which justice would be done to the poor.

3. Poverty and Discipleship

Jesus was poor and he showed special concern for the poor. Does that mean, then, that rich are automatically excluded from the Kingdom of God? Is poverty an unavoidable condition for Christian discipleship?

In Luke 14:33 the renunciation of all possessions appears as a straightforward demand Jesus makes to those who want to follow him: "So, therefore, whoever of you does not renounce all that he has cannot be my disciple." This is the price that one must count as part of the cost of discipleship, together with the bearing of one's cross and the breaking away from one's family (Lk. 14:26-32). Evidently the Twelve accepted that demand in a literal sense, as Peter pointed out when Jesus spoke about the hindrance of riches in relation to entering the Kingdom: "Lo, we have left everything and followed you" (Mk. 10:20; cf. Mk. 1:10ff. and par.; Lk. 5:11, 28). When Jesus sent out his disciples, he sent them out in complete poverty (Lk. 9:3; 10:4; cf. Mk. 6:7ff.). On another occasion he told them to sell their possessions and give alms, thus providing themselves with "purses that do not grow old" (Lk. 12:33). In the same direction goes his demand to the rich young ruler: "You lack one thing; go sell what you have, and give to the poor, and you will have treasure in heaven; and come, follow me" (Mk. 10:21 and par.).

In the light of the foregoing passages, the conclusion can hardly be avoided that Jesus regarded poverty as essential to Christian discipleship. The radicality of his position is summed up in his comment, "How hard it will be for those who have riches to enter the kingdom of God!", followed by the well-known simile of the needle's eye: "It is easier for a camel to go through the eye of a needle than for a rich man to enter the kingdom of God" (Mk. 10:23f.). Quite clearly this saying was toned down in some manuscripts through the addition of words that leave the way open for the rich to enter the Kingdom without necessarily giving up his riches: "how hard it is *for those who trust in riches* to enter the kingdom of God." Such an addition provides a comforting interpretation of Jesus' saying, but it must not be allowed to take away the bite inherent to Jesus' demand concerning earthly possessions. If the disciples were "exceedingly astonished" after Jesus told them how difficult it is for a rich man to enter the Kingdom, it is quite clear that they did not understand him to be saying the obvious, i.e. that trust in riches is incompatible with life in the Kingdom. Their astonishment was rather their response to an affirmation which stood in total opposition to the common belief, that it is relatively easy to combine riches and piety; that as long as one is willing to give alms to the poor, one must not worry about how much one keeps for oneself. In contrast with this opinion, Jesus saw riches as a real obstacle to the germination of God's Word in the human heart (Mt. 13:22), discarded the attempt to serve God and money (Mt. 6:24) and warned against the foolish accumulation of wealth for the sake of securing one's future (Lk. 12:13-20). Therefore it is not surprising that he should regard salvation as practically impossible for the rich.

Jesus' demand to the rich young ruler, to sell everything he had and give it to the poor, applies to one individual the general call addressed to the multitudes, to renounce all in order to fol-

low him. It is at root a call to be like him in his solidarity with
the poor for the sake of the Gospel. It is therefore a call to
servanthood and it can be understood only in the context of discipleship. We should not, however, assume that Jesus' words to
the rich young ruler, "You lack one thing; go, sell what you
have, and give to the poor", have nothing to do with us, nor
that his demand to renounce all things should not be interpreted
in a literal sense but simply as a demand for inward detachment
from earthly possessions. If it is clear that Jesus did at times
demand literal poverty as a condition of discipleship, why
should we take it for granted that in our case his demand to
renounce all possessions should be interpreted figuratively?
True inward detachment from riches can be experienced only by
those who are willing literally to give all they have for the sake
of the Gospel. The renunciation of all we have is genuine to the
extent to which *it can be concretely expressed*, even as it was
expressed in the case of Jesus and his disciples. Such a renunciation is a *sine qua non* of spiritual poverty and it derives its significance from its connection to personal commitment to him
who being rich, for our sake became poor, so that by his
poverty we may become rich.

II. The Primitive Church and the Poor

1. The Constituency of the Primitive Church

A number of pointers given by the New Testament indicate that
the Christian communities which were formed from Pentecost
on were predominantly made up of poor people. Paul's words
addressed to the Corinthian church, for instance, suggest that
only a few members of it may have belonged to the upper
classes: "Consider your call, brethren," he writes, "not many
of you were wise according to worldly standards, not many were
powerful, not many were of noble birth" (1 Cor. 1:26). Some of
the exceptions can be easily detected in Acts and the Pauline
epistles: the "most excellent" Theophilus (Lk. 1:3; Acts 1:1) for
whom Luke writes his two works; the centurion Cornelius (Acts
10:1ff.); Manaen, a member of the court of Herod the tetrarch
(Acts 13:1); Sergius Paulus, proconsul of Cyprus (Acts 13:7);
Dionysius the Areopagite and a woman named Damaris (Acts
17:34); Philemon of Colossae (Philem. 2); Erastus, the city
treasurer (Rom. 16:23) and Crispus, the ruler of the synagogue
in Corinth (Acts 18:8). But it is obvious that the large majority
of Christians came from a humble origin. And this fact was

interpreted by Paul as a way God wanted to use to confound the world, "so that no human being might boast in the presence of God" (1 Cor. 1:27ff.). Jesus Christ is a crucified Messiah; his church is the church of the weak and the poor.

2. Concern for the Poor in the Primitive Church

Jesus' concern for the poor was reproduced in the early church, especially in the context of the Christian community. Obviously, they conceived themselves as the community modelled on the Messiah-Servant.

Luke shows the effect of Jesus' message and lifestyle on the Church in Jerusalem, whose "love communism" (described in Acts 2:40-47; 4:32-37) has attracted the attention of friends and foes down through the centuries. According to Luke's report, "all who believed were together and had all things in common; and they sold their possessions and goods and distributed them to all, as any had need" (2:44, 45); "no one said that any of the things which he possessed was his own but had everything in common" (4:32). How are we to understand this "love communism"?

The common ownership of goods was one of the results of the outpouring of the Holy Spirit on the day of Pentecost. It was not an accomplishment made possible through human engineering but the outflow of spiritual life which welded the believers together in "one heart and soul" (4:32).

The sharing of goods was also practised by the Essenes, but in their case it was strictly enforced by law.[9] By contrast, in the early community it was entirely on a voluntary basis. The sin of Ananias and Sapphira was not that they kept a part of the proceeds of the sale of their land for themselves, but that they brought only a part as if it had been all. Sharing was not compulsory; therefore, as Peter made clear, they did not have to sell their land, and after selling it, they were free to use the money as they wished (5:4). Private property was not totally eliminated (Mary the mother of John Mark, for instance, kept her house as a meeting place, according to 12:12), but it was made subservient to the needs of the whole community.

The basic criterion for the distribution of the goods was that each person receive according to his or her needs (2:45; 4:35), and the immediate result was the elimination of poverty, so that "there was not a needy person among them" (4:34). The age-long ideal that there be no poor among God's people (Deut. 15:4) was thus fulfilled. In the dawn of "the Age of the Spirit" the barriers of possessions had been broken down and the New Society had come into existence. Consequently, "the Lord was adding to their number day by day those who were being saved" (2:47).

Neither Acts of the Apostles nor the New Testament epistles ever refer to the "love communism" of the early Jerusalem church as normative for the church throughout the ages. It is quite clear, however, that the concern for the poor was for the early Christians an essential aspect of the life and mission of the church. When the church in Jerusalem faced economic distress because of the great famine which took place under Claudius in the forties, the church in Antioch sent relief by the hand of Barnabas and Saul (Acts 11:29f.). Later on Paul organized a great collection in the Gentile churches for the purpose of helping "the poor among the saints in Jerusalem" (Rom. 15:26; cf. Gal. 1:10). The careful instructions which the apostle lays down for the collection, especially in 2 Corinthians 8 and 9, show the great significance that he attaches to economic sharing as an expression of Christian unity across racial and national boundaries. He sees material contributions as concrete "fellowship" (*koinonia,* Rom. 15:26) and as a means to respond to the grace of God manifest in Jesus Christ (2 Cor. 8:8f.). Money is thus divested of its demonic power and turned into an instrument of service which supplies the needs of the poor and brings glory to God (2 Cor. 9:11ff.).

Concern for the poor in the primitive church is a normal aspect of Christian discipleship. Translated into action, it makes visible the life of the Kingdom inaugurated by Jesus Christ. Its root is neither in the idealization of poverty nor in the desire to gain merits before God, but in "the grace of our Lord Jesus Christ, that though he was rich, yet for our sake became poor, so that by his poverty you might become rich" (2 Cor. 8:9).

III. Apostolic Teaching Regarding Riches

The same prophetic note present in Jesus' teaching regarding riches as contained in the Gospels can be found also in the apostolic teaching contained in the Epistles. Paul, for instance, includes the greedy among those who will not inherit the Kingdom of God (1 Cor. 6:10; cf. 5:10f.; Rom. 1:29; Eph. 5:5) and describes covetousness as idolatry (Col. 3:5) and the love of money as "the root of all evils" (1 Tim. 6:10). James goes even further and assumes that the wealth of the rich is related to oppression of the poor (Jas. 2:1-7), exploitation of workers and wastefulness (5:1-6). In the same vein the Revelation of John announces the destruction of a civilization dedicated to the consumption of luxuries and indifferent to the Gospel (chapter 18).

All these warnings echo Jesus' injunction on how hard it will be for those who have riches to enter the Kingdom of God. They leave us in no doubt as to the danger facing the rich man of gaining the whole world but forfeiting his life. There is, however, another strand of teaching in the Epistles which allows the possibility of combining riches with Christian discipleship in a lifestyle characterized by inner freedom or detachment with regard to material possessions and by generosity toward the poor.

The most illuminating passage on the question of inner freedom is found in Philippians 4:10-13, in the context of a series of remarks Paul makes concerning the material gift he has received from the church in Philippi. "I have learned," he writes, "in whatever state I am, to be content. I know how to be abased, and I know how to abound; in any and all circumstances I have learned the secret of facing plenty and hunger, abundance and want. I can do all things in him who strengthens me" (4:11f.). The basic attitude described here is one of contentment, inner freedom or detachment (*autarkaia*), which calls for the following comments.

First, it is an ideal held in high regard in Greek popular philosophy in Paul's time[10] and, according to Xenephon, was taught by Socrates, whom he quotes as saying: "My belief is that to have no wants is divine, to have as few as possible comes next to divine."[11] Placed in a Christian context, however, contentment is no more ideal but the faith response to a heavenly Father who knows the needs of his children, as was taught by Jesus Christ (Mt. 6:25-34). True contentment is possible only where both abundance and scarcity can be seen in the light of God's purpose of love. In the final analysis, therefore, anxiety over material things is unbelief, loss of perspective because of the loss of the values derived from the Kingdom.

Second, contentment stands at opposite ends to greed. The latter is unable to recognize limits and boundaries; the former is possible only when the limits and boundaries of the human condition are fully acknowledged. "There is great gain in godliness with contentment; for we brought nothing into the world, and we cannot take anything out of the world" (1 Tim. 6:7). It was this kind of contentment that the rich fool of Jesus' parable lacked. Whenever greed is allowed to take the place of contentment, life itself is under threat of destruction (1 Tim. 6:9). We are exhorted therefore to keep our lives "free from love of money" and to be content with what we have (Heb. 13:5).

Third, contentment is intimately related to sobriety or temperance, one of the marks of the lifestyle for which the grace of God has appeared in Jesus Christ (Titus 1:11) and a fruit of the Spirit (Gal. 5:23). As Paul claims, it is possible through the resurrection power of Christ (Phil. 4:13).

Fourth, contentment is an essential qualification for leadership in the church (1 Tim. 3:2f.; Titus 1:17; 1 P. 5:2).

Generosity toward the poor goes hand in hand with contentment or inner freedom. One can give only to the extent to which one recognizes that all things belong to God and can be possessed only when they are put in relation to the Kingdom of God and his righteousness. In his instructions for rich Christians, therefore, Paul exhorts Timothy to teach them not to be conceited or to fix their hope in the uncertainty of riches, but to show concern for the poor, "to do good, to be rich in good deeds, liberal and generous, thus laying up for themselves a good foundation for the future, so that they may take hold of the life which is life indeed" (1 Tim. 6:17ff.). A clear inference from these injunctions is that rich Christians are to see themselves as no more than stewards of God's gift summoned to live in the light of God's generosity toward all men and his special concern for the poor. The same assumption lies behind John's claim, that the rich man who fails to share with the needy does not know God's love manifest in Jesus Christ (1 Jn. 3:16f.). Solidarity with the poor on the part of the poor is not a mere option but an essential mark of participation in the life of the Kingdom.

Jesus was poor and came to proclaim good news to the poor. His followers are those who in response to his love give up all their possessions and even their lives for the sake of the Kingdom of God. Blessed are the poor and those who share the outlook of the poor, for theirs is the Kingdom of God.

4

Simple Lifestyle and Evangelism

DAVID WATSON

In a moving and disturbing passage from *The New Face of Evangelicalism*[1], Jacob Loewen recounts a discussion between some missionaries and a group of teachers from a tribe in South America. One of the missionaries asked, "What would you consider to be the axle (the centre point of reference) of the missionary's way of life?" Unanimously and unhesitatingly they replied "Money!" Astonished by this, the missionaries asked if they often talked about money. "No," came the reply. "They usually talk about God and religion, but *money is still the most important thing in their way of life.*" They then illustrated this with numerous examples of how, in practice, money was the ultimate yardstick in both the material and spiritual areas of the missionaries' life and culture. If that fact seemed transparently true about Christian workers who had probably accepted a much simpler lifestyle than many others in the church today, how far do our attitudes towards money and possessions seriously hinder and damage the task of world evangelization that has been so solemnly given to us by Jesus Christ?

In studying this subject I want to look first at the qualities that God both looks for and seeks to develop for effective evangelism; and second at the way in which all these qualities may well have to be tested, proved and matured by crucial issues affecting the lifestyle of the evangelist or of those engaged in evangelism. In this discussion I shall deliberately omit the obvious and essential God-given elements in all true evangelism, such as the divine call, the message of the gospel, the convincing power of the Holy Spirit, and the sovereignty of God's working. Instead I shall concentrate on the attitudes and responses on the part of us who are called to be fellow-workers together with Christ.

Qualities required for effective evangelism

Looking at these briefly, the disciples of Jesus were faithful in
their work insofar as at least their lives demonstrated these five
main characteristics.

1. Obedience

From the very beginning Jesus sought to teach his followers the
absolute necessity of total obedience to him as Lord of their
lives. He had come to usher in the kingdom of God, which
involved his reign or rule over every area of their lives, whether
they understood or not, whether they agreed or not. In Luke 5,
when Jesus, the carpenter's son from Nazareth, told Simon, the
experienced Galilean fisherman, to throw his nets into the sea in
broad daylight, we can understand the professional protest:
"Master, we toiled all night and took nothing!" Yet such was the
commanding presence of Jesus in his boat that Simon went on,
"But at your word I will let down the nets." The catch was staggering. Here was the first and foremost lesson for Simon to
learn if he were later to be "catching men": one minute's obedience to Christ is worth infinitely more than striving, even to the
point of exhaustion, in the wisdom and energy of the flesh.

Throughout the short period of discipleship training by the
Master this lesson had to be taught again and again, but we can
see later how effective it became in terms of direct evangelism.
In Acts 4, when Peter and John were "charged not to speak or
teach at all in the name of Jesus", they replied, "Whether it is
right in the sight of God to listen to you rather than to God, you
must judge; for we cannot but speak of what we have seen and
heard." Later they prayed again for boldness to speak the word
of God. And in Acts 5, after further serious threats, Peter and
the apostles answered, "We must obey God rather than men.
The God of our fathers raised Jesus whom you killed by hang-
ing him on a tree . . ." It is no wonder that their opponents
"were enraged and wanted to kill them"; and it is no wonder
that the word of God spread like wildfire through the ancient
world. Those first Christians learnt obedience, whatever the
cost in terms of personal sacrifice. For many it meant literally
laying down their lives for the gospel of Christ.

J. B. Phillips once made this comment: "Perhaps because of
their very simplicity, perhaps because of their readiness to
believe, to obey, to give, to suffer, and if need be to die, the
Spirit of God found what he must always be seeking — a fellowship of men and women so united in love and faith that he can

work in them and through them with the minimum of let or hindrance."[2]

2. Faith

This too is crucial if we are to see the power of God at work. It is "he who believes in me" who "will also do the works that I do," Jesus promised his disciples during his last discourse with them (John 14:12). "Whatever you ask in my name I will do it, that the Father may be glorified in the Son." Those upon whom the Spirit fell at Pentecost and on other occasions were sometimes described as "full of faith and of the Holy Spirit"; and it was "by faith in his name" that God was able to work with unusual power amongst them. We see Philip, later termed the evangelist, acting by faith in the unusual promptings of the Spirit of God in Acts 8, which brought new life to the Samaritans and then to the Ethiopian eunuch. See the faith of Ananias as he went nervously to the feared Saul of Tarsus, arch-enemy of the Christian Church; note the faith of Simon Peter (even if a protesting faith) as he crossed the great divide into the house of Cornelius. The whole story of the early church is one continuous demonstration of active faith in the risen Christ. Their evangelistic enterprise makes a magnificent "Volume two" to the epic stories of the great heroes of faith recorded in Hebrews 11.

3. Integrity

Because of the constant danger of false prophets, whose work was (and is today) marked by deceit and corruption, Paul and the other leaders repeatedly stressed their own complete integrity in all their evangelistic, teaching and pastoral work: "We are not, like so many, peddlers of God's word; but as men of sincerity, as commissioned by God, in the sight of God we speak in Christ . . . We have renounced disgraceful, underhanded ways; we refuse to practise cunning or to tamper with God's word, but by the open statement of the truth we would commend ourselves to every man's conscience in the sight of God . . . We put no obstacle in any one's way, so that no fault may be found with our ministry, but as servants of God we commend ourselves in every way . . . Open your hearts to us: we have wronged no one, we have corrupted no one, we have taken advantage of no one . . ."[3] Without any hint of false humility or arrogant pride, Paul could say, in his open, disarming fashion, "You yourselves know how I lived among you all the time from the first day that I set foot in Asia, serving the Lord with all humility . . . You know what kind of men we proved to be among you for your sake . . . You remember our labour and toil, brethren."[4] So we could multiply examples. The integrity of the messenger is vital for the authority and converting power of the message.

4. Identification

Just as the characteristics of obedience, faith and integrity were, of course, perfectly exemplified in the life and ministry of Jesus, so the model of identification is found in its most sublime form in his incarnation. Here the word of God became a human being and dwelt among us. In Martin Luther's words about Jesus: "He ate, drank, slept, waked; was weary, sorrowful, rejoicing; he wept and he laughed; he knew hunger and thirst and sweat; he talked, he toiled, he prayed . . . so that there was no difference between him and other men, save only this that he was God and had no sin." Although in some circles theological debate continues over the divinity of Jesus, many non-academic and traditional Christians have more difficulty coming to terms with the genuine humanity of Jesus. It is possibly because we tend to think of him as being intrinsically different and separate from ordinary men that the church, as a whole, has often kept to its own religious ghetto and thus failed to be God's agent in the healing of the whole of God's creation. We have wrongly divided the sacred and the secular. In trying to keep ourselves "unstained from the world", we have sometimes kept ourselves from the world altogether. How, then, can we begin to carry out our God-given ministry of reconciliation? Paul rejected such religious detachment. "I have made myself a slave to all, that I might win the more . . . I have become all things to all men, that I might by all means save some. I do it all for the sake of the gospel, that I may share in its blessings."[5] Here is this vital incarnational principle applied in the realm of effective and compassionate evangelism.

5. Love

This is the supreme quality of all, without which all our eloquent preaching would be as a noisy gong or a clanging cymbal. It was, above all, the love of Christ that controlled and compelled that persecuted early church. "So being affectionately desirous of you, we were ready to share with you not only the gospel of God but also our own selves, because you had become very dear to us." It was their infectious love that drew people to them, and to the Lord, like a magnet: the poor and the outcast, the sick and the lame, Jew and Gentile, slave and free, male and female, even a few who were rich and influential — they all came, apart from those whose hearts were inflamed with jealousy or hardened towards God. Insofar as those Christians loved one another, others could see both that they were manifestly the disciples of Jesus and that God was evidently abiding in their midst. That is why John pressed on Christians God's new commandment, to love one another: "As we obey this commandment, to love one another, the darkness in our lives disappears and the new light of life in Christ shines in" (1 John 2:8, Living Bible). Love is always the greatest thing in the world, and it never fails to be the most powerful factor in evangelism.

There are no doubt other qualities that could be listed as desirable if God's people are seriously seeking to make disciples of all nations. But certainly these five hold a place of particular importance: obedience, faith, integrity, identification and, most of all, love.

Qualities tested by simple lifestyle

From this it is fascinating to note that in the training of his own disciples Jesus tested and developed these particular qualities — which were so crucial to the entire growth of the Christian church — by searching and repeated challenges to the whole issue of lifestyle. For Jesus, proclamation and demonstration went hand-in-hand. If his disciples were to proclaim the kingdom of God, they must at the same time demonstrate its reality.

Unless obedience could be seen to be obedience, often in costly and sacrificial terms, the possibilities for self-deception were always present. "Why do you call me 'Lord, Lord', and not do what I tell you?" Jesus once challenged them — a question set, incidentally, in a passage which contains many hard sayings about simplicity of life (Luke 6:20-49).

Unless faith could be proved to be genuine faith, "believing in God" could be little more than a pious sentiment; and time and again Jesus had gently to rebuke his "believing" disciples for their lack of faith — "O you of little faith! Why did you doubt? Have you no faith?" Moreover, their lack of true faith was sometimes revealed when faced with material issues.

Unless love could be demonstrated in down-to-earth sharing, giving and serving, it might be little more than religious and subjective feelings. To make three booths on the mount of transfiguration was not the prime expression of love that Jesus was looking for. What about helping the demon-possessed boy in the valley? Who would wash the feet of the disciples at the Last Supper?

Today there is no shortage of pious words, affirmations of faith, discussions about hunger, or expressions of spirituality. But the world is still waiting for the demonstration, in hard, costly and practical terms, of what we proclaim with our lips. "I was hungry, and you formed a committee to investigate my hunger . . . I was homeless, and you filed a report on my plight . . . I was sick, and you held a seminar on the situation of the underprivileged . . . You have investigated all aspects of my plight. And yet I am still hungry, homeless and sick."

"The life of Jesus and his disciples," writes John Taylor, "was not only eucharistic but also defiant. He knew it was not enough to say these things; the world is waiting for concrete examples and realizations. So in our day it is not enough to point out the contrast between our idolatry of growth and the Bible's theology of enough; we have to opt out of the drift and help one another to live in cheerful protest against it . . ."[6]

The Hindu poet Rabindranath Tagore once said to a Christian leader in India: "On that day when we see Jesus Christ living out his life in you, on that day we Hindus will flock to your Christ, even as doves flock to their feeding ground." Given the poetic licence behind those words, it was precisely for the truth of this general principle that Jesus spent so much time teaching and challenging his disciples on the whole issue of money, possessions and lifestyle. Unless there was some tangible evidence of their obedience, faith and love he knew that he would be building his church as a castle in the air instead of that rock-like reality, against which neither the gates of hell nor any other gates could prevail. How, then, were these vital qualities for effective evangelism proved and developed?

1. Obedience

An effective army will be marked by instant obedience to the word of command, apart from any other fighting qualities. Without such obedience its fighting capacity is considerably diminished. To obtain this obedience many hours of training on seemingly minor issues are necessary.

In order to train his disciples for the greatest spiritual revolution the world has ever known, Jesus likewise tested them over what might have seemed a minor and material issue of possessions.

In Matthew 6:19-24 Jesus puts the issue in a series of sharp contrasts. We must make our choice between two treasures (earthly or heavenly), two conditions (light or darkness), and two masters (God and Mammon). Here there is a clear either-or; we cannot aim at, or serve, both. In other words, we have to face up to the searching question, Who or what comes first in our life? And nowhere is this question more clearly answered than in our whole attitude to possessions.

To maintain a biblical balance, Jesus is not forbidding the ownership of private property. Even when the sharing amongst Christians was at its best and most generous, Peter said to Ananias about the sale of his land, "While it remained unsold, did it not remain your own? And after it was sold, was it not at your disposal?" Several of the disciples had possessions of their own, as is implied by the statement that they went on continuously (Greek imperfect tense) selling what they had to provide for those that had not. Further, Jesus is not against some wise provision for the future. As Paul later wrote: "If any one does not provide for his relatives, and especially for his own family, he has disowned the faith and is worse than an unbeliever" (1 Timothy 5:8). Nor certainly is Jesus encouraging us to ignore or despise the numerous good gifts of God's creation. Matter is not intrinsically evil, as the gnostics wrongly taught. Such teaching is the "doctrine of demons", "for everything created by God is good, and nothing is to be rejected if it is received with thanksgiving" (1 Timothy 4:1-5). Paul knew "how to be abased, and how to abound", and he found the Lord's peace in facing either plenty or hunger, either abundance or want (Philippians 4:12).

What Jesus spoke strongly against was hoarding up treasures *"for yourselves"*. This is not only foolish, for all these earthly treasures will sooner or later decay or disappear; it is selfish in the light of the vast needs of men, women and children throughout the world — a straight denial of the love of God; and, worst of all, it is idolatrous, "for where your treasure is there will your heart be also."

"Worldly possessions tend to turn the hearts of the disciples away from Jesus. What are we really devoted to? That is the question. Are our hearts set on earthly goods? Do we try to combine devotion to them with loyalty to Christ? Or are we devoted exclusively to him? . . . Where our treasure is, there is our trust, our security, our consolation and our God. Hoarding is idolatry . . . Everything which hinders us from loving God above all things . . . is our treasure, and the place where our heart is . . . If our hearts are entirely given to God, it is clear that we *cannot* serve two masters; it is simply impossible . . . Our hearts have room only for one all-embracing devotion, and we can only cleave to one Lord . . ."[7]

"The eye is the lamp of the body" said Jesus. In other words, without the clear vision of the eye my whole body has to walk and move in darkness. It cannot see what it is doing or where it is going. It is only as my "eye" (a biblical synonym for "heart") is set wholly on the light of Christ that my whole life can have clear direction. But if my eye or heart serves another master — for it cannot serve two — then my whole life is left in deep darkness. "The love of money is the root of all evils"; every day reveals the inescapable and ugly truth of that statement.

In calling or selecting his disciples, Jesus allowed therefore no compromise at all. Even with the lovable, talented, promising, seeking rich young ruler, Jesus still told him to "sell all that you have and distribute to the poor, and you will have treasure in heaven". The man went away sad. But Jesus could strike no bargain, for no man can serve two masters.

However, in this well-known incident there are various details that are instructive. First, in a passage cited by Ronald Sider, "When Jesus asked the rich young man to sell his goods and give to the poor, he did not say 'Become destitute and friendless.' Rather he said, 'Come follow me.' In other words, he invited him to join a community of sharing and love, where his security would not be based on individual property holdings, but on openness to the Spirit and on the loving care of new-found brothers and sisters."[8] Second, what Jesus looks for first and foremost is not poverty but obedience. Obedience could lead to poverty, if that is what Jesus requires of us; but choosing poverty in itself could be choosing my own way of life, or some religious ideal, which is not the command of Jesus. Third, having made that point and being aware of the dangers of legalism over this matter of lifestyle, Sider is quite right when he states that "what 99 per cent of all Western Christians need to hear 99 per cent of the time is: 'Give to everyone who begs from you,' and 'Sell your possessions.' " Fourth, we must never minimize the seductive danger of riches (1 Timothy 6:9-10; James 4:1-2; etc.). Covetousness is perhaps the most serious sin in the West (or North) today, and no covetous person will inherit the kingdom of God. The strictures against all forms of covetousness in the scriptures are powerful. Always we come back to this basic issue: Who or what comes first in our life? Only when the Lordship of Christ is clearly recognized — and our attitude to possessions will test this as nothing else — can we truly be his disciples and of any use in evangelism.

2. Faith

Faith in the living God is essential if we are to see the power of his Spirit working through us to glorify Christ and to draw people to him. Once again this quality has to be tested carefully amongst all professing disciples.

When Jesus tells us in Matthew 6:25-34, "Do not be anxious," he is asking us another crucial and penetrating question: Whom or what do you really trust? What is the clear object of your faith? Again the logic is compelling, for we have to face up to this alternative: *either* we are trusting our heavenly Father — for everything — *or* we are ultimately trusting in some form of worldly security.

Dietrich Bonhoeffer puts it arrestingly in this way:

Be not anxious! Earthly possessions dazzle our eyes and delude us into thinking that they can provide security and freedom from anxiety. Yet all the time they are the very source of all anxiety. If our hearts are set on them, our reward is an anxiety whose burden is intolerable. Anxiety creates its own treasures and they in turn beget further care. When we seek for security in possessions we are trying to drive out care with care, and the net result is the precise opposite of our anticipations. The fetters which bind us to our possessions prove to be cares themselves.

The way to misuse our possessions is to use them as an insurance against the morrow. Anxiety is always directed to the morrow, whereas goods are in the strictest sense meant to be used only for today. By trying to insure for the next day we are only creating uncertainty today. Sufficient unto the day is the evil thereof . . . It is not care that frees the disciples from care, but their faith in Jesus Christ.[9]

All this may sound a little pious, naive and irresponsible, until we realize that Jesus is calling us out of the kingdom of this world, with all its cares and anxieties that choke the word of God, into the kingdom of God — a kingdom that is demonstrated by the loving care and generous sharing of the people of God. In this new, alternative, prophetic society, we are to develop "unconditional availability to and unlimited liability for the other sisters and brothers — emotionally, financially, and spiritually", to quote a favourite statement of Sider's. It is especially in this quality of our shared life together that we experience the reality of God's love, and this in turn casts out our fear and enables us to develop true faith in him.

Certainly this was the lifestyle that Jesus adopted for himself, and instructed his disciples to do the same. Indeed, it could almost be said that the power and effectiveness of their ministry depended on their willingness to trust God for everything. Remember his commission to the twelve: "Preach as you go, saying, 'The kingdom of heaven is at hand.' Heal the sick, raise the dead, cleanse lepers, cast out demons. You received without paying, give without pay. Take no gold, nor silver, nor copper in your belts, no bag for your journey, nor two tunics, nor sandals, not a staff . . ." (Matthew 10:7-10). Most of us will readily understand that their faith was at times unable to rise to such levels. How could the 5,000 be fed? What about the time when they were hungry themselves? Jesus simply and gently rebuked them, "O men of little faith!" However much we might sympathize with them, it was their little faith over these material matters that meant little faith in spiritual ministry. When the disciples a little later asked why they could not cast out a demon from a boy, Jesus replied, "Because of your little faith." That is why he constantly tested and stretched their faith over the ordinary, everyday matters of lifestyle; only as their faith developed here would they be able to believe for the much more vital work of the kingdom of God.

Exactly the same testing was given when the seventy were sent out: "Carry no purse, no bag, no sandals . . . Whenever you enter a town and they receive you, eat what is set before you; heal the sick in it and say to them, 'The kingdom of God has come near to you' . . ." Off they went, inexperienced, untaught, but with simple faith; and "they returned with joy, saying, 'Lord, even the demons are subject to us in your name!' " And Jesus too rejoiced, "I thank thee, Father . . . that thou hast hidden these things from the wise and understanding and revealed them to babes" — that is, to those who exercized an unwavering faith in the reality and faithfulness of their heavenly Father (Luke 10:1-21).

Most of us would like to arrive at a happy compromise. Of course we want to seek first the kingdom of God; but earthly treasures continue to attract, tug away at the heart, cause anxiety, and lessen our faith. We may not want to be extravagantly wealthy providing we have clear financial security. However, in wanting the best of both worlds we lose the transforming power of the kingdom of God. Again we must stress that Jesus is not forbidding personal property; but when we in any way start 'craving' for these things we may well wander away from the faith and pierce our hearts with many pangs (1 Timothy 6:10).

"It is want of faith that makes us opt for earthly rather than heavenly treasure. If we really believed in celestial treasure, who among us would be so stupid as to buy gold? We just do not believe. Heaven is a dream, a religious fantasy which we affirm because we are orthodox. If people believed in heaven, they would spend their time preparing for permanent residence there. But nobody does. We just like the assurance that something nice awaits us *when the real life is over*."[10]

This is important. We may glory in the fact that a man is justified by faith. But how real is that faith before we can know that we are justified? John White puts it in this way: "We must be suspicious of any faith about personal justification that is not substantiated by faith in God's power over material things in our everyday life. Faith about pie in the sky when I die cannot be demonstrated. Faith that God can supply my need today *can* be demonstrated."[11]

That is precisely the challenge to the rich young ruler. Having told him to sell what he had and to give to the poor, Jesus promised him that he would have "treasure in heaven". "Come," said Jesus, "follow me." But at that critical point, the young man, with all his good living and religious enthusiasm, did not have true faith in Jesus. He did not believe him: or, if he did, he would not obey him. Jesus admitted to his startled disciples that it is not easy for a rich man to enter the kingdom of heaven. But he gave his promise to those who felt that they had now left everything for his sake: "Every one who has left houses or brothers or sisters or father or mother or children or lands, for my name's sake, will receive a hundredfold, and inherit eternal life."

In some measure the disciples experienced immediately the greater riches that God has in store for us when we put our whole life into his hands. They discovered a depth of relationships in their apostolic band that they had never known before. They shared a common life. They lived together, worked together, prayed together, learnt together. They had given up everything and, as a result, had gained so much more.

So the question is, when it comes to the financial crunch, who or what do we really believe? Do we have faith — true faith — in Jesus? It is by faith that we are justified, and it is by faith that we shall see the power of God in our ministry. It is God's rebuke to us affluent Christians, as we hedge ourselves around with earthly treasures and securities, that God's power is today much more obviously demonstrated amongst those who have little or nothing of this world's goods. But they are rich in faith.

3. *Integrity*

We have already seen that the personal integrity of the messenger is crucial to the authority of his message. Jesus could throw out the challenge to his critics: "Which of you convicts me of sin?" (John 8:46). Although Jesus came from a reasonably secure family business, his family was far from wealthy, and he willingly became poor for us that we through his poverty might become rich. Possibly because of the deceitfulness of riches, Jesus saw that a marked simplicity of lifestyle was a vital part of the credibility of his whole ministry. That is why he insisted that his disciples should live the same way. They shared a common purse; they gave regularly to the poor (as is suggested by John 13:29, et. al.). They denied themselves some of the material possessions and comforts that most of them had been used to. And they taught others to live in the same way: "If we have food and clothing, with these we shall be content. But those who desire to be rich fall into temptation, into a snare, into many senseless and hurtful desires that plunge men into ruin and destruction . . ." (1 Timothy 6:8-9); "Keep your life free from the love of money, and be content with what you have" (Hebrews 13:5).

It was one of the marks of the false prophet that his heart was "trained in greed" (2 Peter 2:14); he would flatter people "to gain advantage" (Jude 16). It was for this reason that any prospective leader in the church must be "no lover of money" (1 Timothy 3:3) and "not greedy for gain" (1 Timothy 3:8; Titus 1:7).

"The poverty of Christ's messengers is the proof of their freedom . . . As they go forth to be the plenipotentiaries of his word, Jesus enjoins strict poverty upon them . . . They are not to go about like beggars and call attention to themselves, nor are they to burden other people like parasites. They are to go forth in the battle-dress of poverty, taking as little with them as a traveller who knows he will get board and lodging with friends at the end of the day. This shall be an expression of their faith, not in men, but in their heavenly father who sent them and will care for them. *It is this that will make their gospel credible.*"[12] (Italics mine.)

Today, some literature from quite a well-known evangelist came in my mail. After an impassioned statement about the needs of "this hour", there was a strong appeal to me to "yield yourself to the Holy Spirit and ask for His guidance in your special thanksgiving gift — for his goodness to you!" And, in case

I had missed the point, there was a postage-paid envelope for my "reply", together with a slip for me to complete, entitled "MY GIFT TO REVERSE THE TREND!" I was encouraged to sign this slip, which says, "Dear Brother (name of evangelist), I am thankful to God for His goodness, His love in choosing me, in challenging me to rise up and become one of His Partners in prophecy for the Healing of the Nations . . . I have felt led of the Holy Spirit to send £____ as my November gift to overtake the Heathen . . ." At the end of the form I was reminded that "this is God's Hour!" No doubt many gullible Christians will respond financially to the challenge. No doubt this evangelist will continue to enjoy "success". Since he seems to preach Christ, it may be that God will bless his efforts in one way or another. But the whole approach tragically lacks the credibility of the Master.

When I am interviewed by secular journalists or broadcasters concerning my work as an evangelist, one inevitable, cynical question is, "What do you get out of it?" They are asking not about job-satisfaction, but about financial reward. To be able to speak truthfully in answer to this question is a vital part of my integrity when it comes to anything else I may want to say. In an age when covetousness is the most common and gross sin, at least in affluent societies, it is more important than ever that the church should guard itself against the strong and subtle pressures of this temptation.

The temptations are possibly greater for those with an independent ministry that is not firmly rooted in the discipline of a local church. Certainly within a local congregation, explicit biblical teaching must be given regularly about the Christian responsibility to give generously to the Lord and to his work. However, the aim of this teaching is both that God may be glorified through the joyful offering of our possessions, and that Christians may be blessed through such giving. With fund-raising techniques, on the other hand, the main aim is obviously the raising of funds. Thus instead of being primarily concerned with the worship of God and the freedom of God's people, the focus shifts onto the economic survival of some religious project. It is at this point that the integrity of the whole project, and of those involved with it, must come under question.

4. Identification

It is sometimes said today that the battle of the '80s will be between Marxism, Islam and Third World Christianity — because

Western Christianity is spiritually too flabby to offer any real help. Certainly the most vibrant and evangelistically effective Christians are on the whole to be found in the poorest areas of the world today. Is it because, in their material poverty, they have become spiritually rich, whereas those who are materially affluent have become spiritually poor?

Throughout the scriptures God is clearly seen to be on the side of the poor. Although he is no respecter of persons, and is rich to all who call upon him, he is a God of justice. Therefore, since by affluence, greed or neglect, the rich oppress the poor and inevitably add to their weight of suffering, God must be on the side of the poor. Moreover, he identifies with the poor. When we are kind to the poor, we lend to the Lord (Proverbs 19:17). When we offer practical help to those who are hungry, thirsty, lonely, naked, sick or in prison, we are doing it as to Jesus (Matthew 25:34-40). The reason why Jesus was loved and welcomed by ordinary and often poor people was partly because he consciously identified himself with them. He had come "to preach good news to the poor", and he could do so because he had "nowhere to lay his head". On the cross he was literally stripped of everything. No one could be more destitute than a naked man fastened to a cross. Yet the apostle Paul repeatedly refers to "the power of the cross" — materially nothing, spiritually everything.

The early church continued the same pattern. Peter and John had neither silver nor gold to offer to the crippled beggar at the Gate Beautiful, but they did have the power of the Spirit of Christ: "In the name of Jesus Christ of Nazareth, walk." When we see also, in this young church, the extraordinary quality of their sharing and the generosity of their giving, it is not surprising that God was able to work through them with "many wonders and signs". It was because God found them faithful in handling the lesser material riches, that he was able to trust them with his much greater spiritual riches. Their willingness to live by the principle of "enough", so that any abundance might be given to every good work, was plain proof of the grace of God amongst them; and that grace clearly mainfested itself in many different ways. It is small wonder that the word of God increased so rapidly, not least amongst the poor and needy of that day.

The church of the West today, however, appeals largely to the affluent middle-class. Is this because we have frequently erected cultural barriers which make it very difficult for many to hear "good news to the poor"? Our church buildings, our vicarages or manses, our styles of dress, language and music — all these can become highly selective factors, determining what sections of the community we are likely to reach for Jesus Christ. It is not that we should aim for damp and depressing buildings instead (some of us have these anyway!); but as soon as we become materially ambitious for our buildings we stand in great danger of shutting the door of the gospel on those who need the Saviour so much. It is sobering to remember that the fastest period of growth in the entire history of the church was almost certainly during the first three centuries when there were no church buildings or material assets at all.

Howard Snyder has rightly commented, "Normal church growth is not really limited by lack of financial resources or physical facilities. We do not find Paul complaining that more could be accomplished if only more funds were available. Nor is there any evidence that the early church was hindered in its growth by its lack of church buildings. If anything, the opposite is true. Heavy financial investment in buildings, property and programmes intended to facilitate church growth often becomes instead a limiting factor. Emphasis is shifted to these things and the vision for ministering the gospel simply and directly to persons is dimmed or lost altogether."[13] If an important mark of the kingdom is that "the poor have the good news preached to them" (Luke 7:22), the kingdom of God will come in power when as a church we identify ourselves with those who are needy and give ourselves unstintingly in service to them.

Chaeok Chun, a Korean missionary in Pakistan, made this comment: "I think it is significant that today's image of the Christian missionary endeavour from the Asian receptor's point of view is an image of comfort and privilege. Hence, Asians tended to reject the missionary and misunderstand his message."[14] We still have much to learn from the incarnation of the Lord of glory.

5. Love

This is the primary and outstanding quality in all true evangelism. Christian love *(agape)*, however, is always marked by sacrificial giving: "God so loved the world that he gave his only Son." There was nothing sentimental about this greatest expression of love of all time. In the same way the evidence and demonstration of love must be much more than the eloquent words of an evangelist. No one can read the first few chapters of Acts without noticing that the amazing sharing of their lives and possessions so demonstrated the love of God amongst them that others were drawn to Jesus Christ almost irresistably.

"All who believed were together, and had all things in common; and they sold their possessions and goods and distributed them to all, as any had need . . . And the Lord added to their number day by day those who were being saved" (Acts 2:44-45, 47).

"Now the company of those who believed were of one heart and soul, and no one said that any of the things which he possessed was his own, but they had everything in common. And with great power the apostles gave their testimony to the resurrection of the Lord Jesus, and great grace was upon them all. There was not a needy person among them, for as many as were possessors of lands or houses sold them, and brought the proceeds of what was sold and laid it at the apostles' feet, and distribution was made to each as any had need" (Acts 4:32-35). It is interesting that the remark about powerful evangelism is sandwiched between the comments about their shared life. In other words, it was precisely in the context of this loving, sacrificial care of one another that the good news of Jesus Christ made such an impact.

In Acts 6 we see the same pattern repeated again. The needs of some Greek widows were not being met. When, however, the apostles took active steps to attend to their material needs by setting aside seven men "full of faith and of the Holy Spirit", we read that "the word of God increased; and the number of disciples multiplied greatly in Jerusalem . . ."

There was no compulsion to sell property or to give money. Nor was there any pressure brought to give up the right to private ownership. It is clear that many Christians kept at least some of their possessions and lands, even though a number of them went on selling what they had as the needs continued. But such was the love of God amongst this new community in Christ that they longed to express this love towards their brothers and sisters according to the obvious needs that arose. "If any one has the world's goods and sees his brother in need, yet closes his heart against him, how does God's love abide in him?" (1 John 3:17). Even when there was a prophecy of famine, the newly formed Gentile church at Antioch responded at once in love towards their Jewish brethren in Judea by sending such money as they could, "every one according to his ability" (Acts 11:27-30).

Paul saw that this loving care for the poor was an essential part of his evangelistic work. When stating that the church leaders in Jerusalem had backed his mission to the Gentiles, he mentioned this one stipulation that they had imposed — "only they would have us remember the poor, which very thing I was eager to do" (Galatians 2:10).

I was asked by a leading Anglican bishop recently if I thought it right to try to reproduce a New Testament church in this highly complex, technological twentieth century. My reply was that I believed the New Testament principles to be timeless, but that the outworkings of them must always be contemporary if relevant to this particular generation. We are not to follow the exact pattern of the early church slavishly. At the same time, when the evangelistic impact of the Western churches is mostly very weak, when the needs of this present day are increasing all the time, and when the crisis of the church today is primarily in its lack of spiritual power and life and love, it is imperative that we examine closely those basic principles that both made the church so effective 2000 years ago and that make the church so effective in some areas today, especially in the Third World.

Undoubtedly one great area concerns the person and work of the Holy Spirit. We desperately need individual Christians and churches continuously filled with the Spirit. Nothing can be a substitute for that. But if the life and love of Jesus are to be clearly manifest — and without this all our gospel words will be empty words — the church must learn again what it means to be the body of Christ on earth. It needs to demonstrate God's new society, marked by love and seen in the costly, practical sharing of lives and possessions together. Money talks — not least in this covetous generation. When others see that our faith really means something, in practical and material ways, then the good news of Jesus Christ will be very much more than religious talk.

James Baxter once wrote: "The first Christians did not start to share their goods in a free and full manner till after the bomb of the Spirit exploded in their souls at Pentecost. Before then, they would be morally incapable of this free and joyful sharing. The acquisitive habit is one of the deepest rooted habits of the human race. To say, 'This is yours, not mine,' and to carry the words into effect, is as much a miracle of God as raising of the dead."[15] It is by such miracles of God's grace that others may catch a glimpse of the realities that we proclaim so loudly with our lips. But without such tangible evidence of the love of God amongst us, we shall have to accept E. M. Forster's rebuke when he referred to "poor, talkative, little Christianity".

"Little children, let us not love in word or speech but in deed and in truth."

5

The International Socio-Economic-Political Order and our Lifestyle

DONALD HAY

The facts of international inequality in living standards are not in serious doubt. We may discuss whether this measure or that measure is most appropriate. But the conclusion is inescapable: the inhabitants of the developed countries (DCs) consume a great deal, while most inhabitants of less developed countries (LDCs) consume very little, even if they are not actually dying of hunger. Most Christian audiences will accept that. Many Christians will also feel mildly guilty about it. But their level of understanding has progressed very little. What, they will ask, is the connection between wealth and prosperity in the DCs and poverty in the LDCs? Sheer geographical distance alone gives the impression that they are not connected. How then, can consumption in the DCs be a cause of the poverty in the LDCs? If, for example, many Christians were to adopt the kind of lifestyle advocated in *Rich Christians in an Age of Hunger* how would that help the starving in the Sahel or Bangladesh? Even more puzzling, especially to those without training in economics, is the charge that international disparities are the consequence of "economic structures" which systematically favour the rich in the DCs. What are these structures? Are the charges levelled against the system true? And, if they are, what can we do about it?

   The purpose of this paper is to try to advance our understanding of these issues a little. The style will be analytic rather than descriptive, though we will base our discussion in the context of the current situation. But the international economic system exhibits a chameleon-like quality, with the problems changing from year to year. In 1973-4 there was a "food crisis". At the time of writing there is an "energy crisis", consequent upon the OPEC decision to restrict oil supplies to the West. In five years time the "crisis" will be quite different, and any description will be out of date. Analysis is more flexible. We can go on applying it as the situation changes. It equips us to win the war, not just local skirmishes. The plan of the paper is as follows. In the first section we set out Christian criteria for economic life. These form the basis for our critique of existing economic relations. They also provide criteria for Christian prescription and action. The second section reviews the current world development situation. Section three is an extended fable, intended to ease the reader into the following three sections on trade, trade barriers and the multinational corporation (MNC). Section seven looks at the Third World's demands for a New International Economic Order. A final section is devoted to the question "Who is responsible for promoting a more just international economic order?"

1. Christian Criteria for Economic Life

(a) The Derivation of Biblical Criteria

Christian criteria are important, not only because they form the basis of criticism and action, but also because they direct our attention to the fundamental questions that need to be asked about the world economic system. As we show below, the Bible does have much to say about work, production and consumption. However, some may object that this teaching applies particularly to the covenant people of God (the Children of Israel in the Old Testament, and the Church in the New Testament) and is not intended to be extensible to mankind in general. This raises major theological issues which lie beyond the scope of this paper. But we may sketch our own response to this argument.

Our method is that adopted by Jesus in his teaching about marriage and divorce in Matthew 19:3-9. Jesus affirms the creation principles (4, 5) with direct quotations from Genesis 1 and 2. A lifelong union between man and wife is God's plan for mankind. This brings the retort that Moses had permitted divorce. How could this be? Jesus replies that divorce is permitted because of their "hardness of heart". The basic difficulty is apparent. God has a creation plan for mankind, but because of the Fall, that plan is not capable of fulfilment. Eden cannot be recreated. We must look for a second best in a sinful world, but at the same time we must continue to affirm God's "first" best.

That the same method is to be adopted in broader economic and political issues is strongly supported by two considerations.

First, the prophets addressed the judgement of God not only to Israel and Judah, but also to the heathen nations around about (Amos is the clearest, but by no means the only example). Their message must imply that there are general social ethical standards that even heathen rulers and nations must strive to attain. Second, the teaching of the New Testament ("render unto Caesar . . .", Romans 13 and so on) suggests that rulers have a specific role, under God, to fulfil in their societies. That role includes the pursuit of peace and justice among their people.

Our starting point for identifying God's creation plan for mankind is Genesis 1 and 2. However, there is no reason to stop there. We must have regard for the whole of biblical teaching in this area. The commandments given to God's covenant people are to be seen as models or examples of how men should live, not only in right relationship with God, but also in relationship with their fellow men. Thus the Old Testament Law, Jesus' teaching about the Kingdom of God and the apostolic teaching about the Body of Christ must all have a place in our consideration of God's ideal for man. This is not to deny the fact of the Fall, nor its consequences, for man in society. However, it is noticeable that some of the key creation promises were reaffirmed *after the Fall* in the covenant with Noah (Genesis 8:22ff). Further the image of God was marred, not destroyed, by the Fall. It is too easy to be so pessimistic about sinful man that one acquiesces in evil. That particularly seems to be the attitude of many Christian people when presented with problems as complex as those described in this paper. One should certainly not cherish utopian hopes about putting the world to rights, but that is no reason for tolerating the evil consequences of sin.

Those who reject this line of argument should think carefully about the consequences of that rejection. If the biblical teaching applies only to the covenant people of God, then they must be careful to avoid any advocacy of Christian criteria in other areas of social life. Their position logically entails that they have nothing to say to their society on such vexed matters as laws concerning abortion, divorce, euthanasia and homosexuality. Yet evangelical leaders have in the past shown a marked lack of reticence in speaking out on these issues.

It is convenient to discuss our criteria under four headings: creation and stewardship, man and work, stewardship and work and the distribution of real consumption.[1]

(b) Creation and Stewardship

The creation story in Genesis emphasizes God's sovereign work in creating the earth within the universe and then filling it with life. It is within this abundant environment that man is placed. He is the image or likeness of God, placed there to show God's sovereign possession, but as a vice-regent with full powers to use and dispose of the resources at hand. Man is given dominion over nature to care for it, and to provide for his existence. After the flood, God promises that the natural cycle of day and night, seedtime and harvest will be maintained (Genesis 8:22). Noah is enjoined to replenish and subdue the earth. The doctrine of God's provision re-appears in Jesus' teaching in the Sermon on the Mount (Matthew 6:25-32). The implications of this teaching are three. First, there can be no pessimism about the ability of the earth to provide adequately for the human race. There is no hint of a niggardly provision that may run out. The emphasis is rather on the abundance of the creation. We would not therefore expect to find that world shortages of resources are the source of international inequality. We do not deny that man can and does waste resources, but properly used there should be enough for all. Second, although the created order is provided for man's use he is in the position of a trustee. Trusteeship or dominion is extended to all men. So the created order is for men in general, to satisfy our needs. Economic activity is justified in that it provides the goods and services necessary for the continuation of man's social existence. Third, man's trusteeship, and the requirement not to waste what God provides, carries with it an obligation to use resources efficiently. The economist's version of this is that man's wants are unlimited, and the resources available at any one time are limited. Hence efficiency in production and distribution is a major preoccupation of much economic analysis. As Christians we may wish to define satisfaction of needs rather than wants as the objective of economic life, but the goal of efficiency in meeting those needs will again be incumbent upon us.

The biblical material also makes it clear that God gives specific dominion or trusteeship to particular people or communities. An obvious example is the provision of the promised land for the Children of Israel. The concept of trusteeship enshrined in that provision is well illustrated by the laws concerning the the land.[2] In Leviticus 25 the land is described as *given* to them by God (not conquered by their armed might). Land was not to be sold to foreigners. Under the Jubilee provisions, land was to be returned to the original families, whatever transactions might have taken place in the intervening period. The families were the trustees for each parcel of land. The idea of personal trusteeship lay behind Naboth's refusal to cede his vineyard to Ahab. Great wealth is also given to individuals such as Abraham, Jacob and Job. Trusteeship is protected by the condemnation of theft, including the eighth commandment and more specific injunctions, e.g. against removing a neighbour's landmark. Theft violates the trusteeship assigned to a particular person. So the penalties provided in the Law involve restoration of that stewardship. However, the right of "property" is subordinated to the obligation to care for others. The Torah exhorts the Israelites to care for the weak, the fatherless and the strangers. Amos condemns the rich for their neglect of the poor. So the trusteeship is conditional. In the New Testament wealth is not condemned in itself, but only when it becomes a hindrance to following Christ. The parable of the stewards in Luke 19:11-27 makes it clear that the resources are given to each individual as a trustee. And each is required to give an account of his dealings. Those who had done well were rewarded with a greater authority over their Lord's possessions. We may note the contrast with the idea of "private property", which involves the right not merely to control the use of resources, but also to consume the product oneself. Instead of the obligation to share which is the corollary of stewardship in the Law, any sharing within the "private property" framework is an act of altruism or charity.

(c) Man and Work

Man's dignity and greatness stems from his creation in the image of God. As we have seen, he has a great stewardship to fulfil in his dominion over the created order. His tragedy is the Fall, which has marred the image, but not destroyed the purposes for which man was created. The contrast between the biblical doctrine of man, and the humanistic conception of man in economic analysis is nowhere more clearly shown than in the values given to work. The usual economic analysis sees work as a necessary evil in order to obtain purchasing power over goods and services. Marx described the worker's role as that of a "wage slave". The biblical view is quite different.[3] First, man has an obligation and a right to work. This is a creation provision, not, as is sometimes erroneously asserted, a result of the Fall. God, in whose image man is created, is described as a worker (Genesis 2,3). Before the Fall, man is created to subdue the earth and replenish it, and to have dominion. He is placed in the Garden of Eden to till it and keep it. The Wisdom literature contains many exhortations to honest labour. Second, work should be meaningful and purposeful. This may be deduced from man's creation in the image of God, and the dominion that is assigned to him. Man's first activity, that of naming the animals, was a purposeful activity. But man is never encouraged to think of himself as creative in the sense that God is. His work is to explore, understand, subdue and use that which is given to him by God in the created order. Man's "creativity" is no more than thinking God's thoughts after him, and humbly using the materials he has provided. The consequences of the Fall for man's work are specifically described in Genesis 3:17-19. Work becomes toil and is subject to a curse. But that is the result of sin and not God's intention. Work remains essential to human dignity, and integral to man's nature. Finally, the biblical view is that work is a social activity. Men should live together in communities and should share in work, each contributing his own particular skills. The New Testament doctrine of the Body of Christ may be taken as a model of how man was intended to live in community. Each one has his own gifts to contribute, all share in the trusteeship over the natural order. Once again, the creation order has been sadly affected by the Fall. No longer in right relationship with God, man finds it difficult to live in right relationship with his fellow man. The result is conflict, not least in the organization of work. However, as Christians we will not accept this situation as God's intention for man.

(d) Stewardship and Work

Although separated for purposes of exposition, the discussions of stewardship and work need to be taken together. In Genesis 1 and 2, man the worker is given the stewardship of the created order. In the parable of the talents (Luke 19:11-27) each steward is given an initial endowment to work with. The basic point is that man cannot work unless he has resources to work with, unless he has the means of production.

This can be illustrated from the Law concerning the land. We know from the account in Joshua 13-19 that each family was provided with a piece of land. This land was to be held by the family in perpetuity. It could not be sold, it could only be rented until the Jubilee. The normal pattern of work was labour on the family farm. Wage labour was regarded as a form of social insurance (Deuteronomy 24:15) for those who had lost possession of their land until the next Jubilee. The prohibition of interest meant that each family had to use its own savings in the family farm. All decisions about the farm were kept within the family.

The returns were earnings representing the labour and initiative of the family, rather than profits. These returns provided the incentives for economic development. Large accumulations of wealth were avoided by provision for inheritance by all the sons rather than just the eldest. Clearly, some aspects of the Law concerning the land relate specifically to the functioning of an agrarian economy (e.g. the injunctions concerning the moving of boundary markers). But there are also some interesting general principles. First, it is clear that work and the stewardship of resources are linked. Man cannot operate without resources: he must have access to land, capital (tools or machinery) and training in the skills required. Second, stewards should control production rather than be dominated or merely "hired" by capital. Not only is this a precondition for the exercize of responsible stewardship: it should also provide incentives by ensuring that those who work share in the prosperity (or lack of prosperity) of the enterprise. Third, work is an enterprise in which man cooperates not only with resources but also with his fellow men. A division of labour in which each person contributes his own particular skills is no bad thing, so long as each can see his own contribution to the whole.

(e) The Distribution of Real Consumption

The third area of biblical teaching which is relevant to our theme concerns the distribution of real consumption. The term "real" here is used to imply the actual goods and services consumed by an individual or household, not the less concrete idea of money expenditure. We have already emphasized the need to distinguish wealth from consumption. A person may have great resources at his disposal, personal abilities, property and technical information. He has the obligation to dispose those resources wisely and fruitfully. But *consumption* of the product of those resources is subject to other biblical teaching. First, the presumption is that every person has the right to share in God's provision for mankind. The creation was for man in general. For the maintenance of human dignity every man needs a minimum standard in food, clothing and housing. God provided food and clothing for Adam and Eve. In the wilderness manna and water are given miraculously, sufficient for each person's needs. In the Law the poor are given the right to a share in the harvest. Exodus 22:26 requires that a man who has pawned his coat should be allowed to have it back for the night to sleep in. In the Sermon on the Mount, Jesus explicitly refers to food and clothing as God's provision for man (Matthew 6:25-32). Paul enjoins Timothy to be content with food and clothing. We observe that everything that is necessary for individuals is also necessary for families. Given the Christian insistence on family life, we are required to see that families have sufficient goods and security for bringing up children.

By contrast with the minimum described, biblical teaching also suggests that there is a maximum standard to which a man should attain. This has been well documented by J. V. Taylor, under the heading *Enough is Enough*[4], setting out the biblical teaching on greed and covetousness. The condemnation of greed and luxury in Amos 6 is paralleled by James 5:1-5 in the New Testament, with the warning of God's impending judgement. When the rich fail in their obligation to the poor, then God's judgement follows (Isaiah 10:1-4; Matthew 25:31-46). As the Magnificat suggests, God is very zealous in his defence of the poor. Covetousness is the precise antithesis of enough is enough: it means "wanting more and more". The seriousness with which God views it is indicated by inclusion of a prohibition of covetousness as the tenth commandment. Jesus puts it into a list of evils as equal with adultery and murder (Mark 7:22) and the warning against covetousness is repeated in Ephesians 5:3. The contrast between the maximum and minimum is sharply drawn in 1 Timothy 6:6-10. The advice to be content with food and clothing is coupled with a warning of spiritual damage resulting from the pursuit of riches.

The teaching concerning a maximum and minimum is fully consistent with the biblical view that personal dominion over resources does not imply the right to consume the entire product of those resources. This is the most satisfactory resolution[5] of two contrasting attitudes in the teaching and life of Jesus. The first is his radical criticism of property. In Luke 12:22-34 he urges his followers to eschew all concern with possessions, and to abandon all cares about their daily needs. They are urged to make do with the absolute minimum (Luke 9:3). Furthermore, Jesus' teaching emphasizes the dangers of possessions. It is impossible to serve God and mammon (Luke 16:13). The rich farmer is condemned for his selfish and thoughtless accumulation (Luke 12:16-21). The rich man who neglects Lazarus lying at his gates ends up in Hades (Luke 16:19-31). On the other hand, Jesus never challenged the ownership of wealth per se, nor did he lead an ascetic life himself. The concern is always for the use which is being made of property. The desire to hold and to use it for oneself becomes a hindrance to knowing God, indeed it may become an idol in itself. The exercize of wise and fruitful stewardship is warmly endorsed and encouraged. But it is paralleled by numerous New Testament injunctions to give. At the feeding of the five thousand, Jesus responds to the disciple's suggestion that the crowd be sent away by challenging them to do something about it. By his subsequent action he shows them that he is concerned for men's bodies as well as their souls, and that God does provide for all men in their basic needs. On other occasions he exhorts the disciples to give generously to others (Luke 6:38), and not to neglect those who ask for material help (Matthew 5:42). The same exhortations are reiterated in the Epistles (e.g. 1 Timothy 6:17,18).

(f) Conclusions

We may summarize the main themes of biblical teaching relevant to our enquiry as follows. The basic concept is of man as a steward or a trustee of God's creation. It is an abundant creation over which man is given dominion, and from which he may derive the means of material life and existence. He exercizes his dominion as a worker, using the resources efficiently and carefully. In that work there is a division of labour, each one contributing the particular skills with which he is endowed. Within the process of production some have larger responsibilities than others. Some may have stewardship responsibility over much and others over little. But the proceeds of production are for mankind as a whole, to meet material needs. Consequently there is a minimum level of provision to which each man is entitled. There is also a maximum level, particularly in these situations where others have too little. There is no necessary connection between a large stewardship responsibility and a large consumption. Ideally the two should be quite distinct. We note that the Fall has had serious consequences in each of these areas. Fallen man has an ambivalent attitude to work. True to his nature he prefers employment to unemployment. But at work, his motivation is as much what he can get as what he can give to his fellow workers. Fallen man desires more and more, and has no wish to share the fruits of production. As a consequence, a fully just human society is beyond our grasp. There is no Christian hope of Utopia. But that should not allow us, as Christians, to acquiesce in evil and injustice. Insofar as human society, at its international level, falls short of God's creation ordinance, we shall strive to get justice done. Our analysis is dominated by that objective, however powerful the forces of evil and injustice may appear to be.

2. World Development Report 1978

Our section heading is the title of an influential report first produced in 1978 by the World Bank[6] as a comprehensive assessment of global development issues. Reports are promised on an annual basis, and are likely to be essential reading for those wishing to keep abreast of the major issues which are the subject of this paper. Here we can only summarize the major themes.

(a) Incomes

The 1978 report divides the world economy (excluding the Communist bloc) into three broad groups. There are 34 low income countries with a total population of 1,220 million in 1976. They include large economies such as India and Indonesia, and very small ones such as Lesotho. They are all characterized by having annual income per capita less than $250 in 1976. Indeed the average for all the countries was $150 per capita. The second group are 58 middle income countries of which the largest are Nigeria and Brazil. With a combined population of 845 million, and average income per capita of $750 per annum, they are considerably better placed than the low income countries. Finally, the industrialized countries, which include USA, Europe, Japan and Australia, constitute a third group with a combined population of 690 million. Their income per capita is on average $6200. These figures can be expressed as multiples of the income per capita in the low income countries. On that basis, the middle income countries' income per capita is five times that of the poorest group and the high income countries' income per capita is a staggering 41 times as great! Putting the low and middle income countries together we find that they represent 75% of the population, but only 21% of the GNP in 1975. So the rich one quarter of the world disposes of nearly four-fifths of the income.

The growth picture is scarely more encouraging. Few would doubt that the past twenty years have seen unprecedented efforts to promote development in the Third World. National income has indeed grown at very high rates. But in the low income countries income per capita grew at only 0.9% p.a. over the period 1960-76, and 2.8% p.a. for middle income countries. (This compares with a comfortable 3.4% p.a. in the industrialized countries.) So the rich get richer and the poor get poorer. One major contributing factor was the faster growth of population in the Third World over this period.

While the GNP per capita figures are useful for global comparison they should be used with caution for a number of reasons. First, the exercise of converting them to dollar measures depends critically on the exchange rate used. These are not always good indicators of the relative costs of living in different countries. Further, there is a certain relativity about what constitutes a reasonable standard in different cultures. A further difficulty is that much production in LDCs is for subsistence. The output is not marketed, and its value is notoriously difficult to estimate. So in that respect the data may be unreliable. The use of per capita figures may also mislead. Most of the poorer countries have a very high proportion of children in their populations. Insofar as the children live with their parents and share housing and other family possessions, their per capita *needs* are probably less. Finally, we should note that averages are not necessarily good indicators. It has been noted that although the GNP per capita in Brazil grew at a rate of 2.5% p.a. in the period 1960-70, the share going to the poorest 40% fell from 10% to 8%. All this suggests that we need to probe the development situation more deeply in order to understand it.

(b) Basic Human Needs

Robert McNamara, the president of the World Bank, described the situation as follows:[7] "What are we to say of a world in which hundreds of millions of people are not only poor in statistical terms but are faced with day to day deprivations that degrade human dignity to levels which no statistics can adequately describe? — A developing world in which children under five account for only 20% of the population but for more than 60% of the deaths — A developing world in which two-thirds of the children who have escaped death will live on, restricted in their growth by malnutrition, a malnutrition that can stunt both bodies and minds alike — A developing world in which there are 100 million more adult illiterates than there were twenty years ago — A developing world, in short, in which death and disease are rampant, education and employment are scarce, squalor and stagnation common, and the opportunity and the realization of personal potential drastically limited."

McNamara's statement reflects a certain disillusion with the results of a policy that has concentrated on improving growth rates of GNP in the hope that benefits will spread to the poorest sections of the world community. Instead there is a new emphasis on "basic human needs" development.[8] The stress is on food, water, clothing, shelter, health and education at minimal levels. One estimate is that more than half the population of LDCs is deprived in at least one of these areas. The approach has much to commend it in terms of the Christian doctrine of man, and his right to sufficient means to maintain human dignity, which was discusssed in the previous section. In terms of priorities, we need to give our attention to those whose share is smallest. The World Development Report puts it in the following terms: ". . . about 800 million people still live in absolute poverty. These people are living at the very margin of existence, with inadequate food, shelter, education and health care. For many of them there has been little improvement in the standard of living, and for some there may have been a deterioration."[9]

The food supply situation in the LDCs showed a marked improvement in the 20 years up to 1973. Production grew at 3% p.a. compared to aggregate population growth of 2.5% p.a. Production has been boosted somewhat by the Green Revolution, the introduction of new seed varieties and other technological advances. However, it has been uneven in its impact. For the most part the small farmer is unable to afford the irrigation, fertilizers and pesticides that are essential to success. Landless peasants may find themselves no longer required as agricultural labourers once mechanization in agriculture is introduced. In addition, the LDCs have been increasing their imports of cereals and other foods. Imports in 1974-5 were 52 million tons, four times their level 25 years before.

Despite the increase in output and food imports, the extent of the problem remains alarming. Early estimates of food requirements have been revised downwards, largely as a result of the discovery by nutrition experts that different elements of the diet are interdependent in their effects. However, a recent estimate was that 30% of the population of the Far Eastern LDCs were below the lower limit of an adequate diet, and 25% of the population of African LDCs. Altogether perhaps 500 million people are in this category. This is however by no means the whole story. Two groups are particularly at risk — the pregnant women and young mothers, whose dietary requirements are higher than average, and young children under two years. D. G. Jones[10] has provided a convenient summary of the effects of malnutrition. About 10,000 die of starvation every week. About 10 million pre-school children are severely malnourished, and as many as 250 million have a diet that is deficient in significant respects. The effects of this are seen in high infant mortality rates, and in brain damage to children from which they probably do not recover, even if a full diet is later provided. Malnutrition also reduced resistance to a wide variety of debilitating or even disabling diseases.

A major feature of virtually all LDCs in the past 25 years has been the rapid growth of the cities. These have been peopled by rural-urban migrants, and by the high birth rates in urban areas. Since 1960, population growth has exceeded 5% in most low income LDCs, and has fallen not far short of that figure in the middle income LDCs. Statistics cannot adequately describe the conditions under which these people live, but no visitor to an LDC can fail to be impressed by the shanty towns that are such a feature of urban life. For the most part urban services such as water, sewerage or electricity are inadequate or non-existent in such areas.

Education is an area where LDCs have made considerable progress since 1960, but the situation in the low income countries is still highly unsatisfactory. Only 23% of adults are literate, only half of the children of primary school age naturally attend school and less than 8% of children have secondary education. In the middle income countries the situation is much more satisfactory, with virtually complete coverage of primary education and nearly two-thirds of the adult population being literate.

There has been similar progress in health, though the disparities between the LDCs and the DCs are still very marked. In low income countries there are 21,000 people per doctor (though the situation is much better in India, for example) compared to 650 per doctor in the industrialized countries. The difference is the more notable when one reflects that life expectancy in the low income countries is 44 years, compared with 72 in the industrialized countries. All the LDCs have experienced a reduction in infant mortality rates since the 1950s, but the average figure is still four times that of the industrial countries. The evidence also suggests that there are great disparities *within* LDCs, with health care being particularly inadequate for the poor, especially in rural areas. The reason is the preference of qualified medical personnel for life in the towns, and the higher income to be earned there, notably in private practice.

Finally we should note the growing problem of urban unemployment in LDCs. This is in one sense an indicator of development. While a large proportion of the population is in the subsistence sector, the possibility of employment does not arise directly. However, once there is a significant work force that depends on wage labour for its livelihood then unemployment becomes a serious possibility. It becomes particularly apparent in urban areas. All statistical data in this area must be suspect, since there is no reason to believe that people will register as unemployed unless there are real prospects of getting a job. However, all LDCs which collect data on unemployment show a sharp rise since the early 1960s. In India, for example, the recorded figure rose from 2 million in 1962 to over 9 million in 1976.

Statistics, however described and interpreted, do not make the most interesting reading. But the message of the World Bank Report is overwhelming. In terms of the criteria set out in Section One above, it is clear that the situation falls short of the ideal in many respects. A very large proportion of mankind lives in conditions of great personal deprivation. By comparison the inhabitants of the industrial countries live in prosperity and luxury. Each deprived person is more than a statistic: he or she is one for whom Christ died. "Then he will say to those on his left hand, 'Depart from me you cursed, into the eternal fire prepared for the devil and his angels; for I was hungry and you gave me no food, I was thirsty and you gave me no drink, I was a stranger and you did not welcome me, naked and you did not clothe me, sick, and in prison, and you did not visit me.' Then they will answer, 'Lord, when did we see thee hungry or thirsty, or a stranger, or naked or sick or in prison and did not minister to thee?' Then he will answer them, 'Truly I say to you, as you did it not to one of the least of these, you did it not to me.' " (Matthew 25:41-45).

3. A Fable

The explanation of this international situation, in which there are great disparities in the distribution of basic human necessities, is inevitably complex. The object of this section is to tell a fable which will enable us to understand the economic relationships that are basic to the analysis of subsequent sections.

The setting of the story is an island, set in the midst of an appropriate ocean, and cut off from all contact with the rest of the world. On the island there are precisely 100 people. Our story is not concerned with their origins. One day a social scientist appeared on the island, perhaps a survivor from a shipwreck. Having no means of escape from the island he settled down to study the customs and was treated as an honoured guest. He was particularly interested in the economy of the island. He observed that the islanders practised division of labour on a considerable scale. Each islander was allotted some land, and each controlled some other resources, in addition to providing his own labour. Some of the islanders were educated, but others had difficulty in reading, and certainly were not able to write. On the island was a central market place. Twice a week all the goods and services on offer were brought to the market place, and under the watchful eye of an "auctioneer" commodities were bought and sold. The task of the auctioneer was to conduct market transactions of behalf of each buyer and seller. He had to ensure that transactions were concluded at a free market price (there is a rudimentary coinage on the island), which reflected the true scarcity of the goods in question. If the price exceeded the cost of making the product, then another supplier was free to enter the market and increase the supply. The auctioneer kept a record of all transactions and the social scientist was able to scrutinize these over a number of weeks. These enabled him to calculate the sales accruing to each person. He discovered that 25 people received at least 85% of the revenue from all sales. Another 30 accounted for an additional 12%, leaving only 3% for the remaining 45 people. Intrigued, he labelled the three groups *R, M* and *P* people and set out to explain the reasons for the differences, and to examine the consequences.

The auctioneer was very helpful in explaining the situation. The *R* people had four important advantages over the other inhabitants. They had a disproportionate share of the best land on the island. However, other parts of the island, which did not belong to the *R* people, also had rich resources, but did not provide as high a return to their owners. One reason was that the *R* people had advanced technological knowledge which enabled them to identify the capabilities of their land. But not only did they have that knowledge, they were also very skilled workers. They had received advanced training that enabled them to put their knowledge to good use. Finally, the auctioneer drew attention to the land belonging to the *R* people. It was very intensively used: there were plenty of machines to increase output per man-hour. Some of the machinery was very sophisticated indeed. By contrast the *M* people had made much less of their land. The land belonging to the *P* people was very difficult to use: besides the *P* people had neither the skill nor the machinery nor the technical knowledge to do much with it. The consequences of the situation were straightforward. The *R* people made a lot to sell so they ended up rather rich. The *M* people had rather less, while the 45 *P* people had so little to sell at the market that it was scarcely worth their while to come once, let alone twice, a week. Having little to sell meant that there was little they could buy, so it cut both ways. Indeed the auctioneer sometimes wished he could exclude them altogether, since recording their transactions was very tedious as the accounts were so small. On occasion they had not come to market at all. It was rumoured that this was because they literally had nothing to sell because their crops had failed. The auctioneer thought that one or two might have died of starvation in consequence but the *P* people bred rapidly so one or two were not missed. On the whole, he would prefer not to investigate. When the social scientist questioned the *R* people about this account, they wanted to deny it. After all, they replied, the market is organized along entirely fair lines; everyone is free to come to market. So the failure of the *P* people to come to market on occasion was their own responsibility. Perhaps they could not be bothered to work.

The social scientist then enquired of the auctioneer how the 25 *R* people had managed to get into such a privileged position, with each one having an income 40 times as great as that of the *P* people. The auctioneer was vague on the historical detail, but from his description the social scientist was able to piece together the reasons for a continuing situation in which the *R* people did well compared to the rest. With their high incomes the *R* people were able to consume at a high level, and still have plenty over for uses which increased their earning capacity. They could afford to keep their children for long years of training in technical matters. They themselves could take time off from actual production to think about new methods, and they could devote some of their output to making newer and better machines. As a result, each generation of *R* people was better off than the last. They too, like the auctioneer, were hazy about their origins. They simply presumed that this pattern of increasing affluence could be traced back through successive previous generations. They were proud of their achievements and believed they deserved the high rewards that their efforts had brought. In their view it was up to the *M* and *P* people to emulate them.

At this point the social scientist decided that he should seek out the *M* and *P* people to see how they interpreted the situation. The *M* people were reasonably easy to find, and they were quite articulate. They were also somewhat bitter about the attitudes of the *R* people. They had observed the *R* people rather carefully, and would indeed like to emulate them, but it was not quite as easy as that. The market, of which the auctioneer was so proud, was less than perfect. A number of the *M* people had found that their resources could be used to make cheaply a number of products which the R people had formerly made and traded among themselves. So the M people had made an effort to produce these products and had taken them along to the twice weekly market. There a strange thing had happened. The R people had not bid for the goods as expected: instead they had continued to buy their own products at a higher price. The explanation seemed to be that the R people were not prepared to accept any disruption of their own production patterns. They had been making these products for some time. They had the skills and the machinery. It was true that they could be better off buying the products more cheaply from the M people. But they were so rich already that it made little difference to them. The M people were naturally rather frustrated by this situation, but there was nothing they could do so long as the R people (who accounted for 85% of the spending power on the island) declined to buy their goods.

The M people also complained about another feature of the situation. There were certain advanced products which they needed, but only the R people could supply. This was mainly because the R people held all the technological knowledge needed, and were not prepared to let anyone else see it. Or if they did offer to share the information, it was on the terms set up by the R people. Mostly, however, the R people kept the information to themselves. The M people suspected that the R people deliberately restricted supplies of these commodities on the market, so that the prices were high. It was very difficult to check this suspicion as no one really knew what the costs of production were.

The social scientist decided to complete his enquiries by seeking out some of the P people. He enquired on which part of the island they were living and made his way there. On arrival he was a little surprised to be greeted by one of the R people, who quickly explained his presence. One of the goods in which he specialized in production required an input which was not to be found in his own land. But there was a very good source in the land belonging to the P people. Unfortunately, the P people lacked the skills, the knowledge and the machinery to do anything about it. So he had made a deal with them, and was doing the job himself. He paid a few P workers to operate his machinery, but much of the returns to the operation came to him. After all he had provided all the skills and the capital, so it was only fair that he should take the largest share. What the P people thought of this, the social scientist was not able to discover. They were rather inarticulate, and it was not clear that they understood what was going on.

Having completed his enquiries, the social scientist sat down to write a report. It contained all the tables and jargon that would have pleased his professional colleagues. But it also included a final section in which he gave his personal judgement on the economic life of the island. Here the social scientist confessed to some puzzlement. He was very uneasy about the distribution of income on the island. How could it be just for one quarter of the inhabitants to have nearly 85%, when the poorest 45 people had only 3%? Yet he had no reason to believe that the R people were wicked or dishonest. On the contrary, they were hardworking, usually sober, and trustworthy traders. They certainly had no *desire* to exploit or oppress the M and the P people. Indeed, they had been known to express sympathy for them in their plight. So the social scientist concluded that it was the whole system which was responsible for the outcome, since no individuals could be blamed. Copies of the report and conclusions were read by the R and M people, but not by the P people as they were not able to read. The M people began to get angry, and there were mutterings at the market that the system should be changed. The R people said very little, but it was apparent that they were working on a new and secret product. The social scientist was invited to the inauguration of this product down on the sea shore. When he arrived, the R people showed him an ocean-going boat they had made. They put him on board, with all the copies of his report, pushed him out to sea and told him to head off in a northeasterly direction. On no account was he to return to disturb the peace of the island.

4. Trade

The first part of the fable explained how the 25 R (rich) people on the island were rich because they were able to bring high priced goods to market, whereas the M (middle income) and the P (poor) groups had much less to offer. Our analysis can be summarized in two propositions. First, income in a market system depends on ability to supply products or services to the market. Our conclusion is that many people in our world do not have access to resources, so they are unable to work effectively and to conform to the biblical norm of responsible stewardship. Second, consumption in a market system depends on income or purchasing power. Those whose incomes are small will consume little. The purpose of this section is to translate this into world terms to explain world disparities. We will then look at the consequences of income disparity for consumption of food.

(a) Ability to Produce

Differences of resource endowment clearly contribute to the disparities between nations. At one extreme, Kuwait and Abu Dhabi are distinguished by a higher income per capita than the USA, based on their ability to produce petroleum. In the same part of the world, the Yemen has no resources and is almost entirely desert, and falls into the lowest income group of nations. *Prima facie* too one would expect climate to be an important feature of agricultural development, taken with the basic fertility of the soil. However the experience of the last 25 years suggests that development is not dependent directly on resources or climate. Japan has developed despite a lack of natural resources, and despite geographical restrictions on the supply of agricultural land. Singapore and Hong Kong have industrialized on a smaller scale, but again without either resources or fertile land, and with the disadvantage of a tropical climate. Equally a number of African and S. American countries are known to be rich in resources, but these have not so far formed the basis for development. The reason is that resources are of no value without the knowledge, the human skills and the capital necessary to make use of them. Human skills are basically developed by education and we have already seen that access to education is restricted in LDCs to a level well below that in the DCs. In addition, the general level of adult literacy is much lower. Estimates of the capital per man in LDCs compared to DCs are not available, since the information is difficult to obtain. However, energy consumption is a useful proxy measure. Very approximately, in 1975, energy consumption per capita was ten times as great in the middle income countries as in the low income countries, and a hundred times as great in the high income countries.[11]

The final ingredient determining the ability to produce is knowledge. Griffin[12] has drawn attention to the geographical concentration of R and D (research and development) expenditures in the DCs. 98% is undertaken in the advanced industrial countries, 78% in the USA alone. The expenditures themselves are heavily biased towards defence, and technologically advanced products such as aircraft. Very little is done on problems arising from production in LDCs. A specific example indicates the scale of the differential. In 1971 the World Bank and the

FAO financed the establishment of a Consultative Group on International Agricultural Research, which set up six research centres to investigate crops and climatic factors relevant to LDCs. But in 1974 the funds available were less than the cost of government supported R and D into agriculture in the UK alone.[13] Given these kinds of disparities it is scarcely surprising that technical progress makes a greater contribution to growth in the DCs than in the LDCs.[14] It is possible to argue that the disparities give the LDCs great scope for improving the position by "catching up" technologically with the DCs. However, technology tends to be very specific to the production conditions of DCs and many economists have doubted whether it is either feasible or wise simply to translate it to the LDCs.

The existing disparities can then be explained in part by the differences in the ability of economies to produce. However, there is some evidence to suggest that the trend is for the disparities to widen. We have already mentioned the differences in expenditure on R and D, and their consequential effects on outputs. However, the sequence does not end at that point. Because of the technological progress in DCs, they are able to pay higher returns to skilled manpower. As a result there is a considerable movement of professionally qualified people from the LDCs to the DCs. Bhagwati and Dellafar[15] found that in the period 1962-9 the US had received as immigrants, 12,800 doctors, dentists and surgeons, 6,500 natural scientists and 19,000 engineers from LDCs. The consequence for the LDCs is a deterioration in their prospects of development.

Furthermore, the DCs are able to attract international capital. Thus of all US direct investment abroad in manufacturing in 1971, 83% was in advanced countries and only 17% in LDCs. It was notable that the LDC investment was also concentrated in the middle income LDCs, and not in the poorest.

A final source of widening disparities identified by some analysts is a long term trend for the relative price of goods produced by LDCs to fall in international markets. This possibility has occasioned much dispute since it was first asserted by Prebisch in the early 1950s. His argument was that the world income and price elasticity of demand for primary commodities tended to be low. So the world market would grow slowly and attempts by the LDCs to sell more would depress the price. He predicted that over time the LDCs would find their primary commodity exports were purchasing less and less in terms of manufactured products. Empirical analysis has produced a mixed verdict on this general hypothesis. Early studies gave it strong support, since they took as their starting point the high prices of commodities that prevailed during the Korean War. Taking a starting point further back, in the 1920s, suggested that there was no long term general decline in the terms of trade. However, the World Development Report points out that much depends on which commodities a country is exporting. Over the period 1960-75 the low income countries did suffer a deterioration in their terms of trade, largely because of their reliance on agricultural export crops. The middle income countries, particularly those producing metals and oil, saw their position improve.

(b) Consumption Depends on Income

What then are the consequences of this pattern of world development? The obvious corollary is that those who produce very little (because they lack the means to produce) will also have low incomes, and consume little. This point has been illustrated dramatically in a study by Sen[16] of the great Bengal famine of 1942-44 during which 3 million people died. The official version is that there was a dramatic fall in the availability of food. However, this is not borne out by the data. Food supplies in 1943 were indeed 5% lower than in the previous year, but they were 13% higher than in 1941. In 1941 there had been no famine. So what was the explanation? It seems that over the period 1940-43, the price of grain rose much faster than the wages of labourers. There was no shortage of food: but the poorest section of the community lacked the income to purchase it. So they starved. Sen also quotes the case of Bangladesh in 1974. Floods reduced the demand for agricultural labour. The result was famine, *before* the harvest failed.

Precisely the same point has been made by Jones[17] in the context of world food supply problems. He points out that all the problem of malnutrition in LDCs would be "solved" with 25 million tons of cereals per annum: perhaps 2% of the world harvest. The difficulty is to get it to the people who need it. They tend to be those with low incomes. So when world production dips a little they are the marginal consumers who are pushed out of the market by higher prices. The situation is eased if the DCs increase food production or decrease consumption since that will moderate the price increases: but that still does not give the poorest section of the world community the income that they would need in order to make purchases.

A parallel case is that of fertilizer. The LDCs imported 6 million tons of fertilizer in 1971-2, and were highly dependent on

DCs for sophisticated chemicals. In 1973, there was a world shortage of fertilizers. Supply tends to be inelastic (plants cannot be built overnight), and industrial demand competes for the basic imputs. The outcome was predictable: the DCs outbid the LDCs for available supplies. The impact on food supplies in LDCs was dramatic, since one ton of fertilizer can boost yields by up to eight tons. In one sense the market "worked" efficiently, since fertilizer is used more effectively in DCs than in LDCs. But unfortunately the food is produced in the wrong place: one ton of additional output in the US does less to relieve malnutrition than a hundredweight in Bangladesh.

No useful purpose is served by extending the examples. The principle is the same in every case. Consumption is possible only if one has income, and income is determined by the resources that one puts onto the market. So world distribution of income is in the first place determined by the world distribution of resources — natural resources, human skills, capital equipment and knowledge. But that distribution is very uneven, and so is the distribution of income. So those who have little to offer must expect to consume very little: that is the essence of the international market system. Note that we are not assigning malevolent motives to anyone in reaching this conclusion. Economic factors are merely reacting to world price signals, and adjusting their behaviour accordingly. There is certainly no desire to exploit the poor: the rich are probably quite unaware of the consequences of the system. However, we cannot deny that the system falls short, in performance, of God's creation ordinance that the creation was for man in general. The major reason for this is the tying together of production and consumption. Production is motivated by the lure of consumption that it brings, rather than by the desire to be fruitful stewards of God's gifts. Consumption is determined by income, rather than by need. So 800 million people still live in absolute poverty, in a world that is fruitful and abundant.

5. Barriers to Trade

(a) Trade and Growth in the LDCs

In our fable the *M* producers were puzzled by the refusal of the *R* people to purchase their goods. The real world analogue is the barriers to trade that exist in all DCs to prevent the access of goods from LDCs. Many LDCs are thereby prevented from earning incomes on products in which their resources give them advantages in production (i.e. they are prevented from acting as responsible stewards). The irony of the situation is that it exists after 30 years of devotion to free trade on the part of OECD countries. A sequence of negotiations under the GATT have enabled world trade in manufactures to grow extremely rapidly. Thus in the period 1965-73 when output of manufactures in DCs grew at a rate of 4.9% p.a. their exports grew at a rate of 10.6% p.a. To an extent the LDCs have shared in that growth, registering high growth rates of both output and exports.[19,20] One estimate is that LDC exports of manufactures to DCs alone have created 3 million jobs in LDCs in the period 1965-74. On current trends the World Bank expects LDC exports to grow at 12% p.a. up to 1985, and to increase their share in the imports of manufactures of DCs from 8.9% in 1975 to 13.6% in 1985. However, there is every sign that this growth may be jeopardized by increased protectionism on the part of the DCs.

What are the products in which the LDCs have a comparative advantage in manufacture? A wide variety of studies have found two features to be important.[21] The LDCs tend to have an advantage in the production of labour intensive goods such as textiles, clothing, footwear and leather, particularly where these are linked to local resources. However, since 1965 the LDCs have diversified production into a much wider range of products, including electronics and electrical machinery, other machinery and transport equipment, basic chemicals and iron and steel products. The common feature of these is that they are products which are late in the product cycle. Either the technology or the product is completely standardized. LDCs often have sufficient skilled labour to produce such goods, even if they do not have the ability to innovate. This is particularly true of a select group of middle income countries, Hong Kong, Taiwan, Korea, Singapore and Brazil, which account for some 60% of LDC manufactured exports to DCs.

(b) Protectionism in Manufactures

The reaction of the DCs to this increasing manufacturing export potential of the LDCs has been broadly negative, particularly since 1973. For example, the Kennedy Round of tariff negotiations under GATT, 1968-72, brought down average tariffs to the range 5% to 11% within the OECD area (the EEC tariff went down to 10.0%). But textiles, footwear, clothing and food products were specifically excluded. The subsequent Tokyo Round has resulted in further cuts in tariffs, though many of the same restrictions applied. It also promoted the Generalized System of Preferences (GSP), whereby DCs grant tariff reductions on designated imports from LDCs on a non-reciprocal basis. This was finally implemented by the USA in 1976, having been implemented earlier elsewhere. However, there are specific exclusions: textiles, leather products, footwear, wood and paper products, certain categories of electrical and electronic equipment, furniture, toys and miscellaneous light manufactures. Alternatively tariffs have been reduced, but quota systems operate instead. Some restrictions are applied to particular countries that happen to be efficient producers: for example, Taiwan has been excluded from at least half of the OECD GSP arrangements. An IMF memorandum[22] comments that for the US and the UK ". . . the structure of effective tariff protection is significantly and positively correlated with the comparative advantage of less developed countries in manufacturing activities . . ." Wolter and Chung[23] reach the conclusion that non-tariff barriers to trade in DCs "tend to be applied most frequently to products in which developing countries presently have or are establishing a competitive advantage in international markets . . . the impact of individual non-tariff barriers tends almost uniformly to bear disproportionately on developing country suppliers . . ." Both of these comments were written before the increase in protection that has been such a feature of the past five years.

A specific example of the restrictions imposed on LDC exporters is the Multifibre Arrangement (MFA). This was originally negotiated as an "orderly marketing arrangement" for LDC clothing and textiles exports to DCs. However, it has rapidly become a restrictive instrument. The most recent Common Market quotas have actually reduced the input levels for Taiwan, Korea and Hong Kong to their 1976 levels. Other leading exporters have seen the growth in their quotas reduced sharply. Since one LDC response in the past has been to diversify production to goods outside the restrictions, the new rules introduce very low "trigger levels" for further quota restrictions to be applied. The USA in its own bilateral agreements on textiles with LDCs, has frozen quotas at their 1977 level. New quantitative restrictions have come into force (in addition to tariffs) on footwear, steel, television sets and shipbuilding. And there is a rising chorus of demands for protection on a wide range of products of interest to LDCs. The implications of these restrictions are very serious for the LDCs; not so much for those LDCs which are already major exporters of manufactures and can diversify reasonably easily as quotas become restrictive, but particularly for the poorer LDCs which are looking for DC markets for their exports as they begin tentatively to industrialize. These include some of the poorest LDCs such as Bangladesh and Sri Lanka.[24] The World Bank estimate is that without further protection the LDCs could increase export earnings from $33 billion in 1975 to $94 billion in 1985. The latter figure could be $118 billion if the OECD dismantled all its restrictions on trade: it would be considerably less if protectionism spreads.

(c) Protectionism in Agriculture

However, the most glaring example of DC protectionism is the area of agriculture.[25] A complete analysis is not possible, so we will take the example of the EEC Common Agricultural Policy, the purpose of which is to ensure security of supplies, to stabilize markets, to keep prices at a reasonable (undefined) level, and to provide a fair (undefined) standard of living to those involved in agriculture. In practice, the policy has been geared to European self-sufficiency in food and the protection of small farms. To achieve this result, livestock farming in Europe has been protected, at a high cost to consumers. So imported meat, poultry, eggs, dairy produce and sugar are kept out. Instead Europe imports cereals to feed its livestock. The inefficiency of producing food this way is well known. The gross ratio of food consumed (as inputs to the process) to food output has been calculated at 30:1 for beef, 20:1 for pork, and 12:1 for chicken. In a more rational world, Europe would import these products from other countries (including LDCs) where livestock farming could be based on natural pastureland. LDCs would be able to use the income so generated to import the cereals that they need from the USA and W. Europe. The main livestock operation remaining in Europe would be dairy farming for milk, for which there is sufficient pasture land available in Europe.

An objection to this which is sometimes voiced, is that it makes no sense to import food for Europe from LDCs which already have insufficient food. The answer is simply that malnutrition results from lack of income rather than inadequate food supplies. LDC production would give them the incomes they now lack. For example, the EEC protection afforded to sugar beet has had detrimental effects on the sugar producers of the Caribbean. Without markets for their sugar, many sugar workers are now unemployed. A sugar worker cannot live on sugar cane alone.

(d) Protectionism and the "Adjustment Problem"

The reason for protectionism in the DCs is not hard to find. In the fable, the *R* people declined to change their pattern of production. They could afford to disdain the opportunity of cheaper goods from the *M* people as they were already well off. Broadly speaking precisely the same thinking affects the DCs in the face of import competition from the LDCs. It has attracted much attention as the "adjustment problem".[26] The difficulty arises because the impact of LDC competition tends to be felt most in a few industries, notably textiles, clothing and footwear, though the list is likely to grow. Import penetration leads to the closure of factories and the displacement of workers. In many countries the impact will be concentrated regionally. So pressure for protection for those employed in the industry is not surprising. What is surprising is the extent to which DC governments have succumbed to such pressures. First, the costs to consumers are often high. They are denied cheap sources of supply. Second, LDC imports are only one of a number of factors that generate changes in employment patterns over time. Technical progress, changes in tastes and trade with other DC countries are others. Every competent study has shown that the employment effects of LDC inputs are truly negligible by comparison with these. One can only suspect that changes arising from LDC exports are singled out for attention because the LDCs have no powerful voice. Third, one presumes that the LDC earnings from new exports will be spent. Most LDCs are extremely short of foreign exchange, and are likely to spend any increment on imports to help their development. LDCs are already an important export market for DC manufacturers. They could be even more important. The conclusion is that workers in DCs will have to switch jobs, not, in aggregate, lose them. And everyone could be better off. Fourth, protection of jobs in DCs has a much greater effect on employment in LDCs. Lydall[27] has calculated some orders of magnitude, for 12 manufactured product groups of particular interest to LDCs. Displacing one worker in the EEC in these sectors would generate on average two jobs in a middle income country and 4.6 jobs in a low income country. The comparable figures for the USA are 2.8 and 6.5 jobs respectively. This is merely the direct employment effects. Multiplier effects of the expansion of activity in LDCs made possible by their additional earnings of foreign exchange could increase these impacts by between 2 and 5 times the figures quoted. Thus in a very poor country the effect could be as high as 20 additional jobs for one worker displaced in Europe or the USA.

The conclusion is inescapable. Analysis of the interests of the LDCs (employment and income) point to the selfishness of protectionism in the DCs. Yet, if anything, it continues to be strengthened.

6. Multinationals

(a) The Growth of Large Firms

In our fable we drew attention to two activities of the *R* people which might be thought to contribute to their enrichment. The first was the terms under which they sold advanced products to the poorer people. The second was their search for essential supplies of materials from the lands of the *P* people. The real analogues are the operations of multinational corporations (MNCs) to which we now direct our attention. Over the last ten years there has been a flood of literature on the subject[28] and their essential features have been delineated. Many of the firms are household names: Exxon (Esso), Shell, Ford, Unilever, IBM, ICI. Others, such as American Telephone and Telegraph will not be so familiar to English readers. Their essential feature is that they operate in a large number of countries, and see their operations in world, rather than national terms. For this reason some writers prefer to call them transnational, emphasizing that their allegiance transcends the nation state. Their prevailing characteristic, and the one which has occasioned the greatest alarm, is bigness. The value added of the ten largest MNCs individually exceeded the GNP of more than 80 countries in 1974. All MNCs accounted for 22% of world output. Their growth is more than double that of world trade. It has been calculated that by the end of the century, if this growth continued, between two and three hundred companies would produce more than half the world's output.

Even now, within particular sectors, very few companies are responsible for most of the world production of essential industrial products. For example, six companies control more than 70% of the world output of aluminium, seven companies produce more than 60% of the world's oil (the proportion was 90% in 1950), and one company holds almost half the world market in computers. MNCs are not easily categorized according to product, since many have diversified their operations. But it is possible to distinguish an older group, in cars, pulp and paper, aluminium, zinc, petroleum, copper and lead, whose grip on world markets has diminished over the past 25 years. The newer

MNCs tend to emphasize high technology products (e.g. computers, pharmaceuticals, transport equipment) and it is notable that they control large research and development budgets. In the United States it has been estimated that MNCs account for about 80% of all private research and development expenditures. The control on world markets of this newer group is growing at present. The origin of the MNCs has been direct investment abroad by firms that have sought investment opportunities outside their national markets. Classifying firms by country of origin, the MNC appears as a distinctively American and British phenomenon, with the USA accounting for 55% of the assets and the UK for 20%. Most of these were formed after the end of the Second World War. But more recently European firms have become multinational and are investing abroad. The only major industrial nation not having substantial involvement in MNCs is now Japan, and there is good reason to believe that that pattern is already changing with Japanese companies showing much more interest in foreign subsidiaries.

(b) Why Multinational?

Why then should a large firm also be a *multinational* firm? Three distinct reasons have been explored in the literature. The first relies on the advantages to be gained from vertical integration. The typical case is the firm that uses as an essential input a resource that is available only in another country. As firms in the industrialized nations of the West exhausted domestic supplies of raw materials they were forced to go further afield for sources of supply: petroleum and primary metals are particular examples of this. It seemed natural to the firms to search out supplies themselves, and then to make the necessary investments. In this way they could ensure their supplies, and benefit the country in which the resource was found by supplying the requisite capital, technological skills and entrepreneurship. The control of supplies also had the indirect benefit, to the firm, of cutting off a source of supply to any potential rival in the market for the finished product.

A second reason for going multinational arises from abundant labour supplies available in less developed countries. Given the high wage costs in the developed nations, firms have found it advantageous to move the more labour intensive parts of their production to low wage countries. This is the phenomenon known as "sourcing". Control over the production and marketing is retained by the headquarters of the MNC, but production itself may take place at a large number of locations with only final assembly taking place in the major markets.

The third reason for multinationalism is likely to be the most important in the next few decades, and is particularly applicable to firms using advanced technology. Suppose such a firm has developed a new product that represents a considerable technical advance. It now wants to gain the maximum, international, market for the product. One way of doing this could be via exports. But that is likely to be unattractive, for two reasons. National markets, particularly in less developed countries, are likely to be heavily protected by tariffs, in an effort to promote industrialization. Further, for many differentiated products, the marketing of the product is essential to its success. This means that it must be adapted to meet local conditions of use. Both these factors weigh in favour of dispersed production, and hence direct investment. The only alternative is to license the technology to a national firm. But that will not always work, since it is hard to exploit the monopoly of knowledge via another firm. For example, the national firm may lack the entrepreneurship to exploit the situation to the full.

(c) Multinationals and the LDCs

Armed with our Christian criteria we will look first at the impact of MNCs on the developing countries, and then at the impact on advanced economies.

The defence of the role of MNCs in less developed countries (LDCs) would emphasize the following points. We live in a world where the facts of deprivation and starvation in many LDCs make development an essential task. MNCs are ideally suited to provide for that development. They have access to large sources of funds, so that they can undertake large projects. They may also be able to mobilize additional aid from their "home" countries to provide for infrastructure investment. They can provide entrepreneurship and managerial skills that are lacking in many LDCs, and their presence can help with the training of a local labour force. They can bring with them valuable technology, and experience of making new products, which an LDC could acquire otherwise only by research and development expenditures that they are in no position to undertake. Finally with their marketing experience, MNCs can do much to improve the distribution network in an LDC. Looked at in this light MNCs would seem to merit approval in that they reflect good stewardship of unused resources.

However, there are other aspects of the situation which give pause for thought. Particular horror stories about the behaviour of MNCs abound.[29] For example, a number of MNCs have been systematically clearing areas of Amazonia for short term cultivation, regardless of warnings that this will affect the soil irreparably in the course of a few years. Other MNCs have deliberately moved toxic processes to LDCs to avoid the more stringent pollution laws that have been enacted in more advanced countries. But our case does not rely on such stories. Rather we emphasize those aspects that are common to direct investment by MNCs regardless of their intentions, good or bad.

First, we should note that the actual new capital provided by MNCs is rather a small part of the total. In a sample of MNCs studied by Streeten and Lall,[30] only 12% of new capital investment represented an inflow of funds. The rest was financed from profit retentions or local savings. More alarmingly, a recent study has shown that net inflows, and the stock of foreign capital are associated with *lower* growth rates in LDCs. This striking result has been explained in the following way. First, the arrival on the scene of a highly efficient MNC producer will tend to eliminate indigenous firms. Local firms will be happy to sell out to the MNC. But inability to compete will stunt the growth of local enterprise, and in particular local savings may diminish as profitable opportunities are not available to national entrepreneurs. Second, a local industrial élite will be prepared to bring pressure on national governments to provide the necessary infrastructure for development. MNCs on the other hand will provide a total investment package, and will be less interested in government action on education, health and other public services. They will provide these for themselves, but restrict them to their own operations. The consequence of the arrival of MNCs is often that production within big sectors in a country is entirely in the hands of a very few MNCs. They may in fact follow each other into a market to preserve their market share, and once established will avoid competing with each other.

Second, within a vertically integrated MNC, it is in the interests of the company to arrange its global operations with a view to maximizing profits. One consequence is that decisions about the level of production in a particular country will be taken at the headquarters of the MNC, and the welfare of that country will not necessarily be taken into account. For example, a MNC with sources of materials in a large number of countries may react to a recession in demand by closing down completely in one or more countries, rather than reducing output equally across all countries. There is a danger of an LDC becoming a "branch plant" economy. Another consequence is the existence of transfer pricing between different sections of the company. To avoid local taxation, or restrictions on remission of profits abroad, the MNC may arrange for its subsidiary in an LDC to charge a low price for its supplies to other parts of the company. The subsidiary's reported profit is reduced thereby. Alternatively the MNC may charge its subsidiary an excessive price for the use of technological information. For example, pharmaceutical firms are often accused of charging very high license fees to their subsidiaries in LDCs. This discussion raises the question of whether MNCs "exploit" LDCs by earning an excessive rate of profit. It should perhaps be noted that one of the severest critics of the MNC, Vernon,[31] thinks this is not proven. An analysis of the rate of return on capital to US owned subsidiaries in LDCs gave a return of 20% after allowing for "transfer pricing" practices. He also suggests that the division of profits between the host country and the MNCs has shifted in favour of the host countries over the period since 1950.

Third, MNCs are frequently criticized for bringing the wrong sort of development to the LDCs. This applies to those MNCs that undertake direct investment in order to exploit the market for some highly differentiated product. They have little interest in making more appropriate mass produced products, since local competition would quickly compete away the profits. So they concentrate on products that will be purchased only by an élite in the range of sophisticated consumer durables. We may rightly doubt whether this represents "development", from the viewpoint of our Christian criteria, in countries where some of the population is destitute of the elementary necessities of life. No sensitive visitor to a LDC can fail to be impressed by this. But it is not merely a matter of appropriate products. MNCs tend also to bring their production technology with them. That technology, having been developed in advanced, high wage countries, tends to be capital intensive and labour saving. It is not appropriate to the conditions of an LDC, with its abundant labour supply. The problem is confounded by the fairly generous incentives to foreign capital that many LDCs have used to attract foreign investment. The MNC is given little incentive to devise technology that is adapted to low wage conditions. On Christian criteria, one of the objectives of development must be to provide men with useful and productive work to do. The path of development via MNCs has proved singularly disappointing in this respect.

There has been much less substantial criticism of the role of MNCs in advanced economies. A comprehensive study of MNCs in the UK economy by M. D. Steuer et al[32] could find no reasons for limiting foreign direct investment, on the basis then available. However we should not be too sanguine about the role of MNCs in the DCs. The reason that they appear to make a positive contribution to those economies is that basically they are creations of the DCs. Consumers within the DCs benefit from their ability to span the world in search of cheap sources of supply. They benefit from the technological advances that they bring. DC balance of payments is aided by the flows of profits from the LDCs. But insofar as DC gains are at the expense of LDCs it is not a situation in which we should acquiesce.

(d) Political Issues in the Assessment of Multinationals

While the economic questions have attracted the most analysis, there can be little doubt that the political issues raised by MNCs have generated the fiercest criticisms of their activities. Vernon sees these as the "real issues". There are two separate aspects of the problem. First, the sheer size of the MNCs turns them into institutions that exceed, in the scope of their operations, many nations. Second, because of their multinational nature, there is likely to be a conflict between their interests, and the interests of nations that host them. We have seen some of these problems in the economic sphere in the case of LDCs.

Looking at the latter problem, a typical criticism of MNCs concerns their relations with national governments in the LDCs. First, it has been well established that MNCs show a distinct preference for stable régimes: in practice this means economies with strong governments of the right. Any hint of a radical government seeking to promote social and economic reform, e.g. land reform, will divert investment to other economies. Second, MNCs have a strong bargaining hand with LDCs seeking foreign investment. This enables them to get generous terms which the LDC government may come to resent once the firm is established. Third, once established, the MNC becomes a positive pressure group for political stability and preferential treatment for foreign firms, but has no particular reason to push the government into social or economic reform. Its interest is to maintain the stability of the status quo. We are not thinking here primarily of the "horror stories" concerning the involvement of American MNCs in Chile. A MNC could be honestly seeking to avoid political involvement and yet be subject to these kinds of criticisms. The political impact of MNCs on advanced countries is again, as in the case of economic issues, less marked than in the LDCs. National governments have stronger bargaining powers, though even they may wilt before the threat of a multinational, as the UK government did in the case of Chrysler. But large firms are much more part of the political structure of advanced countries, and therefore more accepted.

The size of MNCs raises different issues. A number of authors have drawn attention to the way in which MNCs see themselves as alternative organizations to nation states, demanding the loyalty of their employees, and sure of their ability to plan world production and trade rationally within the sectors in which they operate. Their responsibility is described in terms of accountability to their shareholders. But such accountability is, in practice, minimal wherever shareholding is widely spread.

Biblical criteria for evaluating these political issues are not self-evident. That there are authorities in human society, and that they are God's instruments for regulating the affairs of sinful men, is apparent from Romans 13. The association of this teaching with the rulers of the nation state is not too difficult. But what are we to make of the MNC? Is this a new kind of "authority" in human society, seeking to rule men at a different level? The answer must be, I think, in the negative. The reason is that the responsibilites of a MNC cannot be defined except in terms of seeking to promote the interests of a small group in world society, notably their shareholders and managers. Their power is not matched by a multinational or world responsibility. Thus their ability to transcend the controls of national governments, who are recognisable "authorities" in the biblical sense, should be seen as a threat. And co-operation between nations to seek to control them is a proper concern.

7. The New International Economic Order

The New International Economic Order (NIEO) is a series of demands for change in international economic relations enshrined in resolutions of the general assembly of the United Nations in May 1974. In terms of our fable, this was the moment when the *M* people read the social scientist's report on the island's economy and began to mutter angrily in the market place. Within the United Nations, the demands were associated with the LDCs united for this purpose in the so-called Group of 77. If in what follows we are mildly critical of some of the proposals this should not be taken as indication of lack of sympathy with the justified anger that prompted the LDC demands. There is, however, little point in supporting proposals that would fail in the objective of redressing international injustice. That would only store up a rich harvest of frustration for the LDCs later on.

The objectives and proposals of the NIEO have been helpfully summarized by the Commonwealth Secretariat.[33] The starting point is the failure of conventional development programmes to make much progress in alleviating poverty in the LDCs in the past 25 years. The limited objective is to deal with that problem, leaving on one side for the moment the enormous disparities in world income per capita. The requisites are thought to be a shift in the international distribution of economic activity to the LDCs, and the creation of an international economic order that favours development from *within* developing countries, rather than by outside agents such as MNCs. The major areas for action are: markets for primary commodities, manufactured exports, agriculture for food, capital aid to LDCs and technology. We will examine these briefly in turn.

(a) Markets for Primary Commodities

The LDCs wish to improve their earnings from exports of primary commodities. They are concerned by the possibility of a long term decline in the relative price of commodities compared to manufactures. We saw in Section Three above that this is not proven. However, the LDCs would like to improve their position if possible. One suggestion was that the price of commodities should be indexed to prices of manufactured products. However, the UNCTAD proposals are best seen as an attempt to exercize monopoly power against buyers (often MNCs) in the DCs. The basis for such a hope is the success of the OPEC cartel. However, a more careful consideration of the possibilities[34] is not encouraging. Cotton, rubber, jute and sisal are already facing severe price competition from synthetics in DCs. Cane sugar is being replaced by beet sugar. Metals such as copper and tin have high price elasticities of demand in DCs over a two-year period. The best prospects are offered by cocoa, coffee and tea (as a group, to prevent cross substitution). Unfortunately the historical record of attempts at producer cartels with these commodities is not good, and even large price rises (20%) would generate only $600 million revenues for middle income countries and $130 million for the poorest countries.

A further concern with commodities is the tendency for their prices to fluctuate quite widely. Commodities accounting for 35% of LDC exports in 1975 had average annual deviations of more than 10% from a five year moving average price over the previous 20 years.[35] The LDCs argue, not unreasonably, that such fluctuations make for instability in their economies and hence deter development. UNCTAD's proposal is for stabilization of prices in 10 core commodities, the necessary stocks being financed by a $5 billion fund. However, detailed analysis suggests that the gains from stabilization may be quite small compared to the costs of financing and storing the stocks.[36] So there is probably more value in the proposal to improve compensatory financing for countries suffering from short run declines in export earnings due to price fluctuations. The IMF already has such a fund and the EEC set up a similar fund (STABEX) for a number of African LDCs as part of the Lomé Convention. UNCTAD is right to press for the enlargement of these schemes, and for better terms for the poorest countries.

More useful still for many LDCs would be steps to diversify their production of commodities, to encourage more processing of commodities in LDCs, and to improve the marketing and distribution in DCs. The second will depend on the removal of trade barriers. An example can be taken from the EEC: unwrought copper enters duty free, but copper bars, wire and plate attract a 10% tariff, and tubes and pipe fittings a 15% tariff. The point about marketing reflects the concern that highly advertized synthetics are tending to replace natural products in DC markets.

(b) Manufactured Exports

A second demand of the protagonists of NIEO is for better access to DC markets for LDC manufactured exports. This was analyzed in section 5. The demand would seem to be fully justified. Bhagwati[37] has suggested that the appropriate article of GATT should be altered so as to regulate the use of non-tariff barriers to trade. He also proposed that countries which invoke Article XIX of the GATT to prevent "serious injury" to a domestic industry affected by imports from an LDC should be required to pay compensation to LDCs affected by their trade restrictions. This would have the added advantage of encouraging the DC to think seriously of alternative policies, like adjustment assistance.

(c) Transfer of Technology

A third concern of NIEO is with the transfer of technology to the LDCs. There is a general rejection of MNCs for the reasons explained in section 6. The proposal is that they should be replaced by joint ventures from which the DC firm will eventually withdraw, and by technical collaboration agreements. The difficulty with the first is that they are difficult to negotiate, given that the DC firm which holds the technology can see no reason to lose its monopoly rents by giving it to a LDC venture on concessionary terms. The difficulty with the second is that LDCs may not have the necessary human capital to make use of the technological information. The same applies to all radical proposals that LDCs should ignore patent convention, and pirate DC technology. More helpful perhaps would be systematic efforts to translate existing technology into the LDC context. For example, the World Health Organization is working on a list of basic drugs for LDCs on most of which there is not patent protection. This could be used to undermine the marketing policies of MNC pharmaceutical companies, who thrive on the continual introduction of new high priced products, the additional efficacy of which is in some doubt. Finally, there is much to be said for more indigenous R and D within the LDCs, related to the production possibilities of those economies (*not* in basic research).

(d) World Food Supplies

A fourth concern of NIEO is in the area of agriculture, though this has been pursued more in the context of the World Food Council than within UNCTAD. The Council grew out of a world food conference called at Rome in 1974, backed by UNCTAD and FAO, in the wake of the 1973-4 "food crisis".[38] Three issues were discussed. The first concerned the situation of the LDCs. Cereal imports by LDCs stood at 36 million tons in 1972, 52 million tons in 1975 and could reach 100 million tons by 1985. These imports only fill the gap in the market: they do not necessarily do anything to relieve malnutrition and hunger, since the poorest people within LDCs lack the income to make purchases. Importing food makes the LDCs vulnerable to balance of payments problems, especially during food crises. The problem is exacerbated by the tendency of DC producers to put embargoes on exports of grain during world shortages, to keep the price low for their own consumers. The second issue was the need to provide international stocks to prevent a recurrence of "crises". The 1972-3 crisis occurred when world cereal production fell 2% below the level of the previous year. Previous fluctuations in production have been counteracted by US government stockholding. However, the US government made a conscious decision to withdraw from this activity, hoping that private stockholders would fill the role. In the event, they did not do so. A major reason is that the storage and financing costs are too high to make it profitable. There seems little doubt that either national or international official stocks will have to be held, possibly at a loss, if crises and famines are to be averted. A third emphasis of the World Food Council has been on promoting rural development in the poorest areas of LDCs. Infrastructure investment in the Sahel and Bangladesh were singled out for special attention. The need to ensure supplies of fertilizer to LDCs, on concessional terms, was emphasized. Finally, there was the welcome recognition (by an international body at least) that in many LDCs land reform was a prerequisite for agricultural development.

(e) Aid and Other Financial Plans

The last demand of NIEO resolutions concerned the level of Official Development Assistance aid. The influential Pearson Report in 1969 urged the DCs to increase total aid to one per cent of GNP by 1975 of which 0.7% should be official aid. In fact, since then official aid has increased but little in absolute terms, and has not increased at all as a proportion of GNP in DCs. Some of the richest countries are the least generous: in 1976 the US gave 0.22% of GNP, Japan 0.20% and Germany 0.31%. The UK was above average with 0.38%. While much has been written against aid[39] there can be little doubt that the LDCs themselves would like to see the flow increased. However, they would prefer the aid to be channelled via international agencies rather than directly from donor to recipient. Direct aid tends to be tied to procurement in the donor's country, and this can reduce its value by 10-20%. It can also come with unwelcome political strings attached. While some have argued that the World Bank is politically biased in its aid programme, this is certainly less than the bias inherent in direct aid. Further, the LDCs are seeking even more favourable terms on aid. Loans should be made for a term of 40-50 years, with a ten year period of grace on repayment and interest rates less that 1% p.a. They are motivated by the knowledge that Official Development Assistance flows to the LDCs of $9,400 million in 1973 were offset by a flow of $680 million in the reverse direction due to interest payments alone. There is a particular request too for a change in the use of aid. A first priority is to assist those countries which face particular difficulties due to the rise in the price of oil. These tend to be the low income LDCs. Other priorities are identified as investment in rural infrastructure and development, and the promotion of indigenous R and D.

Two other proposals have been linked to the aid issue. The first concerns relief on debts incurred by LDCs in the past. A study of the indebtedness of 67 LDCs showed that their debt rose from $78 billion in 1973 to $123 billion in 1975.[40] Of this, about one seventh was short term debt, mainly from private sources. The interest and amortization in 1976 was some $14 billion. The rapid growth in debt as a whole reflected the difficulties for many LDCs due to the oil price rise of 1973-4. The growth to reliance on private lending reflected the lack of growth of official aid in the 1970s. The situation is now such that many LDCs are in risk of default on their obligations. The proposal is that the debts should be rescheduled to a longer term, and lower interest rates applied (this would involve national governments in the DCs taking over the loans made by the private sector within the DCs). The second proposal is that the issue of Special Drawing Rights (SDRs) by the IMF to finance world trade should be weighted in favour of the LDCs.[41] Until the 1970s world trade was largely financed by US dollars. The United States was able to run a persistent balance of payments deficit (i.e. consumed more than it produced) because the rest of the world was prepared to hold dollars. In the 1970s this was supplemented by the issue of SDR credits by the IMF, but in proportion to the contributions of member countries to the IMF's capital. This system gives the rich countries additional claims on world output. The proposal then is to give these additional claims to the LDCs, perhaps via the World Bank who would ensure that the credits were properly utilized. This proposal for the "link" was discussed within the IMF in the period 1972-4 but was opposed by Germany (who feared inflationary effects of increasing world liquidity) and the US (who did not wish to lose the seigniorage of issuing reserve dollars to finance world trade, and preferred to retain control over aid to LDCs).

This brief summary of the NIEO demands cannot hope to deal exhaustively with the merits of each individual proposal. Some of these have been shown to be misconceived in the sense that they would not work as intended. The commodities programme is an example. But the pleas for removal of trade barriers, for world food stocks, and for more official development aid seem to be justified. There also seems to be a good case for international agreements between the DCs and the LDCs to monitor the activities of MNCs. The only regret one might have is that it is far from obvious that any of these measures, apart from the rural development emphasis on aid, will do anything to improve the lot of the 800 million, who according to the World Development Report, still live in absolute poverty. The strong support for rural and agricultural development in that report is indeed a hopeful sign. But that will require much more aid, not less.

8. Who Bears Responsibility?

The purpose of this paper has been to explore some of the reasons for the present great inequalities in the international distribution of income. The emphasis has been on interdependencies in the world economic system: what happens in New York or London or Paris is not totally unconnected with what happens in Bangladesh or the Sahel region of Africa. There was perhaps a time in the past, when transport costs and other impediments to communications separated the world into local economies. Now, however, the market system has extended its tentacles into the remotest corners. The main consequence is that what a man can consume is largely limited by what he can sell. The rich quarter of the world's population have abundant assets — human skills, knowledge and physical capital; the rest have little of these, and some have almost nothing. It is this distribution which, more than anything else, determines the world distribution of poverty and wealth.

A Christian evaluation would point to two basic ethical defects in this situation. First, the creation ethic views every man as a steward and a worker. But stewardship and work are possible only if one has access to resources, tools and skills. The fact is that many of the poorest in the world have access to none of these. Further, one would wish to ask whether those with many assets have always acquired them justly, whether the stewardship is being properly exercised, and whether some human skills are being wasted for lack of productive opportunities. Second, the automatic link between the ability to earn and the right to consume all that one earns is not consistent with the view that man is a steward, the fruits of his stewardship being for mankind in general and not just for himself.

Then if the working of the *normal* market system is not ethic-ally ideal in its consequences, there is a strong case for saying further that the DCs, operating within the market system, have arranged matters to suit their own interests. In section 5 we dealt with the barriers to trade which effectively debar LDCs from earning as much as they could from their resources. In section 6 we suggested that multinational companies, themselves the creations of the DCs, are on balance detrimental to LDCs. Both barriers to trade and multinational companies are examples of impediments to the exercize of responsible stewardship by people in LDCs.

We conclude then that the explanation of international inequality is to be found in the workings of international economic systems. We do not have to point to the existence of wicked capitalists deliberately setting out to grind the face of the poor, though it would be hard to deny that does sometimes happen. One suspects though that most economic actors in the DCs are blissfully unaware of the consequences of the system, and find the whole question very puzzling. Thus any guilt they may feel about poverty in the LDCs is compounded by a sense of helplessness about what they should do. An immediate personal response, which is being urged on Christians, is to adopt a simple lifestyle and to give away surplus income to missionary societies, and other very worthy charities involved in development and relief. This is to take seriously the Christian doctrine of stewardship which we have emphasized in this paper, and is to be commended.

Two objections are often raised about this personal response. The first objection is the concern that if many consumers in high income countries adopted a simple lifestyle the effect on demand for goods supplied by the Third World could be detrimental. A number of considerations ensure that this is not a serious problem. First, the share of LDC products in the consumption patterns of the high income countries is quite small (for finished manufactures the total was less than 2% in 1976). Second, the kinds of products produced by LDCs are unlikely to be the first targets for elimination in the move to a simpler lifestyle. The sophisticated goods produced in high income countries are more at risk. Third, the restraint on personal consumption does not mean that the income is not spent at all, only that it is spent by the missionary societies, Christian development agencies, etc. There are a number of possibilities. One is expenditure on goods in the high income countries for use in LDCs. This has two effects: it maintains demand and hence employment in the high income countries, and indirectly it maintains demand for Third World exports to provide the basic materials used in that production. Another possibility is that the income is transferred by the agency to a LDC for expenditure in that country. Some may generate local economic activity, some may be used to import tools and equipment from the industrialized countries (where the demand for raw materials from the LDCs will consequently increase). The conclusion is that this objection carries no real weight. An adoption of simple lifestyles could require a different pattern of output in the high income countries, but will not have harmful effects in low income countries.

The second objection is more weighty. It is that charitable aid, far from being beneficial, is positively harmful to the recipients. Here we need to distinguish two types of aid. The first is aid in the form of cash or gifts to a particular needy group, e.g. famine or disaster relief. The difficulty here is that it creates a pattern of dependency. The people involved come to rely on gifts to save them when troubles come. The second type of aid avoids this problem. Its aim is to develop responsible stewardship by providing the basic resources of land, equipment and knowledge so that the people involved can be independent and provide for themselves. The most effective aid of this kind will often come not in the form of cash or goods, but in the form of dedicated expertize. The experts need to be people who can evaluate the development potential, design a viable project and then set it up with the full involvement of the people it is designed to help, so that in due course the expert can withdraw leaving a viable self-supporting community. The role of the Christian development agency in the high income countries is to provide the skilled manpower for such projects. The role of the Church in the low income countries is to identify the local needs, and to be sufficiently aware of development possibilities to know how and when to seek help. Perhaps the principles of local development, both rural and urban, should form part of the training of Christian leaders in low-income countries. It is up to the Church in those countries to set the agenda.

However, we would be mightily deluded if we thought that Christian development efforts were going to do more than scratch the surface of the problem. The real difficulty is the way in which the international system operates. If we are really serious about the problem of international inequality we must be prepared to bring pressure to bear on the system itself to redress the injustices. That means getting involved in the politics of the situation. A hackneyed illustration may help at this point. At the time of the abolition of the slave trade, English Christians could have taken a number of stances. They could have steadfastly refused to have any dealings or interests in the companies that were associated with the trade. They could have paid for evangelistic work among both the slaves and the traders. Or they could have worked to get rid of the whole evil system. Thank God that Wilberforce and his friends had the courage and the vision to dedicate themselves to the last. Are we content to settle for anything less when confronted with the evils of LDC hunger and deprivation?

A radical response is to seek to change the system entirely. One proposal could be to replace the present system of international markets with an internationally planned system. But this is not attractive for a number of reasons. Presumably a world economic plan would require a world authority to implement it. Most large, planned economies (e.g. the USSR) have found difficulties with plan implementation, and are now experimenting with the introduction of market mechanisms. The basic point here is that the price system is a very good information system for regulating economic activity, and much is lost by abandoning it. This is particularly true if one is considering the world economic system. Finally, it is difficult to reconcile a planned system with the exercize of responsible stewardship.

A less radical response is that low income countries should seek to withdraw, partially or completely, from the world economic system, and pursue their own development behind closed economic borders, either on their own or as a group. We do not accept this approach for the following reasons. First, there *are* gains to be obtained through international specialization and trade. Low income countries should not dispense with these lightly. In practice, many of the objections to export development in an open economy are not objections to exporting per se. For example, agriculture for export in the tropics has often been associated with large scale capitalist development, plantations etc. So the gains accrue to the owners of large agricultural enterprises. However, the fault here can be traced to the pattern of ownership, not to trade itself. If large scale operations are required (and frequently they are not), then some form of co-operative enterprise involving a dispersal of ownership and rewards is a feasible alternative. Second, many of the smaller poor nations of the world have a rather limited range of resources. A desire for independence may severely restrict development. For example, a country without iron ore could find itself in considerable difficulties, even if it is relying solely on simple local technology. Third, autarkic development is likely to be slower development. Given the scale of the development problems in many low income nations, rapid progress is essential, even if it brings with it other costs.

Our personal conclusion therefore is that we should seek solutions within the existing framework of international economic relations.

A beginning agenda for political action has already been sketched in our section on the demands of the LDCs for a New International Economic Order. While each proposal requires exhaustive and expert analysis to ensure that it will really serve the purpose for which it is designed, the proposals in the areas of trade liberalization, world food stocks, official development aid and control of the activities of MNCs give the most immediate prospects for effective action. (These need to be matched by an equal concern for the allocation of resources to development *within* low income countries to ensure that the poor and most disadvantaged are given priority. The Church within such countries should also get itself involved in the development debate. We do not pursue this point here, not because it is unimportant, but because we are focusing attention on the specifically international economic issues.)

There remains, however, the problem of how to set about implementation of such proposals. An immediate puzzle is the locus of political action. Political power currently rests with the nation states. Christian doctrine would assign to each set of authorities the responsibility to pursue justice between citizens within their jurisdiction. Who then is responsible for international justice? International bodies such as the UN have no real power to pursue international justice, except by license from their members. Why then should the USA or UK governments (or the EEC) pursue international policies of justice that may be detrimental to the self-interests of some or all of their citizens? The solution of forming a world government to overcome the difficulty seems neither feasible nor attractive. The answer to this puzzle is perhaps provided by O'Donovan's defence of the Just War theory.[42] He suggests that a national government should conduct its international affairs on the basis of what would be required of it by a justice seeking world authority, if such an authority existed. Morally then, a national government should act on the basis of international equity even to the detriment of its own economic interests, and Christians should have no compunction about urging governments to do so.

We should note that the case for DC governments doing more for LDC governments is basically a moral one. MacBean and Balasubramanyam[43] have shown that other motives do not hold up to analysis or experience. Thus the use of aid to gain friends and influence has proved singularly disappointing, as the USA has found. Aid has not been conspicuously successful in preventing local wars between LDCs and, with a few notable exceptions, such wars have not caused serious supply difficulties for DC industry. Nor is there any sign that LDC groupings in international affairs (e.g. the Group of 77 at UNCTAD) have sufficient power to extract concessions from the DCs. The success of OPEC makes it rather conspicuous: we have already seen that it is unlikely to have any equally powerful progeny.

So we are left with moral arguments. But as two economists have pointedly remarked ". . . spontaneous outbursts of sympathy for fellow humans do not appear sufficient to sustain a longer term desire to aid development of poor nations."[44] Can we then hope to succeed where at least two decades of intensive analysis and media coverage of Third World problems have had so little effect? There are three reasons to think that we may.

The first is that much analysis and debate of development problems in international bodies is marked by acrimony and misunderstanding between DCs and LDCs, and between conflicting ideologies. By contrast the Christian church is truly international and united in its concern for man's spiritual and temporal needs. Is it too utopian to hope that we might be able to agree on a common plan of action by sifting the best from the wealth of existing proposals on international economic issues, which we could then press on our own national governments.

Second, we should not underestimate the power of a moral stance which is backed up by real suffering and sacrifice on the part of its advocates. Here the challenge is addressed primarily to Christians in the DCs. Political action to change the system must be linked to personal action in the matter of lifestyles. It *is* an odd way to make a political point: but it is reminiscent of the way the Son of God dealt with a much more serious evil.

Finally, we should not underestimate the ability of small groups to get things done, certainly on a national scale. The modern missionary movement is a story of too few people, pitifully small resources and much prayer. Can anyone looking at Africa today deny the enormous impact that it has had on the nations of that continent? There is no limit to the power of God.

Acknowledgements

The paper has been revised in the light of helpful comments received from a number of people, not least at the Consultation itself. I particuarly benefited from detailed comments submitted by George Monsma Jr. and Ian Davis. In revising the paper, pressure of time and space has prevented me from responding fully to their comments. Both took issue with my use of the terms developing countries (DCs) and less developed countries (LDCs), and wished me to include some discussion of what is meant by "development". In the circumstances I have retained the DC/LDC terminology. However this should not be taken as an indication that I believe that LDCs should necessarily seek to reproduce the economies and cultures of the West. The terminology is intended merely to label different countries, and has no value judgement attached to it. Dan Lam has raised a number of objections to the analysis of MNCs. I have tried in the paper to give adequate coverage to the benefits that MNCs can bring, but I have not been able to alter my overall assessment. The Rev. A. G. Pouncy made a number of suggestions for improved presentation to non-economists: I have incorporated those suggestions wherever possible.

Two issues were raised at the Consultation which are not included in the paper. The first is the production and supply of armaments to Third World countries. The second is the "limits to growth"/ecology/"small is beautiful" school of economics. Both have had to be excluded from the revision for lack of time and space. The paper was written before the publication of the Brandt Commission Report on North-South. Full consideration of that report would require extensive revision, which was not feasible. But it is a very important document.

The paper was written deliberately to give a *personal* assessment of the issues. However I do not think that in any of the economic analyses I have chosen a path that would be rejected by the economics profession as a whole. If the paper does generate disagreement and constructive debate, then the effort will have been well worthwhile.

6

The Church as a New Community Fostering a Simple Lifestyle

GOTTFRIED OSEI-MENSAH

The Community of God's People

The New Testament concept of the Church is rich in its diversity. In the second chapter of Peter's First Letter alone the apostle gives us ten analogies of the Church: a creche of new-born babies at feedtime (v.2), a temple built of living stones (v.5), a college of consecrated priests at temple worship (v.5), a chosen race, a kingdom of priests, a holy nation, the covenant people of God (v.9, cf. Exodus 19:5,6), a community of aliens and refugees in temporary residence (v.11), a brotherhood of privileged sufferers (v.17 and 21, cf. 1 Peter 5:9), and a restored flock of wandering sheep (v.25). Basically, the Church is God's new community, called out of the world into the fellowship of his Son Jesus Christ our Lord (see 1 Cor. 1:9). Every member of the community is freshly inscribed with the divine nature by the Holy Spirit. Corporately, wherever they are, they compose a letter of Christ to be known and read by all (see 2 Cor. 3:2,3). More actively, they are called to be a proclaiming community declaring to the entire universe the excellent virtues of God's character revealed in the wonderful deeds he has done for them (see 1 Peter 2:9,10).

Five essential aspects of the life of God's people, described in the Bible under figures which also clearly indicate the appropriate lifestyle, must receive our attention.

God's Church — A Team of Athletes

The New Testament calls us to run with perseverance (Hebrews 12:1,2). The picture of a walk of faith (see Heb. 11) whereby the Old Testament saints walked with God, responding to his will and pleasure with submission and obedience, now changes slightly to that of a race. But the underlying principles are the same. The prize aimed for is to be pleasing to the Lord as a settled experience, both in this life and the next; to win his approval by doing his will; to share his holy character, and bear the peaceful fruit of righteousness (Heb. 12:10,11). For Paul, "the prize of the upward call of God" was to gain Christ himself, and all there is in him for his people (see Phil. 3:8-14).

Christians, then, are pictured as a team of athletes in the arena, each engaged in a qualifying race. Their competition is not against one another but against certain obstacles which would prevent them from running with perseverance the particular race set before them. The obstacles are real. The cumbersome weight (Heb. 12:1) in the context may well refer to obesity caused by a diet clearly inappropriate for an athlete. Indulgence in the good things of this earth can all too easily lead to the situation where the good has become the enemy of the best. Sin, on the other hand, is pictured as a long, tight skirt which gets in the way and trips us up. It is used comprehensively to denote anything which would keep us from first-class performance. Self-indulgence, indiscipline and vanity are cardinal sins in any athletic camp. A clear vision and commitment to the common objective, coupled with strict self-discipline, are the antidote. Discipline is always acceptable the more we esteem the object we aim for to be both worthwhile and achievable.

In the light of the athletic analogy, we may deduce a threefold mutual responsibility in the community of God's people. First of all, we must admonish and help one another get rid of those things that stand in the way of godly and upright character, behaviour and relationships. We are our brother's and sister's keeper; we belong together. If one member suffers, all suffer together; if one member is honoured, all rejoice together (1 Cor. 12:26). Secondly, we must strengthen and encourage one another to run our particular race of life well, always considering how to stimulate one another to love and good deeds (see Heb. 10:24). It is worth pointing out in our highly individualistic societies that the exhortation "to strengthen the hands that are weak and the knees that are feeble, and make straight paths for your feet . . ." was made to the people of God corporately! (Heb. 12:12,13).

Moreover, we must motivate one another, as we admonish and exhort, with God's promised reward for our submission and obedience. The goodwill and cheer of "the great cloud of witnesses" must be matched by a prayerful concern within the Christian community that "no one may fail to obtain the grace of God" (Heb. 12:15).

God's Church — A Troop of Soldiers

"Fight the good fight of faith" (1 Tim. 6:12). The twentieth century has witnessed two devastating world wars, scores of more localized battles and civil wars, oppressive military regimes and the ever present threat of a third world war in which there may be no winners or survivors. Because of these horrible associations it does sound strange to picture the Church as an army. But the Bible teaches that the Church of Jesus Christ is militant here on earth, and that we are engaged in spiritual warfare on three related fronts.

On the front of personal holiness, purity and faith, we must fight against our own sinful nature to neutralize its appetite for whatever God forbids, while positively, we must cultivate the powers and affections of the Christlike nature. This means also a relentless resistance against the seduction and pressure to conform to the world's false ideologies, distorted values, godless attitudes, and unrighteous way of life (see Rom. 12:2; 1 John 2:15,16). The "god of this world" will do everything to break through our ranks on this front; but we must withstand him in the strength of Christ and in the whole armour of God (see Eph. 6:10-20).

Secondly, on the front of evangelization. Behind human unbelief and disobedience of the gospel stands "the prince of the power of the air, the spirit that is now at work in the sons of disobedience" (Eph. 2:2). Satan "has blinded the minds of the unbelievers to keep them from seeing the light of the gospel of the glory of Christ who is the likeness of God" (2 Cor. 4:4). Our Lord once described himself as the One stronger than the strong man armed, who overpowers and disarms Satan in order to free his captives (Luke 11:21,22). The people of God, clothed with his Spirit and power, are called to repeat Christ's victory by proclaiming the Good News so that the blind may see, and sin's captives may be released (see Luke 4:18). Our weapons for this battle for men and women consist of the Word of God proclaimed in all its purity and relevance, the power of the Holy Spirit appropriated through believing prayer, and the love of Christ demonstrated in a life of service to those we seek to bring into the Kingdom of God's dear Son (see 2 Cor. 4:2; Eph. 6:18, 19; 1 Thes. 2:8).

Thirdly, on the front of justice and peace in human society, the Church is called to be the salt of the earth and the light of the world (Matt. 5:13-16). This implies a painful and costly mission to penetrate every segment of society with a message that will both hurt and heal, convict and convert; a message of hope, that offers a convincing alternative to the life of sin and rebellion against God. The weapons available to us for war on this front consist of a prophetic proclamation and incarnation (by the people of God) of God's requirement of justice; a priestly duty of prayer and intercession for all mankind (see 1 Tim. 2:1-4); and a Christ-like caring love for the casualties of unjust human society.

Of the Church that marches forward courageously under his command, equipped with God's armour for war on these fronts, Christ vows, "the powers of death shall not prevail against it" (Matt. 16:18). The sense of comradeship and solidarity in which the community of God's people should do battle on all three fronts is summed up in Paul's exhortation to the Philippian church: "Only let your manner of life be worthy of the gospel of Christ, so that . . . I may hear of you that you stand firm in one spirit, with one mind striving side by side for the faith of the gospel, and not frightened in anything by your opponents" (Phil. 1:27,28). Because of the enormous challenges, as well as opportunities, we face on the evangelization front, Ralph Winter's call to the people of God to place their economy and entire lifestyle on war footing merits a serious response (see Ralph Winter, *Penetrating the Last Frontiers*, Pasadena, William Carey Library, 1978).

God's Church — A Community of Aliens and Refugees

"Our commonwealth is in heaven, and from it we await a Saviour, the Lord Jesus Christ" (Phil. 3:20). By calling his people out of the world and sending them back into the world, the Lord Jesus constituted his Church as a colony of heaven on earth, but also as a community of aliens and refugees temporarily resident in human society. The Lord was fully aware of the trouble he was thus creating for us in a wicked world (see Matt. 24:9; John 15:18-21), and so he prayed to the Father to keep us from the evil one (see John 17:9-16).

The Bible speaks of the blessedness that comes to the people of God themselves and also to the world in which they live when they come to terms with their new status (cf. the history of Israel). But it also warns of the disastrous consequences of compromise with the world which is tantamount to unfaithfulness to our Sovereign Lord and denial of our heavenly citizenship (see Luke 12:8,9; 2 Tim. 2:12).

There are four specific areas where the effect of our status in the world as a community of aliens and refugees should be felt. The primary concern should be the spiritual health and eternal welfare of the community and its members. We must avoid like the plague the sinful passions and desires that characterize the life of the people of the world. They are like deadly infection to spiritual health (see 1 Peter 2:11). Instead, we must take care to cultivate an ever deepening fellowship with the Lord, deriving our joy and delight in his service and obedience (see John 14:21, 23). The ultimate goal of our pilgrimage must always be kept in focus. It is to enter into the presence of the holy God, the Father of our Lord Jesus Christ, for without holiness no one will see the Lord (see Heb. 12:14).

Our distinctiveness in the world is also indispensable to our witness to the world concerning God's goodness, justice, and saving power (see 1 Peter 2:12-17). We fool ourselves if we think we can influence human society for our Lord by fraternalizing with it in its customs, ways and standards. On the contrary, by submitting our lives to the guidance and direction of God's laws, we show God's goodness which rebukes the ignorance and folly of unbelief and offers a convincing option through faith in Jesus Christ. God's people live upon earth and must take their full share of responsibility for living upon earth, but we are citizens of heaven, and it is by the laws of heaven that we must live.

Our heavenly citizenship must be demonstrated also by the investment of our lives in rigorous service on earth in the interests of heaven. Paul testifies by his own experience how amply God compensates us for the demands of such service (see 2 Cor. 4:10-18): in the salvation of God's elect (v.12, cf. 2 Tim 2:10), the extension of God's reign and worship (v.15), the present enjoyment of resurrection power (v.10,11), and the hope of eternal glory (v.17,18). Moses too got his priorities right. He reckoned it of far greater consequence to be identified with God's people and to share their ill-treatment, as aliens and refugees in Egypt, than to enjoy the fleeting pleasures in sin. He considered the rewards of abuse suffered for Christ infinitely more than all the treasures Egypt could offer him (see Heb. 11:24-26).

The fourth area where a right perception of our status, as aliens and refugees, is bound to make a difference is in the investment of our money and material resources. The Lord Jesus put it bluntly: "Don't lay up for yourselves treasures on earth, where moth and rust consume and where thieves break in and steal, but lay up for yourselves treasures in heaven, where neither moth nor rust consumes and where thieves do not break in and steal" (Matt. 6:19,20). Paul is helpful and practical as to how this may be done (see 1 Tim. 6:17-19). Pride in our wealth or dependence on it is disastrous. Instead, our confidence must be firmly in our Lord, the Giver. To be truly rich is to be rich in good deeds and generous to the poor. How we regard our money and material possessions, and the use to which we are prepared to put them, inevitably reflects the devotion of our lives. "For where your treasure is, there will your heart be also" (Matt. 6:21). When the infant community of believers discerned aright their new solidarity of faith in the Lord Jesus, they voluntarily renounced exclusive rights to their possessions and saw themselves as stewards of whatever they had, for the benefit of the Lord's people (see Acts 2:45; 4:32, 34-37).

The dssire to acquire and hoard is pagan, not Christian (see Luke 12:15-21). The Lord's people are pipelines (channels) to carry his blessings, not reservoirs to retain them! His purpose is to enrich us so that we can give generously to others in need, and in turn bring thanksgiving to God the ultimate Giver (see 2 Cor. 9:8-11).

Foreigners in temporary residence must think twice before investing in immovable property. Exiles and refugees, of necessity, must travel light.

God's Church — A Staff of Stewards

It is required of stewards that they be found faithful (1 Cor. 4:2). The Church may be likened to a household in which we are all servants and stewards. We each have different roles and areas of responsibility for which we have been suitably endowed with gifts and abilities. However, none of us is self-sufficient. In our different areas of responsibility we must depend on the co-operation and shared resources of one another to fulfil our particular roles. The harmonious functioning of the entire household thus requires our unselfish commitment to one another, and the effective coordination of our resources in the Master's service.

The "varied grace of God" of which we are stewards includes both the spiritual and the material: the oracles of God (the gospel of salvation), material possessions, special gifts and ministries, abilities, skills, potentials, time, home and life itself (see Rom. 12:6-8; 1 Cor. 12:4-11; Eph. 4:7, 11-12; 1 Peter 4:9-11).

Our faithfulness as God's stewards has implications in several areas. Primarily, a steward's faithfulness has reference to his master. It is the controlling love of Christ and the solemn sense of accountability to him which lead the Christian to resolve no longer to live for himself but for his Lord who died and was raised to life again for his sake (see 2 Cor. 5:10, 14-15). A deficient sense of stewardship in any Christian community therefore signifies an inadequate grasp of what Christ in love has done for its members and the reality of the day of reckoning.

Stewardship implies creativity and industry in developing our gifts and abilities to the utmost limit of our opportunity and potential in the Lord's service. We learn from the Parable of the Pounds that God's stewards are given *equal opportunity* (everyone was given a pound, see Luke 19:13,16,18 and 20) and from the Parable of the Talents that God recognizes our *different abilities* (He gave to each according to his ability, see Matt. 25:15). But in each case the Lord commended diligence and industry as a measure of his servants' love and loyalty, while he condemned sloth and shirk as a wicked sabotage of his interests.

It is all too easy to reduce our stewardship to diligence in giving to the poor, even the poor of God's people. But we must not create or perpetuate dependence by a patronizing use of the Lord's resources entrusted to us. If any one will not work, let him not eat (2 Thess. 3:10). However, we must ensure that he has the option of work! To help the Lord's people to realize their potential for his service may involve setting up new structures for the purpose. But it is better to help set up fish ponds and train people to fish for themselves than to arrange for regular shipments from abroad!

Every faithful steward must be prepared for the test of greater trust. Under normal circumstances, diligent working coupled with modest living will result in increased resources. The temptation is to upgrade our standard of living accordingly. The luxuries of yesterday become the indispensable necessities of today. What is worse, we may become dependent on (or preoccupied with) our growing wealth. The Lord richly furnishes us with everything to enjoy (1 Tim. 6:17), and expects us to provide adequately for our own needs and that of those closest to us (1 Tim. 5:8). But there is great gain in godliness with contentment which those who set their hearts on riches for riches' sake know nothing about (see 1 Tim. 6:6, 9-10). Increased resources indicate rather increased responsibility to manage our trust for the maximum benefit of our Master and his kingdom. "If your riches increase, don't depend on them" (Psalm 62:10 — Good News Bible). "Everyone to whom much is given, of him will much be required" (Luke 12:48).

The community of God's people must provide the secure caring base from which its members, having discovered their true identity in Christ, can freely dedicate both themselves and all they have to advance the kingly interests of their Lord in the world.

God's Church — A Band of Missionaries

"We beseech you on behalf of Christ, be reconciled to God" (2 Cor. 5:20). The crux of the Church's mission to mankind is the proclamation of the message of reconciliation. God is reconciled to mankind through the atoning sacrifice of himself in the person of Jesus Christ his Son (see 2 Cor. 5:18,19). The people of God are sent to go into all the world and tell this Good News to every people (see Mark 16:15), and to plead with them, on account of God's forgiving love and mercy to quit their rebellion and sin and be reconciled to God. The cross of Christ is at the very centre of the message entrusted to us, to remind us constantly of the costliness of God's redeeming love for mankind. Those to whom we are sent are described as "perishing", indicating how desperately this unique message entrusted to us is needed (see 1 Cor. 1:18). Moreover, there is an inescapable sense of urgency about the Gospel. Man's life is short and uncertain, and there is no second chance beyond the grave (see Heb. 9:27); the day of salvation will not last for ever.

A right understanding of our solemn obligation to God and persons must have far reaching effects on our lives and lifestyle as the people of God. "The cross of Christ must be as central to our lives as it is to our message. A church which preaches the Cross must itself be marked by the cross — self-denial, self-humbling, and self-giving" (John Stott: *The Lausanne Covenant — An Exposition and Commentary* p.32).

The Apostle Paul was a good model of the church in mission. His single-mindedness and utter dedication to his mission stand out everywhere in the New Testament in sharp relief (see Acts 20:24; Rom. 1:14-16; 15:17-19; 1 Thess. 2:2, etc.). But there was nothing rigid or legalistic about Paul's lifestyle; on the contrary, there was a great deal of flexibility, and freedom (see 1 Cor 9:19,23; Phil. 4:12,13). However, all of Paul's flexibility, adaptability and mobility had but one goal, namely to facilitate his mission and ministry. Care was taken that no obstacle was put in any one's way; that no fault be found with his ministry (see 2 Cor. 6:3).

The Church as the community of God's people indirectly fosters a simple Christian lifestyle:

— By a fresh vision of its mission and purpose in the world;

— By cultivating and exercising the gifts and potential (spiritual and material) which the Lord has given to it for its mission and life in the world;
— By fostering the sense of community, solidarity and interdependence in which its members discover themselves and their special gifts, and gladly consecrate both to the service of their Lord.

Authentic Christian lifestyle must flow from inner conviction by the Spirit, and the Word, as part of the process of synchronizing our values and priorities with God's. If the Christian community seeks to achieve this by exerting external moral pressure alone, it will succeed only in fostering legalism and hypocrisy in the camp.

Simple Lifestyle from the Perspective of Church History

TADATAKA MARUYAMA

Prologue

J. Huizinga makes an important point about medieval history: "The picture drawn mainly from official records, though they may be the most reliable sources, will lack one element: that of the vehement passion possessing princes and peoples alike."[1] Huizinga's statement is relevant here as well. The theme before us, "Simple lifestyle for evangelism and justice," especially demands a delicate treatment. Without the slightest doubt the treatment we see in the following pages is destined to suffer from its abstract character. It tries to trace the development of the theme from the early Church down to our days, but it fails to capture the "vehement passion" which characterizes the living saints in their own days. What is only reasonable is its silence on "a cloud of witnesses" who were unaccounted for in the historical records of their days but who had upheld a simple lifestyle as commanded by the living God.

I. Early Church: Simplicity in Conversion and Charity*

1. "He therefore who serves in simplicity shall live to God" (The Shepherd of Hermas, *Mand. 2,6)*

(i) It may not be an overstatement that the Great Commission and the commandment of love had won the ancient world for the early Church. Christ's call, "Go and make disciples of all

---

*In the discussion of this paper Dr. Maruyama explained his broad definition of "simple lifestyle". "I had in mind an all-embracing concept of simple lifestyle including such aspects as justice (not only economic justice but also legal, political, social justice)." Editor's note.

nations" (Mt. 28:19), and his command, "Love your neighbour as yourself" (Mt. 22:39), as well as the ultimate expression of his love on the cross had moved the early Christians and permeated their actions. However, what seems so striking is that these two moving forces were inseparably united. Quoting Jesus' famous saying, "I was hungry, and you fed me . . ." (Mt. 25:35), A. Harnack could say that "these words of Jesus have shone so brilliantly for many generations in his church, and exerted so powerful an influence, that one may further describe the Christian preaching as the preaching of love and charity."[2] There was no polarization between evangelism and social concern.

(ii) In the early Church the aim of evangelism took a pristine form of "conversion". Here a clear-cut dichotomy between God's Kingdom and the world was presumed and simply a radical transformation from a worldly life to a Christian life was often the outcome of evangelism, at least, for three reasons.

First of all, for most of its history, the early Church had to face a world which treated it with hostility and presented many obstacles to its evangelism. "At whatever level in society it was attempted, evangelism in the early Church was a very daunting undertaking. It was a task involving social odium, political danger, the charge of treachery to the gods and the state, the insinuation of horrible crimes and calculated opposition from a combination of sources more powerful, perhaps, than at any time since."[3] Yet, secondly, the church on its part also looked at the world as being hostile to its faith. An obvious evangelistic motive here would be the Christian concern for those who were in the perishing world without Christ. The world was an arena for evangelism where the gospel and the forces of the demons and the pagan gods and customs were two combating forces.[4] Thirdly, there was another but quite important element which made the church an alien in the ancient world. The ancient world knew no religion like Christianity which was an entity with a theology and an organization. The new form of belief which the church presented was not a supplement to the ancestral piety but a radical alternative to it. Therefore, Christianity was a unique religion of "conversion".[5]

(iii) For the individual Christians the practical application of conversion was simply the exercise of Christ's commandment of love. This genuinely Christian expression of charity took place in both their Christian communities and the outside world.

Both before and after the recognition of its faith by the Emperor Constantine the early Church had neither a programme of

reform nor a policy of contemplated revolution. What was prevailing was the spirit of detachment and independence from the
pagan world and as a result, social conservatism which nomin-
ally accepted the existence of the social ordinances in God's
economy yet gave them no intrinsic values independent of its
Christian message. In general the early Christian came into contact with the world only as often as and as much as such contact
was deemed necessary for the purpose of the church's existence
and evangelism.[6]

Nevertheless, the gospel of Jesus was not just word but power
and action. It had to become "a social message" (Harnack) and
its social conservatism conversely accompanied some "revolutionary tendencies" (Troeltsch), and its life-changing power
produced a measurable "effect of Christianity upon its environment" (Latourette). For this reason, on the one hand, many
Christians dissented from prevailing religions, including the imperial cult, as well as many prominent yet morally questionable
practices of the secular life. On the other hand, they gave what
the contemporary world lacked — peace of conscience through
reconciliation with God, a new aim and fresh moral strength.
"The Christian lived for God, for his fellows in the faith and for
humanity at large" (Latourette). This aspect of Christian influence was achieved especially within the church where the Christian ideal of love and its radical negativism toward the world
were combined into a new social order, "the communism of
love" (Troeltsch).[7]

Beside the organization of the church and evangelism, perhaps, the most noticeable social impact of Christianity was its
work of charity. Although the early Church was well aware of
the sufferings and wounds caused by the unjust social-economic
system, Troeltsch says, its reaction to this issue "did not take a
shape of social reform . . . it was simply and solely the work of
charity; the aim of this charity was the revelation and awakening of the spirit of love; its means was restricted to philanthropy, to voluntary contributions, and to the free exercize of
private charity." Harnack further examines ten different types
of charity which include alms in general, the support of teachers
and church officials, widows, orphans, the sick and the dis-
abled, the care of prisoners, the poor, slaves, etc. Naturally the
work of charity was primarily directed to its own number, yet it
often expanded beyond its periphery. Despite all of this, however, what the early Church was concerned with most was
neither the problem of private property nor even the giving of
material help in itself, but simply "the spirit of love and inward

detachment from possessions''. In short, this was "the spirit of simplicity of life in those who give and in those who receive".[8]

2. Sub-Apostolic Period

(i) This was the period of advancing translation of the Christian faith from its Jewish background to the Hellenistic world. We assume, however, that much of the basic apostolic dynamics in both evangelism and social concern was retained in this period. Despite the fact that this Hellenization obviously bore new emphases in evangelism — moralism, sacramental piety, and the growing emphasis on merit — the cardinal elements of the dominical and the apostolic preaching survived vividly in this period. Likewise, surviving well was the apostolic spirit of love with genuine simplicity which is always one result of evangelism. Ignatius pointed to this aspect: "the beginning is faith and the end is love, and when the two are joined together in unity it is God" (Ephesians 14:1).

(ii) During this period, Christianity was yet a minor religious group without recognition. Its expansion was primarily limited to the Empire's urban centres and the evangelistic task was largely borne by the lay people.[9] In addition to this the fact that the church scored success chiefly among the lower classes of the social order left upon its evangelism a mark of simplicity. "The lower classes which do the really creative work, forming communities on a genuine religious basis alone unite imagination and simplicity of feeling with a non-reflective habit of mind, a primitive energy, and an urgent sense of need."[10]

(iii) The following words of the Apostolic Fathers clearly witness the ongoing simplicity in the work of charity:

Give to everyone that asks thee, and do not refuse, for the Father's will is that we give to all from the gifts we have received (Didache 1:5).

They offer free hospitality, but guard their purity. They love all men and are persecuted by all men. They are poor and make many rich; they lack all things and have all things in abundance. . . . To put it shortly what the soul is in the body, that the Christians are in the world (Epistle to Diognetus 5-6).

The call to the work of love was to overcome the unjust and hostile world. Along with this emphasis, however, there appeared an increasing association of voluntary charity with the merits of salvation and the ethical concern for rewards and punishments. "Almsgiving is therefore good even as penitence for sin; fasting is better than prayer, but the giving of alms is

better than both" (II Clement 16:4). Thus, charity was introverted to a salvific mechanism. This pointed to a danger of neg-
lecting both the Christian commitment of love and the world as
the aim of charity as well as to a direction toward asceticism
which would become more noticeable in the succeeding
periods.[11]

3. Early Catholicism

(i) The period under consideration covers the emergence and
the triumph of the early Catholic Church, beginning in the mid-
second century and climaxing at Constantine's recognition of
the Christian faith. In general the early Catholic Church maintained the basic trend of the apostolic and sub-apostolic evangelism and social concern. For example, H. Lietzmann comments on this period and says that "the church spread without
exercising any outer pressure, or any mass suggestion, but simply by a total of purely individual conversions."[12] Furthermore,
as much as the church's awareness of, and concern for, the peril-
ous state of the unconverted was genuine, so was its concern for
both their religious and social well-being. For Tertullian this
concern was simply for the Christians to aim at "a perfection"
and seek "something of a higher type than the commonplace
goodness of the world" for "it is peculiar to Christians alone to
love those that hate them" (*To Scapula* 1)[13].

(ii) As a rich source of the emerging Catholic Church's docu-
ments and the apologists' writings show, this period had witnessed freedom and variety in the evangelistic messages, aims,
and methods. On the one hand, the apologists could make free
use of philosophers, religions, sciences, laws, arts and letters of
the secular world in order to demonstrate the finality of Jesus
Christ and to win new converts. On the other hand, the simple
Christians inherited the apostolic simplicity of personal evangelism in their day to day life and indeed won many converts.
Nevertheless, some changes were inevitable. As the official,
ministerial order had become a "mark" of the Catholic Church,
for example, evangelism had become more "clerically" controlled. Cyprian's famous dictum *extra ecclesiam nulla salus est*,
was only a manifestation of this tendency. Furthermore, the
apostolic hope of the coming Kingdom was gradually replaced
by the desire to pile up merits and good works for the reward of
eternal life and, thus, instead of the freedom of salvation, asceticism was regarded as a high goal of evangelism.[14]

(iii) The apostolic simplicity of charity had also acquired

some new elements. For instance, Christian charity had become a well organized and efficient work of the Catholic Church. For Tertullian "the bond of hospitality" (*The Prescription* 20) was what made the churches into the unity of the Catholic Church. "The deposits of piety" (*The Apology* 39) were individual contributions collected by the church for its work of charity. In this connection, "the office of the diaconate, which was dedicated to works of charity, was made subordinate to the episcopal office."[15] Another element to appear was a double morality among the Christians. The growing worldliness of the church had caused many Christians to compromise, for example, on the problem of material possessions. Others saw denouncing possessions as a good work for one's salvation. Thus, a widening gap between the less meritorious compromise and the more meritorious ideal became noticeable. The latter tendency especially provided a basis for the development of monasticism in the post-Constantine era.[16]

4. After Constantine

(i) The imperial recognition of the Christian faith had transformed not only the life of the church but also the apostolic simplicity in both evangelism and charity. On the one hand, as the sphere of the church had become co-existent with that of the Empire, many new converts began to join the church not always on the religious basis. Thus, the focus of evangelism shifted from the life-changing gospel message to the institutional church as the bulwark of the orthodox gospel. On the other hand, as the church had to give the world some positive Christian meaning and to encourage Christian participation in various aspects of the secular life, those who were not satisfied with the secularized church and its excessive contacts with society had increasingly begun to seek their Christian ideal in the closed community of monasteries. The contrast between the two tendencies can be illustrated by the following sayings of Augustine, an ardent admirer of the monastic life but also a leader of the Catholic Church, and Anthony, a founder of the monastic tradition: "The love of truth doth ask holy quiet, and the necessity of love doth accept a righteous busyness" (*The City of God* 19:19); "The spaces of our human life set against eternity are most brief and poor" (*The Life of St. Anthony* 15).[17]

(ii) During this period Christian evangelism won first the Mediterranean world of the Roman Empire and then territories beyond the Roman boundaries:

The fourth and fifth centuries witnessed the transition of Christianity from the position of a minority religion, well organized and vigorous but persecuted, to the faith of the majority of the Mediterranean basin. It thus became the professed religion of the most powerful of the civilized areas of the globe.[18]

As the state-religion Christianity had increasingly become identified with the Graeco-Roman culture, the religious factor and evangelistic enthusiasm had lost some of its earlier impact to the political and cultural factors. It was in this way that conversion acquired a new meaning, i.e. conversion to the politico-cultural faith of the church.

(iii) More than ever the Catholic Church emerged as "a new class within the social order," but this time as the prestigious class which had such privileges and rights as acquiring property, accepting legacies, and mediation in the judicial disputes. As its social function became immense, naturally, its opportunity of exercizing its influence increased. It could have some say on such social issues as prostitution, the abandonment of children, the manumission of slaves and so forth. Especially "public judicial authority in all matters which concerned the care of the poor and social welfare as a whole" was given to the church and the church exhorted its faithful to exercize these influences as "good work" of asceticism.[19] The church's operation was so efficient that even an enemy like Julian the Apostate tried to copy it for the state. Nevertheless, a new problem was clearly in the offing. "Charity became depersonalized," says Troeltsch, "and Christian philanthropy lost its earlier spirit . . . of overcoming social distress, of equalizing the distribution of wealth, and of the increase of the spirit of fellowship within the church itself."[20] In short, the church as simply another institution alongside the state had failed to exercize its ideal of social reform.

II. The Middle Ages: Simplicity within the Universal Values

1. *"There is nothing freer, nothing more safe, than holy poverty"*

(i) The period under consideration (500-1500) roughly corresponds to what is called in the West the "Middle Ages". What had emerged through a long historical course of the Middle Ages was the *corpus christianum*. This was a universalistic Christian society which adopted the Christian norm for both religion and society. The *corpus christianum* had finally replaced the antinomy between the church and the world. In this context of universalism both the church's evangelism and its social concern were more closely identified in a way which the church had never experienced before.

(ii) One form of the simplicity in evangelism and social concern was expressed by "conformity" to the universalistic values which the Christian sociey imposed upon the faithful. Naturally this kind of conformity could come into conflict with the radical individualism of the apostolic simplicity; yet this was a reality of life in these centuries. As the whole society was governed by one universalistic order, every individual, whether a nobleman, a knight, a priest, a monk or a serf, had to follow what his religious or social status demanded of him for the sake of the whole society. Echoing Christ's call to a simple life, "I was hungry, and you fed me . . .", a 13th century Cistercian monk could speak on the monastic life:

O holy band of men living at unity with one another, what can I say that is worthy of you? You hunger and thirst and suffer penury for the name of Jesus. But it is an honourable and sober poverty, not compulsory but freely chosen . . . There is nothing freer, nothing more safe, than holy poverty.[21]

2. Early Middle Ages

(i) The period from the 6th through the 10th century can be properly called "the darkest hours" in church history. Christendom was in a state of disruption. After the beginning of the invasion of the Germanic tribes in the 5th century, the church suffered the loss of almost half of Christendom to the Moslems, while the Vikings proceeded to plague Europe. Even in the 11th century Europe was in a state of siege. But these losses were countered by some gains; most notably, the conversion of the European heartland. Ireland, Gaul, the British Isles, Germany, Denmark, Moravia, Norway and Russia were won one after another.[22] The Papacy and monasticism were mostly responsible for the gains; the Papacy provided a cohesive mission strategy and the monasteries provided many missionary monks.

"For five hundred years the major task of the Western Church was that of wrestling with barbarians and with barbarism in the effort to make their conversion something more than nominal; in the process, it found itself transformed from an imperial into a feudal church."[23] In this way a system of territorial churches was developed.

(ii) The territorial church system had some lasting impact on the church's evangelism. While the early Church inherited a rather pessimistic view of the state, the territorial churches were often based upon the Germanic idea of the monarchy, more specifically, the idea of the divine right of kings. When a king was converted, therefore, the result was often mass conversion. Moreover, sometimes mass conversion was hastened by the use of force. Of course the actual task of instructing the faith to the throngs of new Christians was the work of missionaries. However, the faith transmitted in this way often included the tribal and pagan customs and beliefs. Although the church tried to either remove or christen them, many of them remained in the veins of the medieval church life.

During these disruptive centuries the Christian ideal of simplicity was measured in terms of the supernatural values it represented and it was believed to be embodied in the ascetic life of the Benedictine monasteries. "The Benedictine monasteries were the symbol of eternity and immutability in a world of flux; they were the gate to heaven; they were a replica of heaven on earth." In this world view an individual was of little value and was likely "swallowed up in his community or in his office. And both community and office drew their strength from the supernatural."[24]

(iii) The church's social concern became subservient to society. This was especially true of the monastic system which was definitely placed at the service of civilization.[25] Missionaries, often provided by monasteries, were political and civilizing agents as well. Furthermore, the church and monasteries fulfilled another important role in the feudalistic society. As they were land owners themselves, they were responsible for their tenant-farmers and vassals. In the territorial church system they were the instigators of charity where it was the congregation which fulfilled the same role in the early Church. Thus, the object of the church's social concern was introverted: Christ's command, "Love your enemy," had to be understood as "Love your own fold."

3. High Middle Ages

(i) The period from the 11th to the 13th century saw the highest manifestation of medieval universalism. After winning Europe's heartland, the West gained momentum and launched the counter-advance against Islam. Spain and then Sicily were freed and even a series of Crusades (1096-1270) was launched from the West to regain the lost territories by force. The tremendous forces of such a movement as the Crusades were not only directed at the external enemy but also used to challenge the internal forces of the territorial church system. For example, the Papacy headed by Gregory VII was not content with a nominal and spiritual role but began to assume a more aggressive role vis-à-vis the Holy Roman Emperor, kings, princes and their territorial churches. In the following centuries this universal claim was backed by the church's doctrinal development: the dogma of the universal episcopate of the Pope, that of the supremacy of the spiritual power over the temporal, and that of the impartation of grace through the seven sacraments. All of this helped the church to consolidate sociologically the *corpus christianum*.[26]

In the *corpus christianum* the bonds of society were tight and were often provided by the Christian ideals and virtues, such as service, humility, charity, hope and love. All of them, however, were directed toward one final goal of the salvation of one's soul. For this reason the church was to provide the faithful with an elaborate system of merits for salvation. For the sake of merits a serf should serve his lord and the lord would care for him and free him by manumission. Christian simplicity was expressed in this form of bondage.

(ii) Again and introvertedly, simplicity in evangelism was confined to the context of the *corpus christianum*. With a few notable exceptions (missions in the Ukraine and Russia and among the Mongols which were opened as the result of the Crusades), the western Church's witnessing to and conversion of the heathen to the Christian faith was replaced by the serious quests for higher virtues within the church and all these quests were controlled by the theocratic church centred around the Papacy.[27]

Throughout the Middle Ages the religious life meant primarily the ascetic life of monasteries. Unlike the original form of Christian monasticism, the Western monasticism of this period was not "a flight into desert places undertaken by individuals . . . it was the expression of the corporate religious ideals and needs of a whole community."[28] Also the monastic ideal was to be hierarchically communicated to and faithfully copied by the cathedral churches and then the parish churches, and finally the laity. "It was from the monasteries that the countryside learned its religion."[29]

Perhaps, the most exceptional and, therefore, non-conformist figure in the general picture was Francis of Assisi. In 1208 he heard the Lord's bidding to apostolic poverty and devoted the rest of his life to ascetic goals. All his passionate devotion to God and man, his love of nature, his constant search for simplicity and humility undoubtedly pointed to the radical simplicity of the apostolic period. Combined with these was his evangelistic zeal for the conversion of the Moslems. He even went personally to both Spain and Egypt for this purpose. When, despite Francis' original intention, the Franciscan order came into being, the whole movement started by Francis was transformed to operate within, and not against, the universal context of the *corpus christianum.*

(iii) Without any doubt the high medieval church had inherited the spirit of charity from the early Church. Many religious orders had been established for the purpose of helping the underprivileged, the sick, and the abnormal.[30] But all the charitable efforts were aimed at the attainment of an other-worldly, and not a this-worldly, salvation. Manumission, for example, was encouraged for the lord to pile up merits, but slavery itself was regarded as necessary for the sake of the whole society. Social injustices were considered normal and even inevitable in this world since they provided an opportunity for the church to exercize charity. The powerful Popes proclaimed "the Truce of God" and "the Peace of God" in order to quell the war-prone Christian princes, but the feudalistic social system upon which the church was built had never given up the warlike spirit and the feudal principle of honour which sharply came into conflict with the Christian ideals of humility and love as well as the doctrine of non-resistance.[31] The more the Christians found these unjust yet normal practices in society, the more the conscientious sought to hide themselves behind the walls of cloisters where they hoped to find the Christian simplicity of love. Nevertheless, monasticism was not expected to be independent of the whole society. Even the original ideal of the Franciscan order with its radically spiritualistic view of the church could not establish an independent system of charity apart from the state.

4. Late Middle Ages

(i) As J. Huizinga vividly portrays, "the last three centuries of the Middle Ages were the time of the great party struggles" and as a result an immense impression of pessimism, "the decline of the world and despair of justice and of peace," settled in.[32] The universalistic values of the high Middle Ages came under attack. The Renaissance of Humanism in the arts and science and Nominalism in philosophy and theology challenged the universalism of the 13th century. Especially, the Papacy, the symbol of universalism, was clearly in decline. Conciliarism and various reform movements attacked its universalistic claim. Among these reform movements, in particular, there appeared what Troeltsch calls "sect-type Christianity" which refused to compromise with the church and radically proclaimed the primitive Christian tradition:

The asceticism of the sects is merely the simple principle of detachment from the world . . . The sects take the Sermon on the Mount as their ideal; they lay stress on the simple but radical opposition of the Kingdom of God to all secular interests and institutions.[33]

In this category, one may include the heretical Catharis, the Poor Men of Lyon and those of Lombardy, Wycliff and the Lollards, the Hussites and others.

(ii) Among these sect-type movements, simplicity in evangelism took a form of a radical return to evangelical Christianity. Its context was the secularized and corrupt Roman Catholic Church and its goal was the reform of that church. In the case of Wycliff, for example, it meant the acceptance of both "Scripture as the final authority in all matters of faith and practice," and "the supremacy of the first three centuries of the church".[34] In the case of Huss, furthermore, it was the return to the "truth", namely Scripture. He urged his followers to "seek the truth, hear the truth, learn the truth, love the truth, speak the truth, adhere to the truth to death . . ."[35] Here was the root for the radical individualism of the gospel. "The sects," says Troeltsch, "start from the teaching and the example of Jesus, from the subjective work of the apostles and the pattern of their life of poverty, and unite the religious individualism preached by the gospel with religious fellowship."[36] In one way or another they all tried to reform the church and in the process they introduced some important elements in the stream of later medieval Christianity, such as the emphasis on a lay Christianity (the Catharis), the "home mission" movement (the Waldensians and the Lollards), the idea of the "poor" church (Wycliff) and, in a sense, paved the way for the Reformation of the 16th century. The simplicity of the gospel, the church, and the Christian life was indeed the watchword for them.

(iii) The sect-type movements' concern for social justice was but a simple application of their evangelical orientation. In most cases this concern was expressed in a negative way, i.e. departing from the secularized church and the world and returning to the apostolic simplicity. Wycliff's message to his contemporary priests, "Imitate Christ in this evangelical poverty," for example, was an accusation for their departure from the apostolic church.[37] Except for a radical wing of the Hussite movement which advocated armed revolution, their movements generally made no attempt to form a new social order. Instead, they tried to realize their evangelical ideal of love and holiness in their own circles.[38]

III. Protestant Reformation: Simplicity in the Responses to the Word of God

1. *"Faith is a sure, firm and solid foundation"*

(i) The Reformation in its central thrust was the restoration of the Word of God within the church. Nurtured in the spirit of Renaissance-humanism's "return to the originals (*ad fontes*)", the Reformers discarded much of the tradition of the Middle Ages and even considered the Church Fathers secondary to the primary importance of Scripture. The principle of *sola scriptura*, therefore, was the main reforming force of both the church's doctrine and life. This recovery of the Word not only shattered the framework of the *corpus christianum* and split the monolithic structure of the Middle Ages into the Roman Catholic and the Protestant camps, but also produced a variety of responses to the Word within the Protestant Reformation. In this respect simplicity in both evangelism and social concern can be also examined as various responses to the Word.

(ii) In the context of the Protestant Reformation evangelism simply meant a reform of the church. In essence it was to change drastically the complex system of medieval Catholicism into the simple system of grace realized in Protestantism. During the Middle Ages the Catholic Church had evolved into an elaborate institution based upon the hierarchical priesthood and the sacramental system of merit. The Reformers found in Scripture the principle of *sola gratia* which they employed as an axe to cut the root of that monumental structure. As a result the simplification in both doctrine and life took place. As one of the Protestant creeds said, "this faith is a sure, firm and solid foundation for and a laying hold of all those things for which one hopes from God" (*The First Helvetic Confession* 13). Such simplicity in evangelism meant the application of the *sola gratia* principle to the entire scope of the Christian religion.

(iii) The Protestant Reformation took the principle of *soli deo gloria* very seriously. For the main stream Reformers, with the chief exception of the Radical Reformation, the sphere in which God's glory was to be manifest encompassed not only the small communities of Christians but also the entire society. Distinguishing between the sect-type and the church-type Christianity, Troeltsch notes some affinities which the main-stream Reformers had with the late medieval sectarian movements (e.g. its individualism, its lay religion, its appeal to the authority of the Bible, its emphasis upon subjective realization of salvation in personal and inward Christian piety, and on the restitution of the true church) but says that "in spite of all this it regarded the church-type as the only Christian type of ecclesiastical organization."[39] Thus, Protestantism had to accept seriously the life of the world and tried to apply to it the ethic of a universal Christian society. In short, both the church's evangelism and social concern had to come under the evangelical reorientation of the Word of God.

2. Luther and Lutheranism

(i) Among many themes which can help us comprehend the dynamic thought of Martin Luther, the one which best sheds light upon the subject before us is his teaching of "gospel and law" and its corollaries, i.e. the two-kingdom theory and Christian liberty.

The dialectic relationship between gospel and law lies in the heart of Luther's theology, especially of his doctrine of justification by faith. In a book, *Temporal Authority: To What Extent It Should Be Obeyed* (1523), he advanced the so-called two-kingdom theory as an application of this gospel-law dialectic and said that "God has ordained two governments: the spiritual, by which the Holy Spirit produces Christians and righteous people under Christ; and the temporal, which restrains the un-Christian and wicked so that they are obliged to keep still and to maintain an outward peace." It is important to distinguish them and maintain them for "neither one is sufficient in the world without the other."[40] In another work, *The Freedom of a Christian* (1520), Luther applied this gospel-law relationship to yet another area, namely, Christian liberty. True Christian living, he said, must simultaneously incarnate the following two theses: "a Christian is a perfectly free lord of all, subject to none" and "a Christian is a perfectly dutiful servant of all, subject to all." The first thesis states what a Christian receives from the gospel. The second shows how a Christian freely obeys the law. Indeed, Luther could say both of the following sentences: "a Christian is free from all things and over all things so that he needs no works to make him righteous and save him" and "we should devote all our works to the welfare of others, since each has such abundant riches in his faith that all his other works and his whole life are a surplus with which he can by voluntary benevolence serve and do good to his neighbour."[41] Here is Luther's answer to Christ's call, "I was hungry and you fed me . . ."

(ii) Simplicity in evangelism meant, first of all, an optimism for what the gospel and faith could bring forth for the Christians. Luther called faith "the inestimable power and liberty of Christians" and said that "true faith in Christ is a treasure beyond comparison which brings with it complete salvation and saves man from every evil."[42] This optimism was further extended to his view on the church reform: "the doctrine of faith and justification . . . drives out all false gods and idolatry; and when that is driven out, the foundation of the Papacy falls, whereon it is built."[43] Secondly, simplicity in evangelism was to let the Word of God rule and reform the church. The basic doctrinal standard of the Lutheran Church, the Augsburg Confession, attested to this: "it is sufficient for the true unity of the Christian Church that the gospel be preached in conformity with a pure understanding of it and that the sacraments be administered in accordance with the divine Word."[44] This was a kind of optimism which was to produce a conviction that the Word must bear its fruits which were necessary, but not essential, for the life of the church.

(iii) For Luther, simplicity in social concern was to acknowledge God's rule over the entire creation. His *Small Catechism* (1529) illustrates this aspect. On the fourth petition of the Lord's Prayer he explained "our daily bread" as "everything required to satisfy our bodily needs, such as food and clothing, house and home, fields and flocks, money and property; a pious spouse and good children, trustworthy servants, godly and faithful rulers, good government; seasonable weather, peace and health, order and honour; true friends, faithful neighbours, and the like."[45] The scope of this description encompassed law, politics, economics and ethics.

However, it has been commonly suggested[46] with a certain degree of justification that by drawing the dividing line between the spiritual and the secular realms too sharply and by leaving the whole area of social justice to the hands of princes, Luther secularized the world by making it independent of the rule of the gospel. (For example, Luther left it to the state to handle the task of human well-being.) Nevertheless this accusation misses the mark at a very crucial point of Christian liberty. Certainly Luther adamantly refused to cross the boundary and to mix the two realms. He could say to the leaders of the Peasants' War in his *Admonition to Peace* (1525): "Suffering! suffering! Cross! cross! This and nothing else is the Christian law."[47] He authorized no forceful attempts to remedy social injustices "in the name of the gospel". However, he believed that those who were under the realm of the gospel could most clearly see, through their faith, the reality of life, the existence of sin, misery, death and injustice in the society. On the one hand, certainly, they would refuse to exercize their Christian liberty to do vengeance against social injustice for they trust in God's word, "Vengeance is mine, I will repay, says the Lord" (Deut. 32:35; Rom. 12:19). On the other hand, however, they would take full advantage of their Christian liberty in serving their neighbours and remedying the social injustices as love called them. Thus it is faith working in love which makes the Christians to recognize "this vile world as God's creation despite its depravity, . . . to believe in merciful, forgiving love in spite of our enslavement in sin, . . . to comfort ourselves with the hope of life eternal in spite of death."[48]

3. *Calvin and the Reformed Tradition*

(i) Like Luther's reform, Calvin and the Reformed tradition accepted the basic platform of the *corpus christianum* and, thus, their reform was a modification of the medieval unity between the spiritual and the secular realms. This modification, however, proved to be more extensive and aggressive than Luther's two-kingdom theory envisioned. While Luther tended to separate the two realms, the Reformed tradition tried to integrate them and to realize the harmonious combination of the two under the common authority of God's Word. From the earliest reformatory attempts of Zwingli in Zurich and of Calvin in Geneva, through the Reformed movements in France, the Netherlands, Germany, East Europe, Scotland and England, to Cromwell's Puritan Revolution, the various expressions of the pan-European Reformed movement tried to realize the "Christocracy" or "Bibliocracy", subjecting the two realms to Christ and his Word.

What was peculiar to the Reformed movement in this connection, however, was the means to realize this combination. Unlike the Roman Catholic Church which insisted on the sacerdotal supremacy, unlike the Erastian Church of England with its doctrine of secular supremacy in church reform, unlike the Lutheran Church which left social justice mostly to the prince, and unlike the Radical Reformation which strictly separated the spiritual from the secular, the Reformed movement was the first to "switch the emphasis of political thought from the prince to the saint (or the band of saints)" who were committed to "the literal reformation of human society, to the creation of a Holy Commonwealth."[49] In short, the saints were God's instruments in the transformation of the entire society. In this sense the church's efforts in both evangelism and social concern were organically united.

(ii) Simplicity in evangelism was nothing but the realization of this Christocracy within the church. This was called a reform of the church yet this reform did not stop at the expulsion of the unscriptural doctrine and customs but was extended to the transformation of the present order according to God's purpose. The church was an instrument for this transformation.[50] In Calvin's view of salvation history, for example, the original order of the creation was manifested in the areas of nature, the political order and in man himself. After the Fall, however, it was corrupted and for the purpose of its restoration God ordained the church to exist.[51] To establish a true church was the beginning of restoring the social order.

(iii) From the above discussion it becomes obvious that the church must work seriously at the task of service to the world and society. In other words, simplicity in social concern is measured by how well and far the church can extend Christ's rule in the society. As Martin Bucer had already done in *Of the Kingdom of Christ* which was dedicated to the young King Edward VI for the reformation of England, Calvin achieved the reform of the entire city of Geneva. In the Geneva of Calvin's days, obviously, the welfare of the Republic and its citizens was under the care of the magistracy. Unlike the Lutheran territorial churches, however, the Genevan church was supposed to contribute positively to the magisterial efforts of social justice. For example, the church was to pray for the magistrates, to remind them of their divine mission, to admonish them in the abuse of their power, to protect the poor against the rich, and especially to request the authority to enforce ecclesiastical discipline.[52] Commenting on Rom. 13:4 Calvin could say, "They are not to rule on their own account, but for the public good. Nor do they have unbridled power, but power that is restricted to the welfare of their subjects."[53] In short, both the spiritual and the secular authorities were to achieve social justice under the common reign of Christ.

4. Radical Reformation

(i) The reform movement which categorically rejected the medieval starting point of the *corpus christianum* has been called "the Left-wing of the Reformation" or more recently "the Radical Reformation". In this movement, there were typologically several groups, namely, the Anabaptists, the Spiritualists, and the Evangelical Rationalists or the Anti-Trinitarians.[54] Since, strictly speaking, only the first group held the biblicist inheritance and was church-oriented, we focus on Anabaptism.

For the understanding of Anabaptism the doctrine of the church is crucially important. The Anabaptists were the Christian Primitivists believing that a pure and true church existed in the early Church, the "Golden Age of the Church". This church was marked by the apostolic simplicity of free religious associations, missions and charity. Then there came the catastrophic Fall of the church. It came with Constantine's recognition of the Christian faith. As the church became a state-church, apostolic simplicity was destroyed. From this viewpoint they rejected the medieval church as the "fallen" church and even considered the Protestant Reformation of Luther, Zwingli and Calvin "magisterial" and "incomplete" because of its close affiliation with the state.[55]

(ii) For them, first of all, evangelism simply meant the restoration of the primitive and true church. Following the late medieval "sect-type" Christianity, they separated themselves from the mainstream Protestant churches and formed their own small communities as voluntary associations. Their true church was to be marked by believers' baptism, spiritual government, communal fellowship, discipline and passive obedience to the civil authority.[56]

Secondly, partly due to their sectarianism and non-conformity, their restitutional work had to bear the mark of suffering. The "suffering church" or the "church under the cross" was their evangelism in action. "True Christian believers are sheep among wolves, sheep for the slaughter," wrote Conrad Grebel in 1524. "They must be baptized in anguish and affliction, tribulation, persecution, suffering and death."[57] Indeed, many historians have considered "martyrdom" and "discipleship" as the very essence of the Anabaptist spirituality.[58]

Lastly, simplicity in evangelism was a sincere and radical re-

sponse to Christ's Great Commission and their vivid eschatological expectation. In the final analysis their expectation encouraged them to "break completely from the inherent idea in . . .
the medieval *corpus christianum*" and to "confirm them in
their conviction that they were at once pilgrims toward, missionaries of, and martyrs for that City which would momentarily
descend from heaven or emerge messianically from the debris of
an age that was breaking asunder."[59]

(iii) A Mennonite scholar says that "in sixteenth-century
Anabaptism there was no organized mission or service programme."[60] Strictly speaking, therefore, the Anabaptists' dual-
istic separation of the spiritual and the secular could leave no
room for the idea of "social" concern. The kingdom of this
world in general and the state in particular had a totally different origin, namely the Fall, from the kingdom of Christ. Certainly they admitted the state had a legitimate place, "to keep
order, to punish the evil, and to protect the good," yet they adamantly insisted that it had no authority in matters of faith.[61]
Their pessimism toward the world forced them to realize introvertedly their ideal of love within the closed communions of the
true believers.

Nevertheless, one aspect of their social ethic was noteworthy.
This was the simplicity of their lifestyle upon which both their
apologists as well as their prejudiced opponents must agree. One
of the opponents, a Roman Catholic, wrote in 1582:

Among the existing heretical sects there is none which in appearance
leads a more modest or pious life than the Anabaptists. As concerns
their outward public life they are irreproachable. No lying, deception,
swearing, strife, harsh language, no intemperate eating and drinking,
no outward personal display is found among them but humility,
patience, uprightness, neatness, honesty, temperance, straight-
forwardness in such measure that one would suppose that they had the
Holy Spirit of God.[62]

In addition, their ethic of love, non-resistance, and radical obedience have made their movement long remembered as well as
an inspiration for many of us and especially for those who call
themselves today "Evangelical Radicals".[63]

IV. Modern Protestantism: Simplicity in the Polarized Society

1. "They call us to deliver their land from error's chain"

At the end of the Thirty Years' War (1618-48) the Christian
churches stepped into the modern period in which the political,

social and cultural structures began to be fashioned apart from Christian values. That was the first major break from the *corpus christianum*. An historian of modern Christianity summarizes the history since then:

The modern Christian churches inherited the great new enterprise of medieval and the Reformation Christianity, the endeavour to penetrate and "Christianize" civilization. For three hundred years they continued this attempt, yet on the whole, with ever less success . . . The great forces and structures of modern civilization have increasingly eluded Christian guidance and have pursued new gods, tribal or utopian.[64]

More than any other realm of the Christian world Protestantism has been most severely affected by the modern age. The Enlightenment, the repercussions of the originally anti-Catholic French revolution, modern scientific thought, Darwinism, liberal theology etc. have helped already confessionally divided Protestantism to polarize further along theological, social, and national lines. Even the great expansion of Western Christianity through missions and immigration has not changed, but only complicated, this picture. To search for simplicity in evangelism and social concern is extremely difficult and can be conducted only against this background of a rapidly changing and polarizing world. The situation is further complicated by the fact that the modern world has increasingly viewed Christianity as a fallible institution. To be sure, not all the Protestant attempts in evangelism and social concern could be called genuinely Christian. In this respect, the call "To deliver their land from error's chain" from Reginald Heber's famous missionary hymn, "From Greenland's Icy Mountains" (1819), could be applied not only to "heathen lands" but also to the polarized Protestant areas.

2. Pietism, Evangelicalism, and the Great Awakening

(i) From the mid-17th to the mid-18th century, the most dynamic Protestant movement was the evangelical revivals in both the Old and the New World.

Philip J. Spener's *Pia desideria* (1675) marked a symbolic end of the age of Protestant Orthodoxy and a beginning of that of Pietism. Although Pietism had predecessors in the "Reformed" pietism of the English Puritans and the Dutch Precisianists of the Jean de Labadie type, its stage was set against the background of Lutheran Orthodoxy. In a word, it was a reform movement aiming to establish "ecclesiola in ecclesiam", i.e. religious fellowship within the Lutheran territorial church system. Since the Protestant Reformation had bogged down in the dogmatics, polemics and institutionalism of Orthodoxy, Pietism claimed to reform the practice and life of the church by emphasizing the devotional use of Scripture, organizing Bible studies, conventicles, and increasing lay participation.[65]

Although sharing many motifs with Pietism, John Wesley and Methodism was a unique evangelical movement within the context of Anglicanism. Its reform was to create in the Church of England *"ecclesiolae"* of the true believers who had had conversion experiences and were exercizing the "able practical religion" toward the goal of Christian perfection.

Both Pietism and English Evangelicalism had greatly influenced the emergence of the Great Awakening in New England. Jonathan Edwards' epoch-making sermon, "Justification by Faith," in December 1734 was only a beginning. The revival was soon to spread to the Middle Colonies and to the South, affecting such denominations as Presbyterians, Baptists, the Anglicans and eventually establishing the Methodist Church in the New World.[66]

(ii) Through these revivals evangelism seemed to have two areas of concentration: one was the reform of the established churches and the other foreign missions.

Concerning the first area, there appeared two emphases, namely, practical religion and orthodoxy. Against Protestant orthodoxy, firstly, Pietism emphasized practical religion as the focus of its reform. "It is by no means enough to have knowledge of the Christian faith," said *Pia desideria*, "for Christianity consists rather of practice."[67] Secondly, English Evangelicalism and the Great Awakening emerged when the traditional Christian doctrines came under the rigorous attacks of the Enlightenment, and therefore a new need arose to emphasize traditional orthodox doctrines. For Wesley, Evangelicalism was "in no small part a reaction against rationalism in all its forms," and for Edwards it was "an apology for experiential religion".[68]

Concerning the second area, the modern impetus for Protestant missions decisively came from Pietism and was further enforced by English and American Evangelicalism. "The history of missions supported by churches on the European continent," says S. Neill, "begins only with the emergence of the movement called Pietism."[69] From the earliest Pietist missions in Tranquebar in India and the Moravian work under Zinzendorf, to Edwards' missionary programme expressed in his book whose title in part reads, *"A Humble Attempt to Promote . . .*

the Advancement of Christ's Kingdom on Earth" (1748), the missionary outreach was a genuine consequence of the revivals.[70]

(iii) The rather modern concept of "progress in humanity" began to be widely used in the Enlightenment. As the 18th century thinkers began to bring down the "heavenly City" of universal Christian values in order to rebuild it on earth, C. L. Becker notes, they began to think that "the salvation of mankind must be attained, not by some outside, miraculous, catastrophic agency, but by man himself, by the progressive improvement made by the efforts of successive generations of men."[71] Diametrically opposite to the Enlightenment's optimistic and deistic concept of the universe, however, the Evangelicals seemed to have approached the issue of charity and social concern from the pessimistic, yet genuinely Christian, perspective of the Fall. It was not simply that the Evangelicals were sharing the "same spirit of the century and a new enthusiasm for humanity" with rationalists and deists, as McGiffert pretends, but actually that they directly associated the necessity of salvation with Christian service and missions to the fallen world.[72] So the Pietists expressed "their love for the world through works of mercy and their hope for the world through an eschatology which expected a revolutionary transformation of the world to be accomplished by God's work in changing human lives." Wesley and Methodism "consciously directed itself to the poor and unchurched and it was a great home missions movement." "In New England as elsewhere the revivals became a major means by which people of many diverse types responded to changing moral, religious, intellectual and social conditions."[73] Perhaps, their idea of simplicity in social concern was largely due to this "directness" of the connection between regeneration on the one hand and missions and social concern on the other. As E. Beyreuther says on Francke: "Conversion and regeneration should lead man into service on behalf of the social betterment of the world."[74]

3. 19th Century

(i) The period under consideration actually extends beyond the chronological limit of the 19th century and covers a period between the French Revolution (1789) and the beginning of the First World War (1914).

As far as our topic is concerned, it can be said that the century began with a sort of harmony between the Protestant churches' evangelism and their social concern, but ended with

both breaking asunder. As we have previously noted, the
Pietistic-Evangelical thrust had maintained the direct connection between the reform-mission aspect and the social concern
aspect. However naive it may have been, this connection proved
to be very productive especially in the first half of this period.
As the century advanced, however, this connection came under
scrutiny.

(ii) In the early decades of the 19th century, an ongoing
thrust of the evangelical revivals stirred many European
churches where Enlightenment Christianity had formerly prevailed. In many different places, evangelical reformers were
active: the awakenings in the Church of Scotland (Thomas
Chalmers of Glasgow), the Reformed Church of Geneva (a
travelling evangelist from England, Robert Haldane and Merle
d'Aubigné), the Reformed Church of France (Caesar Malan,
Felix Neff), the Reformed Church of the Netherlands (Groen
Van Prinsterer), the Lutheran Church of Prussia (under a
statesman, Baron Stein, later an O.T. scholar, Hengstenberg).
The Awakening found its chief stimulus especially in British
Evangelicalism. It encouraged the growth of Free Churches but
also had an impact on the Church of England. Its characteristic
fruit was the emergence of voluntary societies, for example,
missionary societies such as the English Baptist Missionary
Society (1792), the London Missionary Society (1795), the
(Anglican) Church Missionary Society (1799), the British and
Foreign Tract Society (1804), the Society of the Suppression of
Vice (1802), the British and Foreign School Society (1807) and
so forth. A similar development was seen in America and other
European countries.[75]

The great historian of missions, Kenneth Scott Latourette,
calls this period "the great century"; indeed "the age of the
most extensive geographical spread of Christianity." This
achievement was largely due to "a new burst of religious life"
animated by the Awakening.[76] Despite all its enthusiasm, nevertheless, the 19th century Protestant mission as a whole bore the
mark of both strength and weakness exactly because it was
closely associated with the expansion of the European colonial
powers. As long as the *pax Britannica* lasted and was welcome,
the popular slogan "evangelization of the world in this generation," was a possibility. When colonialism began to be looked
at as a force of political and social aggression, however, the
Christian mission became culture-Christianity at best and out-
right religious aggression at worst. At this time, simplicity in
evangelism was indeed at the crossroad.

(iii) It may not be an overstatement that "throughout the world Protestantism had made more significant contributions to social reform, education, medicine and ministered more to cultures in transition than had Roman Catholic missions."[77] Indeed, wherever the advance in evangelism was made in home missions and foreign missions alike, there was genuine social concern manifested. Simplicity in the spirit of love and service was at work.

The early 19th century's response to social injustice was mostly charity. When the capitalist system of *laissez-faire* came under strong attack by Marxist Socialism which regarded established Christianity as a collaborator of the system, however, the Christian responses became more complicated. In the face of the challenge, for example, the Continent's Christian Socialism, England's Church Social Union, the "Settlement movement", the "Neighbourhood Houses", the YMCA-YWCA, and the Salvation Army, all recognized the serious nature of the problem and tried to offer Christian solutions. William Booth's *In Darkest England and the Way Out* (1890) was an excellent example of this agonizing recognition. On the American scene, however, the social gospel completely gave up the traditional approach of charity and challenged the social structure itself. Walter Rauschenbusch's *A Theology for the Social Gospel* (1917), for example, was to show "that the social gospel is a vital part of the Christian conception of sin and salvation, and that any teaching on the sinful condition of the race and on its redemption from evil which fails to do justice to the social factors and processes in sin and redemption, must be incomplete, unreal, and misleading."[78] Influenced by the German liberalism of A. Ritschl, the social gospel reinterpreted the Kingdom of God in terms of social reform and progress. Charity and social concern no longer meant the same thing, and, above all, evangelism was not identified with, but replaced by, social concern.

4. 20th Century

(i) No century before our own had experienced the devastating power of war that our century has known. The electrifying shock of the First World War decisively wiped out the optimism of the 19th century as an overwhelming air of doubt and pessimism set in. "The moral pretensions of the West were shown to be a sham; 'Christendom' was exposed as being no more than a myth; it was no longer possible to speak of 'the Christian West'."[79] The succeeding developments had adverse effects upon Christianity and its missionary expansion: a socialist state produced by the Russian Revolution (1917) became a great anti-Christian force; the rise of nationalism, usually a reaction against the West, had been seen on many continents; and the increasingly self-assured secular states had assumed a greater control over the social and the religious life of the people. Surrounded by these adversaries, for example, mid-century European Protestantism was described as "the Protestant Diaspora".[80] Then, the Second World War, triggered by the rise of totalitarianism in Germany, Italy, and Japan, dramatically manifested the tragedy of modern humanity. After the mid-century point Protestantism was to recover from the nightmare of war and to search for its Christian identity. The national churches, the confessional groups, the World Council of Churches, the international missionary organizations and, certainly, Lausanne '74 have had to share this fate in the rapidly changing world.

(ii) Despite all adverse forces, evangelism in the Protestant world has not been muted but it has certainly been in dispute. Among many areas which have been the focal points of discussion, for example, we may choose two, namely, the nature of the gospel and the field of missions. First of all, the question, "What is the gospel truth?" has produced a host of responses — 19th century liberalism and the social gospel, the Fundamentalist controversy, the dialectic theology of Barth, the demythologization of Bultmann and the post-Bultmannians, the death-of-God theology, liberation theology etc. All may claim to seek the simplicity of the gospel. Commenting on Evangelical responsibility in this area, however, J. W. Montgomery says that the question which the world is asking Evangelicals is, "Do you have the truth?"[81] Their answer, certainly, will determine the attitude toward simplicity in evangelism. Secondly, in the field of missions, Protestantism has still continued its rapid growth outside Europe and the United States and this perhaps validates Latourette's description of this period, "Advance through Storm".[82] Uncertainties about the 19th century missionary method became manifest and accordingly nationalism and totalitarianism have posed a great danger to the future of missions. Also the emphasis on evangelism declined in the ecumenical missionary movement. The Evanston Conference of the WCC (1954) still maintained "mission" as a mark of the church, but the Conference from New Delhi to Uppsala (1961-8) abandoned this mark and instead emphasized that the church's existence is not an end in itself, but is the servant of

God's mission to the world.[83] The increasing chasm between the "Ecumenicals" and the "Evangelicals" became almost un-bridgeable. In this historical context, the World Congress on Evangelism in Berlin (1966) and that in Lausanne (1974) should be assessed.

(iii) In the entire history of the Christian era, perhaps, no century has been more conscious of social justice than the 20th century. The world has been challenging Christianity on this very count and Christianity has been obliged to take this challenge seriously. The church's success or failure will be determined by the next century, but for the moment, it seems that the measure of the Christian response to the challenge has been somewhat mediocre.

First of all, we should note the awesome immensity of the problem of social justice. The conscience of the world which witnessed the Nazi holocaust, Hiroshima and Nagasaki, and the ongoing wars in Indochina cannot be easily soothed. Even a problem within a national boundary is usually too immense for the national church to tackle, and more than ever, the welfare state is assuming a greater control over the problem. Earlier attempts, for example, the Conference on Politics, Economics, and Citizenship (COPEC) which tried to formulate "Christian" answers to the social problems, were only token gestures. The later decline of liberalism and the social gospel was a serious reminder to us of the immensity of the problem. Secondly, an unfortunate division between the "liberal-radical" and the "Evangelical" and between social concern and evangelism has been a hindrance to a stronger Christian approach to the problem. The realization of this failure at Lausanne was a welcomed sign but the remedy for this shortcoming is yet to be seen. Now knowing the direction which the WCC is taking afer New Delhi and Nairobi, thirdly, it seems that the Evangelicals have an opportunity to make a realistic assessment of the problem and to realize how much they can do or are asked to do by the command of the gospel, and to attempt an integral programme uniting both the Great Commission and the commandment of love in order to remedy social injustice. Some positive and serious re-examinations are in the offing with the Christian attitude toward possessions and hunger as an example. One hopes that an accusation such as this, "the majority of affluent 'Christians' of all theological labels have bowed the knee to Mammon,"[84] will not fall on deaf ears and that Lausanne's search for "a simple lifestyle" will not be too late.

Section Three
Testimonies

8

Cross-Bearing In India

VISHAL MANGALWADI

I must start out with a couple of negative statements. Perhaps the most serious one is that very often my wife and I don't like our style of life. I suppose the significance of this will become clear at the end. *Secondly*, I do not like describing our lifestyles in economic terms such as a "simple lifestyle". If a description has to be given then I would like to call it a cross-bearing life-style. At least that is what I hope our lives are. *Thirdly*, I did not really come here to work out a theology for simple living. For our need in India is to create wealth and as such, what we need to do is to discover the dynamic of Christian theology which created wealth in the western world.

As I see it, for those of you in the affluent western countries, the issue of simple lifestyle resembles the picture of the rich young ruler and Zaccheus in the biblical times. It has to begin at the point of economic repentance — they have to repent of the wealth which has been accumulated unjustly, and give it to those from whom the wealth had originally come.

We, in India, have to come to simple lifestyle from the position of Peter and John — those simple, poor fishermen. As I was saying in the Theology of Development consultation, Peter became a disciple of Christ, not at the point of simplicity but abundance.

Peter had worked the whole night and caught nothing. He faced the sad prospect of going home empty-handed, to his hungry wife and children. Then came along Jesus, hired his boat for a preaching session, and took him out into the deep. There Jesus gave him the charges for hiring the boat — two boat loads of fish. Even if it were £5 per fish, for two hundred fish, it would be £1000. When Peter went back home, he didn't just take fish. He took new dresses for his wife, perhaps lipsticks and perfumes too. No wonder, therefore, that when he said to his wife, "I'm not going to fish anymore, I'm going to follow this carpenter," his wife replied, "Sure, no problem. Your giving up boat and nets does not make me insecure."

Move to the scene at Cana: in another situation of need, Jesus created six hundred litres of wine. That is at least £3,000—worth of wine for free distribution! What abundance!

Look again at the shores of the Galilean lake. Five thousand people are fed and twelve baskets are picked up. Didn't the feast cost over £10,000! It was this air of abundance which made it possible for poor people to give up their security and follow Jesus. The poor people were able to see that God is a rich God. He fights for the helpless, the hopeless, the powerless, the oppressed — the poor. But he is not a poor God. This God who is concerned for their poverty is a rich God. They were able to see this and therefore trust him.

Faith was their prerequisite for simple lifestyle, and that is true in our case too. My wife and I were able to venture out as we did, refusing all jobs and offers, because while we were still students we had personally proven the all-sufficiency of our God. I am not giving a testimony of the simplicity of our life-style but a witness that we have found him to be all-sufficient, which makes it possible for us to share our all with others. After creating an air of abundance, Jesus did two important things in the minds of his disciples. He taught them not to trust their human leader (Jesus himself) but their own Father in heaven. "He cares for you," Jesus taught, "therefore trust him for your needs." Jesus also taught them to develop a carefree attitude towards wealth, or a non-materialistic perspective on life. That is why the abundance neither made them greedy, nor dependent on Jesus, in a human sense. They learnt to trust God on their own.

I grew up in a poor home. There were nine of us, and my father was the only wage earner. He earned enough for us to have about £3 per person per month. My wife grew up in different circumstances. I went to very simple schools, but because I was fairly good at my studies, my parents wanted me to get into some profession where I would earn a good salary. When I decided to serve the Lord instead, they seemed disappointed. Because I was not going to be an economic asset to the family, I felt that I had no right to study at their cost. So, at the age of nineteen I left home, to serve the Lord, trusting him to meet my needs. For two years I worked as an evangelist amongst students. Then at twenty-one, I decided to go back to the university. It was easy to trust God to support an evangelist. Could he support a student in a secular college too? He did. It was great to know a God who could meet my needs, feed me, clothe me, give me shoes to wear and money to travel on.

It was in Wheaton College, while studying theology, that my wife learned to trust God for her daily needs. She returned with a clear desire to serve God amongst the poor people in rural India. When we decided to get married neither of us had a job. I was on a scholarship, doing research on Hindu Gurus. But my scholarship was due to end on June 31st and we were getting married on the 21st.

Neither of us had jobs nor were we looking for them. Ruth's parents were therefore a bit apprehensive about the economic viability of our marriage, but they couldn't prevent us from getting married because Ruth was firm in her faith. We decided that after marriage we would move to a village and try to understand the needs and problems of poor people and see if God could make some use of our lives.

Even though we had practically nothing, we decided to have a home open to practically anyone who needed us. The Lord began to bring people to us initially from cities. As we trusted him for our own needs, we started trusting him for their needs too, and therefore shared whatever we had with them.

Then one old man, who had become a Christian thirty years ago and then reverted to Hinduism, decided to come back to Jesus, after I confronted him with the gospel. Without talking to me, he also decided to give up his job at the residence of the district collector, and serve God full-time with us. After quitting his job he came to me and announced: "Now I am free and I am going to serve the Lord full-time with you."

What do you do when all of a sudden you've got to support a family with your own resources? At first I tried to persuade him to stay on the job and come out for evangelism and service part-time with us. But he said: "I have prayed for three days and now there is no turning back." So we just had to say: "Well, as we trust God for our own needs, we'll trust him for this family too." When we began sharing our all, which was very little, with this family, a missionary brother came up and said his organization would finance a regular team including this family. So support started coming for six evangelists. When the World Vision of India heard of and saw what was happening, they came in with a bigger support, for community development work.

We prove the sufficiency of God by giving our all to him. Last year when the monsoons failed and two successive crops failed, we found ourselves in the midst of a people, some of whom literally did not have anything to eat. What do you do when you are surrounded with such need? We passed the word around that we would not let anyone starve to death in our area. We would share our last grain with those who had nothing. With that kind of a commitment behind you, when you pray the Lord has to listen. Now we do have a food-for-work programme going and nobody around needs to die of starvation. Right now we have almost a thousand people who are being fed or given work on a temporary basis, because some of us were able to trust God that he is sufficient. This available manpower is being used for development work.

When I say that I do not like to describe our lifestyle as "simple lifestyle" but a cross-bearing lifestyle, what I mean is that we have not just turned our faces from money or jobs. We have given ourselves totally to God so that he may give us to others as an expression of his love. In our case this commitment has meant many things. Our home had to be opened for many different kinds of people, from criminals to emotionally disturbed people. We had a businessman who broke his marriage, lost his business and made a mess of his life, a nurse who attempted suicide, was thrown out of her job and had no place to go to, another nurse who had several abortions, then an illegitimate child; this made her insane, she killed the child and was in prison for two years. We bailed her out, kept her in our home and got her treated. All of this often put unbearable pressure on us. Just before coming here, we were feeding fifteen people in our home. I hope you can see why we don't like our lifestyle at times.

In the last couple of months when some criminals have been converted, we have been faced with another situation. These people can't go on living off crime; nobody would employ them. What do you do? You just have to open your home to them, and trust God to provide for them too.

When the Lord began to bring so many people to us, even when we had the money we couldn't spend it on ourselves. I am not giving a testimony on how poor we are, but perhaps I could mention just a few things to illustrate that cross-bearing has meant simplicity: We have been married now for five years, but I do not think I have been able to buy a single sari for my wife, not because we do not want to or cannot afford it, but because when we have the money, there are other more pressing needs. For example, when our first baby was going to be born, one brother came to us who had been going out to witness with us. He was a very old man, who supported his family by sitting on the pavement and selling clothes. He came and said that he had used up his capital to repair his roof. Now he didn't have money to buy enough clothes. Could we therefore give him a loan of Rs. 100/- to help improve his business?

My wife and I said that we didn't have money, but that we would pray for him. We were really praying for him. Then on Good Friday morning the Lord said: "I gave my life for you and you say that you do not have money for this brother. What about the money you are saving to repair your watch, Vishal, and what about the money you are saving for your baby's delivery Ruth? Watch can wait, Baby has two more months. Is it more important to save for your tomorrow, or it is more important to meet the need of this family for bread today?"

So, we said: "OK Lord we shall not repair the watch and will not save for our tomorrow. We will rather meet the need of this brother today." This sort of thing has had to continue all along the way. As I was saying earlier in the day, eight people have to share one motorcycle. Ten or fifteen people have had to share our home with people sleeping on the dining table, the office table and all over the floors.

In the early days we were too generous, we even gave our bed to others and slept on the floor. When we realized that we can't really cope with the emotional pressures this kind of sharing puts on us, we stopped going to such lengths. But the hard question remains: Do you spend on things you want for your personal enjoyment, or do you share to meet the needs of those whom the Lord brings to you?

Our real experiment with simple living and common purse came ten months ago, when the organization which had been financing our evangelists could not continue it because of its own financial problems. The question arose, should they go back or should we continue to trust the Lord for their support? Prayerfully, we decided that our six families would have a common purse. Ruth and I were the only ones getting salaries at that time. But we decided that we would share our entire salaries with these families. We also decided that we would not keep the purse in our hands but put it into their hands. For that is exactly what Jesus did. The money that came to him was put into the hands of his disciples. That, we felt, would be the only way to avoid dependence.

When your salary has been put into the hands of a simple, poor, illiterate brother, and your wife has to go to him to ask if it is possible to buy fish today, then you really get down to living simply. The needs of these families were obviously bigger than our small family's needs. Proportionately more money had to be given for them than to us. The experiment worked for six months. During this time we reached a degree of love and commitment we would not have reached under normal conditions.

During this time we were able to train some of these people and put them in different jobs. Then we all went back to salaries. Well, not quite actually, because it was then that these criminals were converted, and their economic rehabilitation meant that our salaries have to be shared with them.

It is not easy for a woman to go to an illiterate brother who is handling her own salary, and ask his permission to buy fish. It is hard. That is why I said that we don't really like it at times. But that is what cross-bearing has meant for us. The cross is not something one runs to. Jesus said: "Father, if it is possible, let this cup pass from me. I don't want it. But not my will but thine be done." The cross means powerlessness, to choose to become powerless, so that you cannot really do things, buy things that you normally would, to make yourself vulnerable, dependent on others, at times dragged and forced against your will, but accepting it all with courage, and offering it all to God. Let me give another very simple illustration: When we go to cities, to our relatives, we are always ashamed that our children are most poorly dressed. And we invariably hear comments. But when we come back to the village then we are always ashamed that our children have so many good clothes, and we invariably hear comments on how much we own! For us to live in that tension is cross-bearing.

To become powerless is not a pleasant experience, but as we continue to walk with the Lord, giving ourselves to him to be given to others by him, we see his blessings. We are working in an area, where an American evangelical mission has worked hard, but in eighty years they have not seen as much fruit as the Lord has given us in three years. I believe one of the basic reasons behind our fruitfulness has been that people have been able to see, through our sharing of our lives with them, that we are committed to them, and we want to raise them, even above ourselves.

We had a Brahmin young man living with us for a couple of months, at the time when we were living out of a common purse. He was interested in studying Christianity but not in becoming a Christian. Because he was very defensive we did not evangelize him, but allowed him to live in our home and see. At the end of his time I asked him: "What do you feel about what you have seen?" He, a person from the highest caste said: "What has impressed me most is that in your Christian community everyone is potentially equal." It was a tremendous experience for him to see that some educated, economically strong people could choose to become poor, so that others may become rich. He saw that in Jesus even a low caste illiterate person had great dignity.

Christian life is cross-bearing life, because it does not just lose us money, but privacy, time, emotional strength, and has even the potential of costing our lives. We live in a crime-infested area. It breeds criminals as dirty water breeds mosquitoes. Farmers never live on the farm because they know that they will be looted in no time. When we went out to live on the farm, everyone warned us not to do so. We were afraid too. Every noise at night raised the question: "Have they come?" But through it all, we were able to trust and prove God. Each night we prayed that God would protect us, and trusted him for protection as we trusted him for finances. During the last three years at least three attempts were made to harm us physically but God has protected us each time.

As we face the future, we feel that the Lord is leading us into a much deeper and fuller involvement with people, through free legal aid to the poor, and local politics. This to my wife means the possibility of being a widow. Obviously no one cherishes such a call or service. We would be happy if the cup were removed and a comfortable lifestyle were given to us instead. But since the cross or self-giving is the Master's way of service and blessings, we continue to follow.

9

From Galloping Gourmet
to Serving the Poor

GRAHAM KERR

I've had the chance to talk many times, but I have never had such an impression from the Lord that this is vital.

I was a wealthy man. I owned, possessed or had an anticipation of about four and three-quarter million dollars when I was saved. That was five years ago yesterday. I am now, as a result of becoming a Christian, exactly 4.3 million dollars down. There is a great deal being spoken about Christian prosperity nowadays, so I am rather unsettling to that group because I seem to contradict the view that faith leads to material prosperity.

I would like to share with you a little of how that happened and then go on to a vision that God has given me. I would like to lay it out and say: "It hasn't been done, it's a vision, so let's test it together."

I was born 24 miles from here some 45 years ago (Brondesbury, London). I had a good start, for my father was a brewery surveyor and I later entered into the hotel business as a result of his earlier occupation. I was brought up in the hotel business; I never made my own bed or washed my own plate. I ordered from the menu — that was my lifestyle. If I wanted a fillet of sole stuffed with a lobster claw, I would have it. As a young man I began to drink wine and to understand the nuances between a Chateau Lafite Rothschild and a Chateau Margaux. I wore good clothes because my parents wanted me to wear good clothes. There was nobody to play with since I was the only child.

Our customers included the Chief Justice of Britain — he used to stop and talk to me in the cocktail bar from my 12th birthday onward. Sir Winston Churchill and J. Paul Getty were also clients. These were the kinds of people with whom I conversed. A certain gift of the gab was developed rather early!

I was captivated with the idea of the hotel business, largely because I was a frightful scholar at school, and it didn't seem likely that I would be able to earn a living at anything else.

I started by scrubbing out the gentlemen's toilet; I still remember the mosaic pattern on the floor to this day. I went on to filleting fish, scrubbing potatoes — going all the way through.

At eighteen I was "donated" to the British army. I wanted to be an officer but ended up scrubbing the kitchen again. God obviously knew what I needed! I washed pans in an eighteen hundred-man kitchen until my skin was so laden with cook's mistakes that I couldn't go out because I smelled so bad.

I was eventually commissioned and served a total of five years before returning once again to the hotel business where I became the general manager of the Royal Ascot Hotel, which was a good hotel at that time. I didn't know what I was doing, so I used bravado. I had the right clothes, spoke with the right accent and people accepted me, or what they supposed was me!

My wife Treena and I were married just before I left the army. I married my childhood sweetheart whom I met at school when I was twelve. I fell in love with her instantly — so great was my love that I gave up soccer. We were badly bruised by the experience of working 16 hours a day and Treena became ill. We lost our second child and decided to go to New Zealand to recover our life. We rented a flat for seven dollars a week complete with rats and perforated floorboards. The stove leaned over at an angle of fifteen degrees; it was here that I discovered fat-free frying.

I was chief catering adviser to the New Zealand Air Force. I introduced saving plans and became quite unpopular because I was told that the Air Force didn't like to request a certain amount of money and then have me underspend it. "It is all very embarrassing, would you please stop saving money." I couldn't understand it — I thought they might be able to buy a new aeroplane, which they needed, but apparently that wasn't possible. I was ordered to go on television during my Air Force service. I didn't want to go on, I was put on. I made many mistakes in five minutes, covering it up with my gift for small talk.

People thought I was the funniest thing that had ever been seen on television. This wasn't surprising because I appeared on the first formal day of television in New Zealand.

The broadcasting service asked the New Zealand Air Force whether I could be seconded to the broadcasting corporation in order that I might do a regular programme. The Air Force agreed. I didn't, but I was asked to go on because it was good public relations.

I obeyed and continued to make mistakes, but people continued to laugh. I wasn't always pleased but at least it filled in the cracks. What I didn't know, people could laugh at. So I was able to get by. A few people appreciated my cooking and others my humour and I got stuck with the combination!

They heard about me in Australia and asked that I go there. I went and became a sort of "overnight success". From there I went to Canada, and from Canada to the United States. From there I returned to Britain, and then went all the way around the world. I had, in the end, ratings that totalled 200 million viewers every week. Apparently, that made it the most widely viewed single television programme, done by one person, on one subject, since the beginning of the world — whatever that means!

I became wealthy and quite powerful in my own field — and terribly unhappy. I had heard of poverty and grinding poverty; well, I had grinding success. Everything I touched went right. I was offered 30-second commercials for $100,000. I could do two in an afternoon. I had long since said to my agent, "I've had enough; I've got enough; I don't need any more." And he said, "That's not the point, you signed the contract; people expect you to finish it." Whatever I did, I was a slave to the system. I was simply being buried by money.

When you're buried by money, it has a remarkable effect on your morals. Since everything I touched turned to gold, perhaps I could touch human beings with the same success? So I touched human beings, became an adulterer, and failed as husband, father . . . human being.

The tenderness of that situation — it's too sad a story to discuss any more, so I won't. I've got out of the dirty bathwater and I've no intention of getting back into it again, even for witness' sake (except on a one to one basis where it's directly applicable). My wife couldn't forgive me. For eight years we tried every single religion, every single possibility. We travelled everywhere. We tried to use our money to buy an alternative to misery.

In the end, my wife was approached by a black servant girl who worked in our house and was to be a missionary in Haiti and was trying to get the money together to go. You might think that I would have given her the money — I had it, and I knew she was working for that purpose, but it seemed right to me that she should have to work for it even if it took her three years!

Treena was at the point of being voluntarily admitted to a

mental institution. She couldn't forgive; we had tried so hard but she just couldn't do it. She was taking up to fourteen Valium a day; five milligrams of Valium fourteen times a day to try to stay sane. She would try to run through plate glass windows and cut herself with shards of glass. She was in a terrible, terrible mess and it hurt me more that I can tell you to see my love so totally wiped out. We had at this time just returned from a two-year trip around the world in a four hundred and sixty thousand dollar yacht which I had had built to try to get everything together. We had given that up and bought a huge white clapboard Southern Colonial mansion on the Chesapeake Bay. Here we would try to get peace.

Ruthie said: "Mrs. Kerr, why don't you give your problems to God?" Unknown to Treena, Ruthie had been praying for her for three months, not on her own, but with the entire congregation of a black Pentecostal Holiness church in Bethlehem, Maryland. That small church prayed for her constantly. They fasted for her: they loved her with all of their hearts and believed God for my wife — not me, but my wife. They didn't care who I was; they just knew that she was hurt and she needed help. All she could say to Treena was, "Why don't you give your problems to God?" After three months of praying, that's all she dared to say. And Treena said, "Alright, God, if you're so clever, you do it, because I can't." Those were her exact words.

One week later, she went to the church in the same way that some people go to Baden-Baden to take the water. She thought, "Well, if I go it might do me some good." She didn't know about Jesus, she'd never read the Bible, she had no idea — we were esoteric Buddhists. So she went. Everybody was having a fabulous time, all rejoicing. They had sent a bus for over 100 miles around the area to bring in the relatives and everybody else to see this white woman saved as a result of their prayer. She was right up front, and suddenly with all this praise going on she fell to her knees. Remember that this is someone who knows nothing at all about Jesus. She started to weep; it wasn't sobs, it was tears that ran out of her eyes like fountains of water. She was saying: "I'm sorry, Jesus; forgive me; I'm sorry, Jesus; forgive me . . ." She rose, changed and got into the water — it was December 17 and it was unheated, very cold water. She was understandably somewhat invigorated by the experience! When she got out the Pastor said, "Do you want to tarry?" She said, "What does that mean?" He said, "It means waiting for the baptism of the Holy Ghost." She said, "I might as well, as

I'm here." She knelt down and prayed, and everybody was banging her on the head and shouting a lot. She didn't know what was going on, her back hurt, and she was getting quite hot.

She opened her eyes and there was a man standing in front of her. He was dressed in a long, white robe and he smiled at her — that's all she could remember, that he smiled at her. It was a comforting, loving "yes, I know" kind of smile. He leaned forward, touched her heart and said, "It's all right now," and she said, "Yes, I know." She got up from that place, went straight back home, threw all her pills away, and *changed* that night, totally and completely. I know that this doesn't always happen, but in my wife's case, it did. I came back after about five days and saw it. Two weeks later I found out what had happened from a girl in a supermarket.

Treena had been told by the Lord to keep her mouth shut. She kept it shut. She was a perfect witness — I slid her under my microscope and watched her. I was totally convinced that I had a miracle on my hands.

Three months later, I was so hungry and thirsty for God because of what I had seen taking place in my wife's life, that I got down on my knees and said, "I don't know how to do this", and I didn't because nobody had witnessed to us. We used to receive thousands of letters every month but nobody ever wrote about Jesus. Lots of people told me later that they prayed for me by laying hands on the TV set, but nobody actually wrote and told me about him. So I knelt down and said: "I don't know how to get in touch with you, but I want what Treena's got and I'd like it now." Since God does not operate room service (I was in a hotel at the time), nothing happened! I shook my fists in agitation at the ceiling and said: "What do I have to say to you to get to know you like Treena does?" The next words out of my mouth were: "Jesus, I love you." It was as if I had been building a giant card castle and it just dropped. I felt utter relief, an incredible relief, and I felt loved for the very first time in my life.

I went back home and held Treena's hand and we knelt together at the side of our bed and I remember praying: "Father, I don't know how to do this, but I presume you know, so if you don't mind, would you just give me a hand, because I know I've got to be a proper husband." Treena was crying and we prayed together and I've never felt anything in my whole life like that union that I felt holding her hand. God gave me back my girlfriend at twelve, and I had the same kind of feeling for her that I had years before — and I still do. She's a fabulous person; God has really anointed her in so many ways.

And so, all I can tell you is that I was very grateful, as we sat in a great big house saying, "What next?" We didn't have a pastor, we didn't have a church, we didn't have anything. Lots of things took place. We got on the celebrity circuit, we were used and abused. We were used by the Lord and we were abused by people. God protected us somehow; everytime we did anything we said: "Lord, it's got to be your will; we don't know what's going on, but would you mind leading us, please?" For a while, that was neat and everything went well. Then I got into a potentially compromising situation. All I need tell you is this: I was told, I believe by the Lord, to put a Scripture on the end of my T.V. programme. A little citation on the bottom of the screen — it would be for on less than one second. God seemed to say: "I want a credit on your television programme." J. Walter Thompson, a huge advertising agency, said: "You take that off the air or we'll take *you* off the air." It's interesting how powerful the word of God is; it was in the credits and was on for only one second. I was told that someone had commented: "He can't have cheap plugs for God. If he wants to join in this evangelical stuff, then he can pay for the time himself like all the rest of them do." (Half a billion dollars are spent on North American television every year for the Gospel.)

I prayed about that and said: "What do I do?" God said: "I told you what to do." So I said to them: "I'm awfully sorry (I was very nice about it), but God's told me to do this," and they said: "Oh, come on. This is *business*." And I said: "Well, I think he means business, so if you don't mind, I'll keep it on" and then, quietly, "Is this how you get me out of television, Lord, because I want to serve you full-time? I don't want to be stirring a pot on television. I want to go out and be Billy Graham or someone like that!"

They told me: "All right, have your little God-thing, then!" And we thought, "Greater is he that is in me than he that is in Madison Avenue." That was neat. Then, a little later when I had done the programmes (sixty-five of them) they turned around and edited the Scripture out. They electronically removed the Scripture. I prayed about that and God said I could not continue to work with them, so I resigned.

My business manager called and said: "If you resign, will you tell me what will happen to my company? Because if you resign, I shall go bankrupt, and all of the people who helped you become a millionaire will go bankrupt!" I lowered the phone and together with Treena I prayed: "What do I do now,

Father?'' And he said: ''Give them what you anticipate getting as a result of being who you are — give it to him.'' I couldn't believe my ears. I prayed again with Treena about it and it was confirmed. So that day we forgave debts and handed over all royalties for T V, radio, commercials and TV cookbooks, including the full rights to merchandise without any strings attached — under the title Galloping Gourmet — a package worth at least three million dollars. I know that's a mind-bender and it is for me now. But we were utterly grateful for what God had done in our lives and totally believed in him to lead us step by step. We simply handed it over. I don't want you to get the wrong impression. I was not doing anything special or spiritual, but simply being obedient in that situation.

From there we went to the mountains, and started building a retreat centre, partially finished it, handed it over to someone else and wound up with Youth with a Mission. Treena and I had the chance to join a three-month Discipleship Training School and find out who God is. I'd been following him all over the place, doing whatever I could obediently, but now I had the chance to come apart and learn how to be a disciple. So we were discipled for this three-month period, and I really, really fell in love with Jesus. What he had done for me, and I had never realized it! I was being obedient . . . giving away all the money and yet I really never knew who it was for. I just knew that it seemed to be right. And then I fell in love.

Then I began to see that there was a styling that God had done in my life and that he wanted me to work for the very, very hungry. I had never known what it meant to be hungry. I said to God: ''I don't know what it means to be hungry or poor like that.'' God gave me a heart of compassion. I have been surprised by the pain that I have felt for the poor. I have sat down and wept, for no apparent reason — suddenly. On one of these occasions after hearing about God, we had our faces in the carpet, praying and seeking God about what he wanted us to do with our lives. This came after many weeks and lots of teaching in this area. As I waited there, I had a vision (see diagram). I'm going to discuss it in terms of a vision because I believe I have the fear of the Lord upon me as I share. I believe that a vision is the same as a prophetic word, and I need to be very careful that I don't add a single plan of my own other than what I saw and heard the Lord tell me.

The Vision

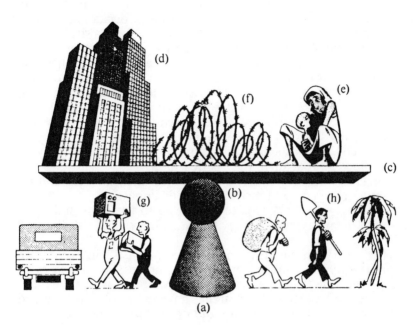

The Interpretation

a. *The Base* (A manufactured wooden model — or prototype) "You are not to be the overall ministry but rather a prototype . . . modelling a simple procedure so that others may use it."

b. *The Circle* (A stainless steel ballbearing) "This is your aim — as a Base you are to lift up Jesus who is shown as a ballbearing — always the same regardless of how you turn him, always making things run smoothly when he is Lord."

c. *The Plank* (A "policy" plank) "This is my policy — that there be equality and that the City of New York is equal in my eyes to the plight of a single dying child in Calcutta."

d. *The Buildings* (New York City). New York City represents the developed nations.

e. *Human Figures* — Mother cradles a dying child in backstreets of Calcutta.

f. *Barbed Wire Loops* — "This represents the view that a businessman, in his 26th floor office in Madison Avenue, has of the mother and child in Calcutta. His compassion is aroused but he sees that his dollar would be substantially ripped to shreds by the time it reached the need. The businessman decides to give without hope (and therefore without joy) in order to alleviate his feeling of guilt; or he decides not to give at all rather than waste his funds on a hopeless situation.'' N.B. The writer experienced, at this point, a revelation of God's heart breaking — not so much for the mother and child as for the businessman. ''The enemy has made a mockery of my Word . . . I have said that it is more blessed to give than to receive — yet because of circumstance this man gives without happiness when he could have great joy and prove my Word to be true . . . therefore I shall give you a plan whereby the barbed wire insinuations of the enemy may be avoided so that there may be joy in giving.''

g. Figures — left: ''This team will go to affluent areas and instruct my people in methods of reducing waste.''

h. Figures — right: ''This team will go to the poor and work with them so that they may know my mercy and have hope.''

It's a very simple idea, and we feel it that it will become an opportunity for churches, even small churches, because we hope to present the whole teaching on videotape as we gain experience. We'll be able to let churches have the whole teaching and then they'll be able to raise up, *out of their own waste*, a team to minister to the poor.

What is so important is this: if we don't do something to bring the recipient and the donor closer together, we'll lose the whole purpose that God has for us — the modelling of a Jesus way of giving and receiving. We begin the process by giving what we would otherwise waste — in doing so we modify our lifestyle. The recipient sees the way we do it. Then, when his microfarm starts to generate a small surplus, his great joy will be in taking from his surplus and passing it on to a neighbour in need. That's the way that justice can be established where there has never been hope. It's a marvellous circle of opportunity to represent God's love on earth today.

We can do something that the high technologists can never do, we can actually exhibit the love of God by giving a part of our lives to somebody else. When we do the possible, I believe, with all my heart, that God will give us the increase and many people, like Treena and me, our children and parents, will come to love God with all their hearts, souls, minds and strength and as they do, they will be loving their neighbours and even, eventually — themselves!

10

Extended Household

DAVID WATSON

A British Journey

I am hesitant to give a testimony on simple lifestyle, almost as hesitant as I would be if asked to speak on "Humility and How I Attained It". Over seven years ago my wife and I felt that God was calling us to live as an extended household. I think this was the first stage for us towards any real understanding of a simpler lifestyle. We have two children, presently aged thirteen and ten, and when we felt this calling to open up our home and live as a small community we were not influenced at that point by any experiment in any other church. For example, one other Anglican church that is well-known to have developed this pattern is the Church of the Holy Redeemer in Houston, Texas, but we hadn't heard of them at the time we opened up our house in this way.

We had three main purposes in our household. First, we wanted to learn more about the Body of Christ, because for some time we had seen that we should be as deeply committed in the church to one another as we are to Christ. Community life seemed to be one relevant expression of such a commitment within the Body of Christ. Second, we were concerned to release both money and manpower for the work of the Kingdom of God. The church everywhere, and certainly in the West, is crying out for more money and more manpower; and this seemed to be one way by which we could release both. Third, we were concerned to provide the context of a loving, caring family for the growing amount of loneliness that I see as one of the major problems of society at the moment, not only among elderly people, but also many younger people, single people, divorced people, as well as widows, widowers, and so on. When we began to ask people to come and join us, not to live as lodgers or guests, but as part of our whole family, we found considerable resistance to the idea from others within our congregation. One reason was that some families were threatened lest I implied that this was the best way for a Christian to live. I was careful not to say that. I said that we felt that God was calling us into this, but it's only one valid way of expressing the family of God; it's not the only way or the best way. Part of the resistance might also have been because we made many, many mistakes. I tend to think that we must have made every mistake that exists, but I daresay there are more mistakes that we have yet to discover! For example, in the early days we invited too many disturbed people to join us. When our children were under the age of twelve that was not right. We had to spend nearly all our time counselling those who had just come off drugs or whatever, and our children began to show signs of suffering because of the lack of attention that we were giving to them and too great attention to others. We began to learn one of the main principles of the households: that you shouldn't take in a really disturbed person unless the children in the household are twelve years of age and over, if the parents are the leaders of the household. That's a good general principle. We didn't know about these things; we learned the hard way because there seemed to be no literature to guide us at that time. We're still learning by mistakes.

After two years of caution and opposition, a few others saw some value in what we were trying to do, and about six or seven other households came into being very quickly in two or three months. Of the households that have come into being in our church, it is fair to say that some have not been successful; and one or two have disbanded and returned to the nuclear unit. Nearly all, even those that are still in existence, have had many painful experiences. I now understand why Jesus taught so much about the need for forgiveness — seventy times seven. As soon as we started, we saw how painful it is when you open your lives to one another. I want to stress that one of the most important things has been not just the sharing of our possessions in the sharing of our home, but the sharing of our lives. In some ways it is easier to share possessions, to share money and to share homes, but when you open up your life to somebody, when you open up your heart, you're making yourself vulnerable, you're likely to be crucified in one form or another. We are still sinful people; we still hurt and get hurt, and that's why we need to forgive one another seventy times seven. But we have found, as we're willing to be really vulnerable and open to pain, that we have tasted something more of the Risen Christ through it all. A fresh experience of his resurrection life nearly always comes through pain, suffering and tears.

All this has been fruitful along a number of ways. First, we have learned as a whole church much faster what it means to be the Body of Christ. The households have been a catalyst to speed up the reaction of a deeper commitment all round. Second, we have learned to share our lives and possessions more freely. In our own household we have had a common purse for about five years. At present, I am the only wage-earner in our household, and we have no private bank account at all. We're normally about eight or nine in the household, and apart from our immediate needs being met (our food, light and heat) we each have a fixed amount. It happens to be £3 per week, out of which we have to buy all our clothes and our presents for birthdays and Christmas etc. I have found this a healthy discipline because it means that when I need another coat, pair of shoes or trousers, I have to save or go to the shops which sell second-hand articles. It is one small way by which we have been able to release more money for the work of the church. Possibly resulting from this, there has been much more sharing and giving of money and possessions throughout the whole of our church. We have also been able to release a lot of people for full-time work. We're an Anglican church and officially in the Anglican terms we have three full-time workers, but for the past four or five years now at least we have had approximately thirty full-time workers, partly because of this way of releasing people. We work on a simple principle of "pay according to need", so we don't have fixed salaries or wages according to the world's standard. We have been able to "level down" considerably and will probably do so even more in spite of inflation and rising costs. That has been, of course, a factor which has enabled us to be much more involved as a church in the life of the city in various ways and released people for full-time pastoral, evangelistic and social work.

Again, partly through the creative expressions of extended households, we have been able to develop several significant groups in our church. For example, it was in this way that our singing and dancing groups were born which opened up a whole area of worship in our church. That has been a very significant factor. Now, the basis of all worship is that of sacrifice. In the New Testament there are various sacrifices which are part of our total worship of God, for example, the sacrifice of our praise (Hebrews 13:15); the sacrifice of our bodies (Romans 12:1) which is part of our spiritual worship, and the sacrifice of our

possessions (Hebrews 13:16) — these are different areas of our
worship. Worship is not just singing, nor is it just serving; it is a
great variety of ways in which we offer the whole of our being to
God and give him his worth.

Anyway, new expressions of worship were born from our
households. A drama group also developed. We must be concerned about the whole question of relevant communication in
this day and age, particularly in countries where television dom-
inates so powerfully. We have seen the immense value of drama
in Christian communication. This was initially possible only
because we were able to invite some people who were professional actors and actresses into our households. We now have a
professional theatre company, called "Riding Lights", which
seeks to communicate the Gospel effectively in dramatic terms,
and is also trying to break into the scene of secular drama. In
the leading British arts festival, the Edinburgh Festival, "Riding
Lights" was one of the very few companies which received an
award for its involvement as a secular theatre company,
although it has a strong Christian basis.

Further, for seven months of the year I lead Christian missions and festivals, always travelling with a small team. This
team has been possible only because of the households. Our
threefold aim, in various towns and cities, is evangelism,
renewal and reconciliation. We find that this is meeting a tremendous need in this country and abroad. This team has been
entirely supported by our own church (partly through the
household arrangement), so that when we go to any area there
are no costs involved, apart from travelling expenses and
accommodation in people's homes. We believe this is important
in view of the tremendous financial budget of some of the evangelistic crusades that take place throughout the world at the
moment.

There are many other spin-offs from these households that I
could mention. My sadness is that I wish we had more households than we have at the moment. The areas of need are vast.
However, there are not more households partly because of the
problems that have developed. You see, when you live in extended households, your whole life is in public — it's like being
in a shop window. Everybody knows about everything. There
are many problems in many nuclear families, but on the whole
they're private, behind closed doors. When it is an extended
household, your whole life is open for the rest of the church and
others around to see, and to criticize if they want to.

Another sadness is that we are not actively involved in areas of social justice in ways that I would like. I think it's partly because this city of York is an attractive tourist city without huge areas of obvious political-social need as there are in most larger cities. Also, I believe that I am primarily called to be an evangelist, and although I would not want to polarize evangelism and social justice, we do have to specialize — you can't do everything, all at once, at the same time. Perhaps we have specialized too much in evangelism, and missed out on social and political involvement.

My third sadness is that, as a church, we haven't moved very far with this whole question of lifestyle, though I think church members now increasingly accept the biblical principles involved. Yes, there are moments of real pain, but through all this we can know a much greater sense of the reality of God's love.

11

From Evangelist to Restaurateur

GORDON STRACHAN

After some of the testimonies we have heard, mine is very much the testimony of the man who stayed at home because I've come only 400 miles. I am very grateful to have heard from people from all over the world. I think that some of us in Scotland have a siege mentality; it seems to be more difficult for us to come over the border than it is for you to travel to the far corners of the earth. I'm very happy to have a fellow Scotsman with me here — Kwame. My one disappointment is that he takes sugar in his porridge. I stand for the ancient ways, where you take only salt. Otherwise, we have good fellowship and we wish we had brought our kilts with us. Someone said that the only difference between Scotland and other parts of the Commonwealth was that Scotland hasn't yet got its independence!

I'm speaking today as a reluctant restaurateur. The title of my testimony is "Bread of Life, or Refined Loaf". I used to be an evangelist with The Church of Scotland, associated in the early 70's with the Charismatic Movement. I was never quite sure whether I was expected to be a fire-raiser to hot things up, or a fire-engine to dampen things down. We had a certain spin-off from the Jesus movement and it was very exciting to see many people coming into real faith and enjoying various types of Christian experience. Then, in 1974, because of my interest in the arts, I was offered the directorship of The Church's arts and communication centre — a small building in the High Street of Edinburgh, next door to John Knox's House.

The Netherbow was completed in 1972, a very remarkable accomplishment for a theological tradition which has not been noted in former generations for patronage of the arts. John Knox himself was not very keen on the theatre, to put it mildly. Even in the 19th century, you were liable to be had up by the

Presbytery, if not by the Kirk Session, and to lose your job as a minister if you were found to be attending the theatre. There is still a tradition in Scotland which supports that point of view. So, to some extent, our job has been difficult.

I have felt, like so many in this conference, that there is no dimension of life that is unable to be influenced by, and unable to serve, the Kingdom. Just as we have been talking about politics, so I would talk about the arts and how they can be used most marvellously for Christ. We in The Netherbow are trying to form links between the world of the arts and the world of the Church. It is difficult, because so few Christians are involved in this area, but nevertheless we do have times when, through exhibitions, through musicals, through drama, through photography, through film, we feel we are into an area that is of great importance.

In terms of culture, I think it is possible for us to hear what people are saying from other continents and other cultures more clearly if we realize that, in the arts, people have made bridges and have gone on pilgrimage and have respected other cultures much more than politicians or even churchmen. So, we are sympathetic to a very broad position. When I took over the arts centre myself, I realized there was nothing in our own tradition that could form the basis of a spirituality for an arts centre, so I had to go elsewhere.

The specific reason that I have been asked to talk and give my testimony is because of a small contribution we have made to the question of lifestyle. That is because we discovered after the first year that we were losing thousands of pounds by over-emphasizing the arts, and there is very little money in the arts. So we changed our policy and began to emphasize our little restaurant. I realized that I was going to have to become a businessman, so I consciously gave up the idea of being only an evangelist.

I was influenced very much by St. Paul in Thessalonians where he says: "For you remember our labour and toil, brethren; we worked night and day, that we might not burden any of you, while we preached to you the Gospel of God" (1 Thess. 2:9). We were led to take that a stage further, and to say that the Gospel for us was not something external to our business but it was the *way in which we ran our business*. In other words, we were pointed towards books like Schumacher's *Small is Beautiful* and towards other people who were led to Christian discipleship in terms of quality of work, rather than quality of preaching or church life. We found we were having the concept of, not

a house church, but a work church. We had prayer and fellowship every day, and while remaining open to the public in our
restaurant, our theatre and our galleries, became inwardly more
centred on Christ and more sure that this was the way that he
was leading. Immediately our debts stopped, and after losing
£10,000 during the first eighteen months, we broke even the
second year and then gradually began to make a small profit.
Then we asked ourselves the question: "As Christians, running
an arts centre whose economic heart is a restaurant, what should
our food policy be?" We were greatly helped by people who
came in from different parts of the world who were rather
shocked to see what we were serving. We were told that (for instance) white bread isn't as good for you as brown and that it
might well be a commercial rip-off. We examined this and
found that, through groups like Friends of the Earth and the
Soil Association — all motivated by ideology and often committed
Christians — if we were going to be true to the idea of a work
church, we were going to have to change our food policies.

This came as a very great shock and strain, because none of us
had been trained in business. It seemed to us remarkable that we
were able to break even in restaurant work when we had no previous experience. But now we were coping with an inner change,
which was very hard, characterized by the fact that a number of
us were graduates, and I myself being a minister and known as
an evangelist, was now seen to be endlessly clearing tables and
doing the washing-up. Friends and colleagues would come in
and say: "What are you doing, wasting your time running a
restaurant and doing the washing-up when you could be leading
rallies and preaching and teaching around the country?" This
was a very difficult thing to cope with, and especially for my
wife, who served behind the counter. The attitudes of people
who wanted service were such that she wanted to say: "I want to
tell you that I am a graduate, and I could be doing a better
job." In other words, in terms of social status we were on the
way down — and we didn't like it. It was very difficult for us to
admit that working in the church and being seen to be an important evangelist or a good church worker was, to some extent, a
status symbol. This was extremely hard, and still is, because
when the queue is long, and people are irritated by slow service,
or we've run out of food, and somebody gets really stroppy,
what we want to do is take them by the throat and pour the remains of the soup over their head! As you can see, I'm not a
small man, and this work keeps me very fit. Once or twice I've
just been itching for a fight.

As someone said: "Where's your Ph.D now?" We wear our degrees in the Church like aristocratic ermine and like titles behind our names. Many of us are in all this because it is a substitute status hierarchy. We have the suspicion that if we were to go into the world, into real jobs, we might not get quite as high. All these things came out, and we had tremendous discussions and arguments and first-class rows. I don't know how David Watson can manage in his extended family, because we were so thankful at the end of the day to get home and get out of it — it was so strenuous in terms of personal relationships and our new status — or lack of it.

Over the next two years we did feasibility studies; we tried to find out what we should serve, and eventually we made our changes. The big thing we had to prove was not only that we could somehow serve food that was healthier and that was consistent with our understanding of Christian principles, but also that we could make it pay. These were the double criteria: that it was all very well to be ideological, but if it didn't work in practice, then we were finished, because the subsidy that we get from the church is small — valuable, but small — so, to a large extent, we have had to be self-supporting. We finally changed, and became what we now call a "Whole-foods Restaurant". I want to read you our policy statement because this is the controversial aspect of our work. We have now been completely this way for nearly four years, and, interestingly enough, it is only in these last three years that we have begun to show a small profit. We are convinced that it *is* possible to put ideology into business and to see it work. I think this is our main contribution to the debate that has been going on this week — it is not impossible to marry ideology with business ethics. We are now going on to growing our own crops and establishing a link with the farmers who supply our food, but that is another chapter in the story.

This is what we put on our Netherbow Wholefood Restaurant policy statement. First, quotations from Frances Moore Lappe's *Diet for a Small Planet* and from the *New Internationalist* of September 1977:

I have become more confident of the value of seeing the world through food, for when we do, it suddenly becomes clear that any economic system must be judged above all else upon how it produces and uses its food resources. How does our present system stand up, under such scrutiny? That is the question that must be confronted.

. . . most of us daily defend, through ignorance, inertia, or just plain greed, a system which not only permits widespread global hunger, but actually ensures it; a system which steadily and efficiently undermines people's capacity to feed themselves.

Then our own introductory paragraph:-

The Netherbow has decided to put food first. Since the Summer of 1974 our restaurant has been the economic mainstay of most of The Netherbow. It has also become its social centre and more recently its spiritual focus. Over the past year we have come to feel that we must only serve food which is consistent with our Christian faith i.e. food which benefits the health of the eater, the wealth of the grower, and the balance of world trade.

This change is still very much an experiment but we would like to present a few guidelines to the policies we have now adopted.

And then the details:-

Humble Pulses. Pulses and beans such as lentils, split peas and soya beans are very rich in protein, vitamins and iron, and yet low in carbohydrates. Soya beans are richer in protein even than meat, and are much cheaper. Recipes such as Soya Bean Tomato Stew not only taste delicious and are nutritious but also consume a fraction of the resources consumed by meat dishes. In Britain, we give vast quantities of protein-rich grains and pulses to cattle, with very little return. At The Netherbow we have decided to eat the beans and rice ourselves and so keep our food simple and economic.

You see, we were changing from giving people what they wanted to giving them what we thought they ought to have, which was really using our kitchen as a pulpit. People began to recognize there was something clerical and ministerial coming from the sink!

Merciless Meat. Most meat dishes are highly wasteful of primary protein. For instance, a small chicken produced by modern intensive methods and eaten by two people will have used up resources which could have supplied a meal of the same nutritional value for twenty people. One-third of the world consumes half the world's supply of grain and most of this is used for feeding livestock such as beef cattle, pigs and poultry. This is to produce the high quality meat which in the West is considered vital to our diet. However, the remaining two-thirds of the world are starving through lack of grain. Because of its wastefulness of energy and because there are very easy and tasty alternatives, we at The Netherbow have decided to cut down on our personal consumption of meat and to exclude it entirely from our restaurant menu.

We sent this around to all ministers in Scotland and, while some were full of interest, others were sceptical, to say the least. We were accused in the columns of our church magazine of representing a position which said the Gospel was now defined as "left-wing vegetarianism". I didn't mind that because people often say that I look too much like a Tory.

Co-operative Coffee. We serve pure ground Tanzanian coffee because we want to help the coffee growers in Tanzania. They are organized on a co-operative basis which means that each coffee grower receives a percentage of the company's profits. Thus the coffee we sell at The Netherbow directly benefits the people who need our money most. The coffee also tastes excellent!

I was preaching in a boys' school and I said to them: "As a Christian restaurateur, should I serve a product that comes from countries where I feel the workers may not be getting paid enough?" By contrast I drew attention to Tanzania's more humane policy and afterwards in the vestry there was a queue of boys who lobbied me, from Kenya and from other countries. They said (again!) that I was the victim of left-wing propaganda. So we had a meeting in The Netherbow with one of the directors of our coffee company, with members of The World Development Movement, members of the academic community and our own kitchen staff. It was quite a battle; it went on for about three hours. In the end, we still couldn't make up our minds whether we were doing the right thing until the director of the coffee company came up to me on the side and said, "If you really want pure-ground Tanzanian coffee, I could supply it to you, but don't tell anyone." So we *have* told everyone, and we're very pleased also now to be getting consignments of Campaign instant Tanzanian coffee, which others of you probably know about.

Brown is Best. We use unrefined natural food — wholemeal bread, brown rice, brown sugar, brown flour, homemade brown baking. The prime example of the value of wholefoods is bread. Wholemeal bread contains all the grain, i.e. the bran, the endosperm and the germ, so it is rich in all the minerals, vitamins and protein. White bleached bread by contrast has the bran and germ removed and also most of the remaining nutrients destroyed through the bleaching process. We felt that it made more sense to keep the goodness in our food so that we fed our customers food which nourished them as well as filling them.

The Killer Whites. Much of today's food contains too little fibre — e.g. white bread, white sugar, white flour, peeled, over-cooked vegetables. Yet recent research findings indicate a connection between lack of dietary fibre and degenerative disease of the intestine, cancer of the colon, varicose veins, coronary heart disease, and many other diseases. We all know that constipation is due to lack of fibre in our diet but it is more alarming to consider the possibility that heart disease and some cancer might be caused by our bad eating habits. Eating over-refined foods could also lead to obesity, one of Britain's commonest diseases. Because they are less nutritious than wholefoods you must eat more to feel satisfied. Wholefoods we believe are safer, healthier and much tastier!

Goodness Greens! All our soups, hot dishes, salads, desserts and puddings are home-made, on the premises. We use only fresh fruit and vegetables — no tins or instant mixes — because the real thing is so much better for us than the imitation or the over-processed. There is nothing to beat fresh green vegetables and fresh fruit for health-giving food.

Kick the Can! We avoid instant tinned foods where possible. So often they are more expensive than fresh food and, more important, they often have little or no nutritious value. Flavouring, colouring and vitamins have to be added to make up loss during processing. But there is great concern over the health hazards of these additives. At The Netherbow we have decided to eat our food fresh and unprocessed — it's the real thing!

We have distributed thousands of these policy statements. They are enormously popular. We've been asked recently to distribute them to all the convents in England and Wales. That is just a special and unusual example. A Reverend Mother Prioress from Gwent wrote to us for further details. We are catholic, in the broad sense of the word. All over the world, we get responses from this, because it seems to be one little way in, through business, to this whole question of simple lifestyle and food distribution.

I end where I started: with a testimony to Jesus Christ, who is the Bread of Life. If he is, then he certainly isn't a refined white or even a reconstituted brown. He doesn't give us constipation. He is not a rip-off. He is altogether healthy and holy. That is why wholefoods and whole grains are what we must go in for in the Christian food trade.

12

From Privilege Toward Poverty

COLLEEN and VINAY SAMUEL

Vinay: I feel awkward, sharing in a situation like this because a situation like this has so many dynamics. The *Evangelical Review of Theology*, has an article written by an American friend and myself, on the relationship between donors and receptors. In that, we suggest that a donor tries to dominate, but a receptor tries to manipulate. I'm very conscious that there are situations like this that can tempt me subtly to manipulate you. I believe that this exercize is not really to my liking — I'm very effective at manipulating people and I don't really want to manipulate you.

This American friend said to me rather cheerfully and bluntly: "You Indians are very subtle and often devious." I agree. So, if my testimony is recorded and played before my colleagues in my diocese, what will happen to my credibility? I've got to give a testimony which can be played before my people.

I thank God that my wife is here, so she hears what I am saying and I hear what she is saying. We're able at least to be honest with each other. We really have very little to say. We feel it extremely difficult to share what's been going on as both of us come from very middle-class backgrounds; my wife comes from a family that in Indian terms would be described as "well to do". We have not known poverty at all. Strangely enough, the only time that we really felt deprived was when I was a student at Cambridge. We were discussing last night that one weekend we ended up with just 25 pence, and no food, so we said: "What shall we buy?" The only thing we could get was a tin of steak-and-kidney pie. Even freshly-done steak-and-kidney pie is not something we particularly relish. And you can imagine the rest. We *haven't* felt deprivation. We come from middle-class backgrounds — I pastor a very middle-class church, and I sympathize with the difficulties that people in the West have. I went as a curate from the Round Church in Cambridge right to St. John's, and I hardly had any difficulty. There was no particular difficulty in adjusting; the middle-class situation was more or less similar.

When I had nearly completed my studies at Cambridge, I began to realize that I was a creature of the West, of a western middle-class culture. I really did not know my own culture. So I began, in the last five years, converting to my own culture, searching for authenticity as an Asian, as an Indian, as well as a Christian, in my own situation. I must confess that only in the last three or four years have I begun to identify with the deprived. My wife has always related to the poor. I used to wonder why — I thought because her father made money in business she must have been feeling guilty and wanted to help the poor. Her orientation in this area was always a mile or two ahead of mine. For me this direction started in the last three or four years. What have we done in this movement? I want Colleen to tell you.

Colleen: I thought I would not go into too much detail of what we are doing and what things we are involved in. I'm a vicar's wife, a pastor's wife. Our house is like a railway station and airport sometimes. The back door is the official entrance and all sorts of people come through.

I would like to share with you, not what I have been doing or what we have been doing in this particular slum area that we are involved in. I want to share with you what things we have learned from working with the underprivileged — I do not like the word "poor" — *underprivileged* brothers and sisters in Bangalore.

We are part of a ministry in a slum area just outside the city limits of Bangalore. The area is called Lingarajapurum. The work began when two of our church families chose to live just at the edge of the slum. Some children were given help with their studies. Others who had never been to school began attending literacy classes. Through this began a ministry which now includes a school for children from the poorest homes and work with unemployed women providing training and employment opportunities.

As a small girl I used to wake up sometimes in the night when there was a very strong monsoon rain. There has always been something inside which would make me wake up and say: "Now what is happening to those who are in the huts — how are they managing?" Through sheer frustration and being young, I would say: "I don't know" and go back to sleep. It was only when Christ came into my life in the mid-sixties that he began to draw me more and more to those who were unlovely. And slowly he began to draw me into this area where we are working now. Only Christ, not anyone, not my personality, has drawn us into this situation and I know that he will carry us through.

What are the values I have learned? There are so many things I have learned in these two years of going and working with people who come from the poorest of the poor. That means people whose salaries are less than 200 rupees ($30) a month; children who come from homes where there is gambling, alcoholism, prostitution, deserted homes where children are left destitute.

First of all, it has given me a genuinely caring, sharing value to my life. I say "genuine" for the simple fact that unless we genuinely care in this situation, we cannot really share what we have. Coming from a church where we are protected, where when we see a prostitute on the road we immediately dismiss her as a "bad woman", going and working and seeing these women there and realizing *why* they have become like this has been a tremendous help to me. But going and being amongst these people has taught me *why*, and I think that has made me want to care and want to share with them what I have.

Apart from myself, I think that God has used us as a link to our middle-class church. Our women's group used to be a fairly closed group where the first response to "fallen" women was to condemn them. But our ladies in the church are becoming more and more open. I believe there will be a time when our group will open up to the so called "fallen women" so they can come and feel welcomed and loved. When we began to work in this area, we were not aware of why people behave like this. Why is a prostitute a prostitute? Because her husband has left her with five children and she has no training. Why is an alcoholic an alcoholic? Because he lives in a tiny room not only with his family but his relations and the only way to escape is to come home dead drunk.

Going there and seeing these folk has led me to want to lead other Christians in our church into a new concern and involvement. Living and caring and being so involved in this work sometimes gives me a guilt complex. What is it doing to my children? We have three of them: a ten-year-old, five-year-old and a three-year-old. It is marvellous to see the way that they are also becoming caring. It's not that I teach them: "You've got to do this" and "You've got to eat that food because Margaret living in Lingarajapurum doesn't have enough food." I want to learn by watching overactions. And it's marvellous to see that they are learning. I can see it in my eldest girl sometimes when she saves a dress and says: "Do you think it will fit so-and-so over there?" Thank God that he cares for our children even though sometimes we cannot give them enough time.

Secondly, it has taught me to have an honest lifestyle. Living in a land where there is so much corruption, living in a land where there is so much exploitation, to be honest — completely honest — is a very difficult thing. One wants to be honest, to have an openness, to have a transparent lifestyle where people do not see us but rather see our motives which are Christ-centred. This is what one aims at, with the teachers, with friends, with the children. I feel I have to be accountable first to those with whom I am working, with whom I am caring. This is why when overseas visitors come I do not like to take visitors around our school because it makes our children like guinea pigs. When they do come, I never talk to them alone. It is always with our teachers, because I want them to know that what I am telling these people is the truth and the full truth. I want our teachers to be able, when I am not in school, to share with them — not what I say — but what they feel themselves. If they feel that this is not being done, that it should be done, it is completely open for them to say it.

On the other hand, when it comes to finance, not only do our teachers know how much money we have in the bank, but our children know and our parents know. We started it as a free school, but then realized that parents did not take it seriously. They used to send their children when they liked. If the children liked to go fishing, they would go fishing. So we have a small fee of five rupees (75 cents). Seventy-five per cent of our parents could not even pay that because their total income per day is five rupees and all goes toward their food. So we sent a sponsorship book around and our church members sponsored the children. When this money came in we had to tell the children: "Would you kindly see that your mother sends the money in, or a part of the money otherwise the teachers don't get their salaries at the end of the month."

Thirdly, it has helped my faith tremendously. When we were in a pastoral set-up, we did a lot of visiting and we did see God working in the lives of our women, in the lives of our church people. But moving into this underprivileged area and taking up a responsibility in this area has taught me more things about trusting God than I have learned in all those years. We started the school with 200 rupees ($25 dollars) which we borrowed from St. John's Church. Within two months we were able to return that money because the money was coming in from people, from ordinary housewives who were interested and did not have enough time to share, but would pay that money. We've never gone into the red. There are many times on the 20th of the month that I sit with the lady who helps us with the accounts and say: "Do we have enough money to pay the teachers this month?" And sometimes she says: "No" and then we've got to work and we get a little money — we borrow from here and there and we pay it back. That is the way we keep going.

At one Christmas we wanted to give the children a Christmas lunch. Since most of them hardly eat meat — it's mainly vegetables that they live on because they can't afford meat — we said we'd give them a rice and meat Indian dish. I remember that the cost came to 59 rupees. I said to this lady: "We don't have the money but let's go ahead and plan it. We will do it even if we have to get it out of our housekeeping money." Just three or four days before the Christmas lunch, Chris (Sugden) came to me and said: "Do you think that you can use this cheque?" I'm not sure how much it was in sterling, but it came to 64 rupees. It was just enough, not only to give them a good meal, but also a balloon at the end. This is just an example of how faithful God has been.

Another incident that built my faith much, much more, occurred just two weeks before we came to this consultation. One of the young girls came to me to share a desperate problem. What happens in this area is that as soon as a girl reaches maturity — eleven or twelve years of age — the father is either wanting to send her out for prostitution here or the mother is wanting to send her to notorious places like Bombay. I think they get trained in Bombay and then are sent back to Bangalore. This young girl came to me and said: "My mother is planning this. My older sister is already in this," and she was weeping and said: "I don't want to go home tonight — you've got to take me into a hostel." I said: "Now what hostel can I take her into?"

I took her home and kept her with me and while I am here in England one of my friends is looking after her. The miracle about it is that the next day after the girl came to me, we had a call from the head office of the Evangelical Fellowship of India Committee on Relief. They said that they were bringing a Mrs. Rookmaaker (I think she is from Holland). They said that she wants to visit our school. So I said: "Fine, bring her along."

Our class was in session and as I was sharing with her I told her the story of the young girl. She said: "You know we support boarding homes in India. Would you like to start a boarding home?" Just the day before that I was saying: "If only we had enough money to rent a two-room house, we could keep these girls and protect them." Here the next day this lady came and said: "You produce the case studies for me and I'll look after them — I'll be able to help out right up until they are twenty-three or twenty-four and they are on their feet." If that is not God working, then what is it? This is the sort of thing that has been going on and on. We see how God takes care of situations.

For the past two years, Vinay has been regularly telling our pastoral committee: "We do not want to stay in this church. We may be associated, but we want to live in Lingarajapurum." Again before he came, at the last meeting of the pastoral committee, he made it clear that in one year's time we will move out and live amongst these underprivileged people. It is easy for us to stand up and talk when we just go there and work for a few hours and then leave the situation and then come out. God is drawing us — and I knew it — to live there, to be a part of these people. You see, in all these discussions about lifestyle this week that have been very theological and going above my head (most of them), my one prayer has been: "God, don't let me get so confused that my faith gets all muddled." If you have your security and you have your faith in God, you won't have to worry about what kind of lifestyle you live, because he is going to show you where you are going to live. Whether he leads you to live in a mansion, or he leads you to live in a hut — if you are secure in him and know that you are in the centre of his will, surely he will lead you on.

It is with this faith that we are going. Thank God, it's not just one of us who wants to live there, but I think God has given us both the desire to live in the place where there will be no sanitation; there will be no water. When the monsoons come it's going to be muddy . . . But, just in case some of you are planning to come out there and want to know, "Should I go stay with them?" please don't get worried; we'll put you up in a hotel close to us! We do want to go, and we feel that God is sending us there because there is a tremendous amount of work to be done.

God helps us, who have a little power, to help the powerless. We can't teach our children in isolation from their problems. When a child comes in hungry, by 10:00 a.m. he can't learn anything more, because he's too hungry (he has a meal once a day, which is at night when the father brings the money home and the mother cooks). God has opened a way. When the Roman Catholics came in and said: "How many of your children are Roman Catholic?" and I said: "Roman Catholics, stand up", they were surprised to see that 25% of them were Roman Catholic. They said: "What can we do for you?" I said: "We don't have food for the afternoon meal and many of the children are very hungry." They gave us oil and wheat and we put in the rest and give them what we call "upahmah" so they have some food.

For their medical needs, we have been sending them to a clinic. The children have been coming in with sores, with runny ears. They are sick; you can't do anything with them, so you send them to the clinic, and the doctor just cleans their ears and sends them back after charging them two rupees. They actually should be getting antiobiotics but they don't get them and so they must go back again and pay another two rupees. God gave us an opening in a free rural health clinic. Because we were able to talk to them, it is open for our children to go there. If our children went on their own there, they would not get admission. But because we can speak, we are able to help them out.

In all these things we see that one cannot do it on one's own. We do want your prayers as we go to live in Lingarajapuram. We want your prayers for our children because it is so easy to get so emotionally involved in the work that we forget our children. I believe that God will take care of them, and he has. We see the interest they have in caring and praying, and we see that our children *are* being taken care of by God. I believe as the hymn says, that God does hold the key of all unknown, and really, I am glad that he does. If we should hold the key of what is going to happen to us in Lingarajapuram, I think we would be terribly afraid. Please do pray for us.

Vinay: Just a few words to conclude. While we are going through this process, we recognize that God has been leading us, even these last four years, to try to have an extended family. At present we do have such an extended family. Sometimes it is very costly and dangerous — when suddenly your child is down with encephalitis and you realize that you brought in a child who is destitute and may be the carrier of many kinds of diseases. Suddenly you have this toxic child — there is a complete darkness of the face and you don't know what happened — and you pray and the next day it's all right, and the doctor says: "It's a miracle and how did it happen?" We thank God it did. The next day we had to send the child away, because I was so scared. I think some of you have given up much, much more than we have given up. Some of you have deprived yourself by providing for the poor much more than we have. Considering our background, and especially the context in which we live, it is very hard for us. But we are trying to do that. It is a step-by-step thing — we are trying the total immersion situation. We hope the Lord will continue to guide and help us.

We don't have a tremendous testimony to give except our struggles, and the joy of these struggles, and the confirmation that the Lord is in the midst of them.

13
Saying No to Upward Mobility

DOLPHUS WEARY

A few days ago I felt I was in the wrong place. I heard a lot of discussion here about the simple lifestyle, the longing to be poor, to be in poverty, and I said: "Wait a minute — I'm in the wrong place." I grew up in a family of ten children and one mother. My father left home when I was about four. All of us lived in a three-room house. I'm not talking about three bedrooms; I'm talking about three rooms! Working on the farm was always a struggle on my part, saying to myself: "How in the world can I get off this farm? How in the world can I get out of this economic poverty? How in the world can I become one of those owners, one of those who control some economic wealth?" I'm convinced that the average person who grows up in a poor community has those same dreams and aspirations and asks himself: "How in the world can I get out of this situation and begin to move in a different direction?"

Integration in Mississippi, in the South, and throughout America, has always been a movement from the poor community to the more affluent community. Integration has seldom ever been from the more affluent down to the poor community. Maybe that's what we've been talking about; maybe that's a direction we need to go. If it is, I think it can be a beautiful one, if I'm willing, somehow or other, to move from a more affluent community to a very poor one.

Growing up in deprived circumstances, one of the things that happened to me was that I ended up being a very religious person. I joined the church when I was eight; it was the right thing to be a church member. I remember joining the church, shaking the preacher's hand and being baptized. The only thing that the leadership of the church told me was: "Dolphus, as long as you come to church, be active, become a junior deacon, a Sunday

School teacher, you're going to be okay. But, if you ever leave the church, you're going to be lost, and you're gonna go to hell.''

So, my whole concept was how could I be good enough to fit into God's plan. I remember at the age of fifteen, I went to a church revival, and while I was there, the preacher finished speaking and said: "All those who are not Christians, I would like for you to raise your hand." I remember that night, raising my hand, with my eyes closed, and the next I heard was: "If you are not a Christian, come join the church." But, I was already a member of the church! Nobody ever told me: "Dolphus, you're lost; you need Jesus Christ as your Saviour. Dolphus, you need something else besides working and trying to be good enough, in order to fit into God's plan."

It was not until I was seventeen, that a friend invited me to a tent meeing, which was sponsored by Voice of Calvary and John Perkins. There, for the first time, I heard the gospel of Jesus Christ. I heard that God loved me just like I was, and that I didn't have to do anything extraordinary to fit into God's plan. The message came from Psalm 116:12, where it says: "What shall I render unto the Lord for all his benefit toward me?" I realized then that all I was trying to reach and work so hard to get was there in God's infinite mercy and love, which he was so willing to give me.

I began to go to some of the Bible classes that were sponsored by the Voice of Calvary.

After my graduation from high school, God had put within me a desire to go to a Christian college. I didn't want to go to a Bible institute, because I knew that here I would be taught one thing — how to be a preacher. What I had seen, personally, in the established black religion in Mississippi, I totally rebelled against. The established black church in Mendenhall, Simpson County, Mississippi, consisted of something like thirty-two black churches, with not a single church having a full-time pastor. In fact, 95% of all the ministers that preached in Simpson County in those thirty-two churches lived fifty to a hundred miles away. Somehow or another, those individuals would come into the community, preach a sermon once or twice a month, and take away with them the resources of that community. At once, I saw that the whole concept was one of exploitation, rather than being concerned with the people that lived in that community.

During the Civil Rights Movement, when we began to get involved in Mendenhall and Simpson County, the preachers would come in and say: "Don't worry about voting, don't worry that you are second-class citizens, that you have to go to segregated restrooms and water fountains, segregated cafes and hotels. Don't let these things bother you, because when you get to heaven, everything's going to be all right."

The problem that faced me as a young Christian was: "Is God concerned about me only in the heavenlies or is God concerned about me right now? Am I one of God's children now, or am I going to become one of his children in eternity?" I learned from Scripture that God was concerned about me at the present moment, and I began to rebel against the established black religious system that I saw all around me.

In 1965, after I graduated from high school, I really wanted to go to a Christian college, but because of the racial situation in America, the established white Christian colleges were not open to receiving black students. As a result, I went to a private junior college in Mississippi, but God was greater than the circumstances and greater than the racial problem! God worked it out so that a gospel team came from California to Mississippi to the school I was attending. When this group found out that I was a Christian, plus the fact that I played a little basketball, they began to find a way to obtain an athletic scholarship for me at Los Angeles Baptist College in California.

About the time I was to go to this college, a friend of mine, Jimmy Walker, and I began to dialogue. I was going to go to one junior college, and he to another. In our discussion, we said: "If you go, I'll go; if I go, you'll go!" When we finally arrived at the college, we found something very surprising — we were the first black students ever to enroll in Los Angeles Baptist College. We came from segregated Mississippi; we grew up in the black community, went to segregated schools, but all of a sudden, we now were placed in roles as integrators in California. Here's a crucial point: when I left Mississippi, I had drawn this conclusion that there were no Christian whites in the state, based on the fact that everybody was against me. The people who treated me the worst were those who filled the white churches on Sunday morning. Furthermore, those were the people that were deacons, Sunday School teachers, and all of that in the name of the Christian white church. Based on these facts, I felt that I hadn't seen a white Christian when I left Mississippi.

One of the severe jolts that happened to me when I was in California was in 1968 when Martin Luther King was shot. While I was in my dorm room, Christian kids were walking up and down the hallway, talking about how glad they were that this had happened. When King died, there were white Christian kids talking about how glad they were that he had died. I had to make a crucial decision: "Lord, am I going to become a militant? Am I going to become a black-power advocate, or do you want me to do something else?" What God told me in the privacy of my room was that he wanted me to become what I call a "liberating force" to the people who were trapped in racial hatred. Many of the problems people have are that they are trapped in ignorance, racism, and in situations from which they need to be liberated.

It's the same kind of thing that we're talking about here. People are trapped in economics, in education, in the systems. Unless we develop ways to liberate people from their traps, they continue to perpetuate things on an ongoing basis. Instead of becoming somebody who hated, I had to say: "Lord, what do you want me to do about this whole situation?" and God enabled me to be one of those who could help educate people concerning their basic needs and be liberated from themselves.

At the end of my first year of college, I returned to Mississippi. This was in the summer of 1968, when John Perkins and I began to talk about what was wrong with our community. The problem, as we saw it, was the same as that which one finds in almost any poor community, namely, the lack of Christian leadership and inadequate finances. We began to discuss what would happen if we developed a summer programme, whereby I would go to a Christian college, come back in the summertime to work among other young people as a leader in that community. This way young people could begin to see a vision of how God could work in their lives. The only patterns they had were bad ones. We prayed: "Lord, how can we develop good models, so that young people can begin to see God alive in these models and don't have to see just old folks going to church, that they don't have to see just bad models on the street, but that they can see some models setting good examples?"

That summer we started our programme. In 1969 and '70, I returned to work in the summer programme. In 1971, I came back for full-time service.

Prior to my coming back, something tragic happened to John Perkins, who had started the ministry. John was teaching what God says: "You shall know the truth and the truth will make you free!" Because of that, John Perkins was locked up in jail in Brandon, Mississippi and almost beaten to death. This came about because people in the established community did not understand God's promise: "You shall know the truth and the truth will make you free.'' That freedom is not just a heavenly freedom. Freedom is not, "Here, by and by we're gonna be free" — but freedom has to do with *now*. It was his conviction — "I'll stand for civil rights, and I'll stand for the struggle in Mississippi" — that caused John to be locked up in jail and almost beaten to death.

Out of his dark experiences and suffering, John Perkins wrote his book, *Let Justice Roll Down*. Once he was so badly beaten that his head appeared like two heads. To add further to his agony, these Simpson County patrolmen and the county sheriff officers bent two prongs of a fork and rammed it up into his nose until the blood shot out.

Pictures and documentation of this unjust cruelty were taken by the Voice of Calvary staff to the local court system who responded: "We want nothing to do with this. You have no cause for complaint!"

Even when this case was taken to the highest court in New Orleans, no conviction was made, because their justice system said: "You have no case!" Thus, the whole affair was thrown completely out of the court system, with no justice being given.

John Perkins relates in his book that during the time that he was beaten, God was teaching him one thing: "Lord, don't let me hate like the people who are beating me. Lord, something must be drastically wrong with a human being that would cause him to beat me so badly when I've done nothing to him. Are these law officials beating me because of my colour?" Despite all this persecution, John feels that God taught him something beautiful.

I remember having to wrestle with the racism that existed in Mississippi. How in the world could somebody beat someone on Saturday night and be sitting in church on Sunday morning? I had to say: "Lord, what kind of system is this that allows circumstances like this to happen?" These occurrences are common, and it's only been over the last five to ten years that this kind of system has been changing. But do you know something? This system just didn't change of itself — it started to change only because God laid it on John Perkins' heart to go back to Mississippi to work and to do something about it.

After I graduated first from college and then from the seminary, God laid it on my heart to go back to Mississippi to work as a part of this ministry called the Voice of Calvary. I had a lot of friends who said: "Dolphus, why go back?" Immediately after John Perkins had been so cruelly treated, the question was repeated.

Not long after this, I travelled as a member of a basketball team that went to Taiwan, the Philippines, and Hong Kong. The coach of my team said: "Dolphus, we like the way that you're working with people in Taiwan. Why not consider becoming a missionary on the overseas crusade?" I prayed about that, and at the end of the trip, we sat down again to talk, and I said: "Norm, God is telling me: 'Dolphus, what are you doing ten, twelve thousand miles away from home? There are people back in Mississippi who are trapped!' "

When we talk about poverty, we speak about those being in an impoverished situation; we're talking about people who are trapped in religion — religion in Mississippi has black folk trapped. It allows them to go to church, sing, shout, be happy but still go back out and face a world that is dying and going to hell. We have people trapped in economic poverty and in educational poverty. God began to direct us in the kind of ministry that could bring about a liberating effect — not something that deals only with relief.

When we began to think about this liberating effect, one of the first things that God led us to deal with was co-operative development. Getting involved in the co-operative movement, we could work together and pool our resources.

The next step was to become involved in health care because we felt that it was important to challenge the whole system. There are thousands of doctors (even thousands of Christian doctors) in America who have no concept of their responsibility to the poor. There are Christian doctors all over America who are working for their own selfish gain, so God called us to a challenge, to see if it was possible to produce a Christian health clinic in Mendenhall that would deal with the needs of the poor. Today, if you were to go to Mendenhall, you would find a Christian health clinic, with a doctor living in that community.

Not only this, you would also find a thrift store — not one in the normal sense of the word, like a Salvation Army or Goodwill Industries. Our Thrift Store is designed to be a model of progress. It was built to be attractive, and everything we have in that store is really well organized, arranged conveniently, and clearly priced. I said: "Wait a minute. Is there something wrong with the direction in which we are going?" One of the things that happens, not only on the part of Christians, because it's true on the part of government organizations as well, is that we try to dehumanize poor people even more by saying: "Anything is all right for poor folk." Every time we talk about working with poor folk, we've got to talk about giving inferior services, of giving inferior things to them, saying: "Throw it up on a junk pile. Let them come get it, because they're already at the bottom."

When I was going to school in California, I used to go to rummage sales, and I always wondered: "Where in the world are my people? Where are the black folk? At the thrift-type store, where are the black people?" The basic reason that black folk are not at either of these types of sale is that they already feel bad about themselves. It's only the people who feel good about themselves already that take advantage of bargains. It's those who feel good about themselves who will go anywhere to shop to try to find bargains. If people already feel bad about themselves and you offer them a bargain, somehow or other, it makes them feel even worse.

So, God has called John Perkins, others, and me in Mississippi to a ministry that is concerned about the total needs of people. We have a congregation, a radio ministry and evangelism. Besides we have a health clinic, a kindergarten, and an adult education programme. Ours is a wholistic ministry that reaches out to the needs of people in Mendenhall, and because of this, we feel that God has given us something unique.

14

The Non-Essentials of Life

ROBERTA WINTER

Ralph Winter planned to attend the consultation and share his testimony, but had to cancel at the last moment. Instead the Winters' testimony was shared in this form. It is reprinted from *Moody Monthly*, Feb., 1980, with permission.

Scene 1: Summer 1951

(It was our second date. Ralph and I were sitting on the grass close to the Rose Bowl, getting acquainted. We had first met just two weeks before.)

"I want you to know I'm a rather . . . uh . . . radical person," Ralph told me. "My mother has often despaired of me. At one point I even refused to wear dress clothes to church."

I waited for explanation. He seemed to be dressed like everyone else — sport shirt and slacks. Nothing elaborate, but nothing weird.

"Some of my friends and I had been reading about various saints down through history, and we just couldn't see why God would not expect as much of us as of them. Take neckties, for example. It didn't seem right to buy neckties when people elsewhere were starving. I figure Americans must own $500,000,000 worth of neckties."

"But you wear them now, don't you?" I asked.

"Yes, but not for the usual reasons. I wear them only to keep from scaring away the natives." And he laughed as he motioned with his hand to some people sitting a little ways away.

I didn't fully understand what he was saying. Gradually I realized that, as Paul said, we don't live to ourselves alone (1 Cor. 10). Our conviction of how the Lord wants us to live must be balanced by its effects on others. Does our style of living lead others to Christ or become a barrier to keep them from him? As

I came to understand, I was more able to enunciate what for us both has become a basic principle of life:

Principle One

Our lifestyle must please the Lord, yet it should not in small matters be so shockingly different from those among whom we walk as to make unintelligible the message we wish to convey.

That day in the park was certainly not *my* first exposure to a simple lifestyle. Born during the depression, I could remember birthdays celebrated with one lead pencil. Yet we now could have meat every day. If I needed a dress, I could get one. Furthermore, long before I met Ralph, God had touched my lifestyle when I asked myself, "Would I follow what the Lord wanted me to do if no one understood?"

As we talked that day I knew it would be exciting and challenging to marry this man. He told me of little economies here and there, but mostly he talked of his dreams, his ideals, his goals that had derived from his walk with the Lord.

I was fascinated with those dreams. Some were just dreams. Others were becoming realities. Because of his efforts as a student in seminary, a group of Christians were in "closed" Afghanistan teaching English and starting an engineering school.

He was excited about his doctoral studies in linguistics because he wanted to make the biblical languages more useful to the average pastor and missionary. Already he had a card file of the Greek lexicon which he hoped to arrange in order of the biblical text to avoid the endless flipping of pages to look up a word. In his head were the ideas behind what has recently been published: the *Word Study Concordance* and the *Word Study New Testament*.

I caught a glimpse that day of the excitement he felt in doing something creative for the Lord, something that would make a difference in the spread of the gospel. Any excitement I might have ever felt for new clothes and a beautiful home paled in comparison to his.

Much later I learned that John Wesley had also been caught up in this same kind of excitement and had called it "the expulsive power of a new affection". Wesley could have become wealthy, but he was so excited accomplishing things for the Lord that he could not be bothered. When he died, he owned only two silver spoons, but was known and loved in the smallest towns of England because of the light he had brought.

During the first few years after marriage, our problem was not whether we should live simply. Once we chose the dreams, we had no alternative. Ralph was in graduate school. And though I could have earned a good salary as a registered nurse, I preferred to become a part of those dreams by working with him in his graduate studies.

I would nurse for a while to build up a reserve, then do research for him until the reserve was gone. We repeated the cycle as often as necessary. After he finished his dissertation, our first two children were born. Then I could neither nurse nor do library research.

By now Ralph had returned to seminary, and we had to make ends meet on what he earned as a student pastor and as a part-time engineer. Our income was so meagre that when we became missionaries, it tripled.

Scene 2: June 1957

(We had just arrived at our post in the mountains of Guatemala. Our assignment was to work with a dozen congregations among the Mam Indians, one of the poorest groups of people in this hemisphere.)

I was embarrassed. The truck with all our belongings arrived dust-covered from the trip over the narrow dirt road which led through the mountain pass into our valley. We collected all our barrels and mattresses and our gas-powered wringer washer — something we considered a "must" with our three small children. A crowd of curious onlookers surrounded us — and all that stuff!

"Why do they stare?" I thought with a twinge of irritation. And then, sure enough, a young man asked the question I had been dreading:

"How much did that cost?"

Barefoot, wearing clothes on which even the patches were patched, he pointed to a mattress. He also kept eyeing the washing machine, obviously wondering what on earth *that* could be. Never in all his life had he seen a machine like that! Mattresses he had seen, to be sure — bags stuffed with straw that rustled and pricked with every move and all too soon became infested with vermin.

What could I tell him? We had bought what seemed to us to be so little. Yet I knew that a month's salary for that young man would not begin to buy a mattress. And I felt defensive.

I could have sold all that was luxurious in the eyes of these people. I could more quickly identify with them if I did.

And yet I also knew that without those machines and little "luxuries" I would be tied to housework. These things could allow me to do in an hour what might otherwise take all day. Even hiring outside help would be luxurious in their eyes.

And I didn't want all my missionary experience to be housework. Surely God had called me to more than that! Thus I had to choose between simplicity in how my *money* was spent and simplicity in how my *time* was spent.

Nevertheless, I could not close my eyes to the dire poverty of these dear people. I could not forget that John said: "If someone who is supposed to be a Christian has money enough to live well, and sees a brother in need, and won't help him — how can God's love be within him?" (1 John 3:17, LB).

It took us some months to adjust to the uncomfortable idea that we would always have more "things" than these people. I doubt if we could have survived on their economic level, but in the long run we did everything we could to live in a way to which they could at least aspire.

We bought only the kinds of equipment which they as a group could afford. We even avoided small luxuries like soda pop, a useless temptation they could ill afford.

I learned in those years a new principle:

Principle Two

A simple lifestyle in the U.S. can still seem extravagant to most of the people in the world. Yet our geographic isolation does not reduce our obligation in God's eyes to people at a distance.

Scene 3: Fall 1961

(We had just returned on furlough after our first five years in Guatemala. Ralph and I stepped into an American drug store to fill a prescription. I waited twenty minutes for the druggist and came back to find Ralph standing near the cash register rather bemused, looking back at a long counter filled with pink, fluffy giraffes, purple elephants, and green monkeys.)

"Roberta, I've walked around this entire store, and there's not one thing here I would take home even if they *gave* it to me." He motioned toward the counters filled with bric-a-brac, poorly made furniture, discount jewellery, and endless toys. "Do they really think they can unload this stuff on thinking people?"

We're still not sure.

After Guatemala, the U.S. society seemed so gorged and glutted with trivialities — things that soon would be more junk at garage sales. But our four young daughters were dazzled.

"Daddy, do we have enough money to buy . . . ?" they would ask.

And he would inevitably reply, "Of course we can! But do we *want* it?" A long discussion would follow, setting "things" in their proper perspective without making the girls feel deprived and poor.

Furloughs were always a problem. From being the wealthiest people in our Guatemala community, we became poor missionaries in the eyes of others. Yet our missionary salary had always seemed adequate. It was adjusted year by year to our cost of living.

We were provided with money to cover most of our medical and dental expenses. We even had the unheard-of benefit of a fund set aside to help with the college education of our children. We paid no income tax. Our home was provided.

It was not hard for us to live on our missionary salary because we knew we were here temporarily. Thus we were not tempted to keep up with friends in the States. Back on the field we would neither need nor want a stereo, a television, or the latest fad in kitchen appliances.

We never hesitated to buy something which would simplify our lives, giving us more time to spend on more important things. But *we* determined what we wanted. *We*, not television ads nor social pressure, decided what would help us. And we tried to teach our daughters what to us had become a principle of life:

Principle Three

We don't really need *most of the things our culture would push off on us. Once we learn to resist social pressure, it is far easier to determine what we really want or need.*

Scene 4: Winter 1968

(After our second furlough, due to several pressing circumstances, we remained in the States. Ralph became a professor in the recently established School of World Mission, and we suddenly found ourselves in a different world. Ralph had to attend important functions and entertain visiting dignitaries.

Because they no longer needed a large home, my parents-in-

law moved into an apartment, giving us their home and all its furniture. One day my sister came to see me.)

"Roberta, you're probably going to be in the States for a while. Why don't you buy some new furniture? This heavy Spanish look is really out of date."

I was caught off guard. The furniture was much better than any we had ever owned. True, the sofa needed to be recovered and the table refinished. But I liked the style. Why spend money on something my sister would choose?

Ralph and I discussed her suggestion that night.

"Does the furniture look that bad?" I asked. "Or do you think that we have become unconscious of what looks good?"

"Don't worry, Roberta," he said. "We decided a long time ago not to let others dictate our lifestyle. We have enough money to buy new furniture if we want, but that does not *force* us to buy it. Why can't we continue to live as if we were still missionaries on furlough, buying only what we need? If we let others know that we choose to live that way, maybe they'll quit worrying about us."

Let me state this idea a different way:

Principle Four

There ought not be any connection between what is earned and what needs to be spent. You don't buy things just because you have the money.

With this principle, money inevitably accumulates. We followed this principle while missionaries; so when it seemed necessary to start a new publishing house specializing in books on missions, we were able to do it. That in turn encouraged us in a much greater venture, the U.S. Centre for World Mission.

Not quite the same, a group of 120 people in Minneapolis have lived for years on only a portion of their group income and used the rest to support dozens of their members as missionaries. What would happen to this world if more evangelical Christians were to realize that God blessed them with money in order to make them a blessing, not to pamper them.

What an immense amount of money would be released for highly strategic causes! How much easier it would be to understand that Christ did not ask us to be "successes" but servants (Mark 10:44).

Scene 5: Summer 1978

(We were seated around a long table at the newly established

U.S. Centre for World Mission. There were twenty of us with notebooks of accounting sheets and a copy of our support-raising manual at each elbow.)

"One of the first things you'll have to learn in raising your support is how to live within your income," Ralph told them. "Our support level is basically the same as Campus Crusade's. To those of you who have worked at well-paying jobs, this will seem very meagre.

"To some of you who are just out of college, it may seem like too much. We want all of you to have enough for your needs and a little besides for you to use as the Lord directs. I believe it is an important exercise to give money to someone else.

"Parkinson enunciated a law which says that 'expenses rise to meet income'. I believe there should be another which says 'when income falls, expenses also fall'.

"Most people have no idea where their money goes. Consequently, the thought of living on less scares them. In order to know exactly how we were coming out, our family has used a basic family accounting system.

"Month by month we can tell how our net worth is changing. This helps us decide if we are spending more than we should. We end up each month with both a profit and loss statement and a balance sheet just like a commercial enterprise."

I could tell my husband was beyond most of them. But little by little he explained a simplified process of double entry book-keeping.

The lessons were important, even for those who never really mastered them. For months many of our staff were living on far less than their full support, and they were amazed at how well they got by. God supplied in unusual ways, and they learned how to buy more efficiently.

Very basic, however, was the fact that we were all in this together. Beyond the suggestions and clues we could give each other, we developed a certain sense of comradeship best stated in another principle:

Principle Five

It is much easier to adopt a simple lifestyle if you join a support group which covenants together to live on less.

Among other equally valuable lessons, we learned that God really does take care of us if we make his concerns our highest priority (Luke 12:31, LB).

We learned that simplicity of life means far more than how

we spend our money. It also means being willing to live to the Lord, unworried about making a good impression (Col. 3:12b, LB).

It means being willing to be God's *servants* in the jobs where he has placed us, recognizing that even Christ was under authority to serve rather than to be served. We learned that our money, like our lives, was ours only because he gave it to us; consequently it was at his beck and call whenever he saw fit.

As a group learning how to live in this new way, we came to value what Jesus meant when he said, "Only those who throw away their lives for my sake and for the sake of the Good News will ever know what it means to really live" (Mark 8:35, LB).

Scene 6: March 16, 1979

(Three generations gathered around a book, reading one paragraph at a time. Dr. and Mrs. McGavran in their eighties and highly revered as missionary statesmen, Ralph and myself now in the middle years, and eight young people. The book was John R. Mott's account of the early days of the Student Volunteer Movement for Foreign Missions, written in 1892.)

"Can we do it again?" This was the unspoken question on every heart.

"In 1807 four other students, praying for the world, said, *'We can do it if we will!'* When they said that, there were no mission societies in America and only one or two in England. Almost all of Protestant mission work was still ahead of them.

"Today we have more than 600 mission agencies in America alone," Ralph said. "We also have thousands, perhaps millions, of evangelical young people. Not all will catch the vision of the unreached frontiers, but Singapore alone has 600 Chinese young people now ready to go."

"But look," Brad insisted, "both in 1807 and in 1892 the student had a watchword. We've also got to have something that will challenge the hearts of our generation."

How about *"A Church for Every People by the Year 2000?"* someone said.

The air was electric. Never have I felt such a holy awe as I sensed that night.

Could we do it? Could *they* do it? Dr. McGavran's life was mainly spent, ours perhaps well over. During the next twenty years the job of missions would have to be the responsibility of these young people and thousands more like them.

Others their age were absorbed with getting better paying jobs or with furnishing homes. Not these! They had caught a higher vision. Their hearts were caught up in the awe of knowing God's hand on their shoulders.

Others their age in earlier times had also experienced this awe, this "expulsive power of a new affection" which dwarfed all lesser pursuits.

For Peter, fishing for mere fish lost its attraction.

The very proper young Wesley abandoned his high church connection for the field and mining camps because God's hand was on him.

Carey, just a poor village cobbler, became history's foremost missionary statesman, meddling in everything from education to commerce to law to Bible translation, all for the sake of the gospel.

Wilberforce poured his riches into legislation for the slaves. And the list goes on and on.

I've often wondered, given the chance, what Christ would have done with the rich young ruler — the only one about whom it is written, "Jesus looked at him and loved him" (Mark 10:21, NIV). But he ended up a rich unknown. Could he have become a Paul, a Luther, a Wesley?

But he was rich, and "the attractions of this world and the delights of wealth, and the search for success and lure of nice things came in and crowded out God's message from his heart, so that no crop was produced" (Mark 4:19).

Principle Six

The foundation of the simple lifestyle is "the expulsive power of a new affection".

It is this which dims worldly goals and makes money itself seem unimportant.

It is this love of Christ and his cause which makes life become real living.

It is this Henry Varley spoke of when he said. "The world has yet to see what God can do with a man who is wholly committed to him."

It is this new affection that makes the simplest lifestyle — really glorious!

Section Four
Bible Studies

15

Bible Studies on World Evangelization and the Simple Lifestyle

HARVIE CONN

1. The Promise of Good News for the World
Main Texts:

Isaiah 40:1-11; Isaiah 52:1-10; Isaiah 61:1-9.

Evangelism is the good news of the great victory of God, his accession, his kingly rule, the dawn of the new age. The city of Jerusalem will one day announce it (Isa. 40:9). The herald/messenger preceding the returning exiles will publish it (Isa. 52:7). The promised Messiah will bring it (Isa. 61:1). "Peace and salvation, Jehovah is King" will be the message, echoed by the watchers on the wall. A new era is to begin for the nations (Isa. 40:5; 42:23-25; 49:1,6; 52:10; 61:5,9). They themselves will come to Zion and proclaim the praises of the redeeming Lord (Isa. 60:6).

1. On the basis of the texts below, what were the reasons in contemporary history for Isaiah's expectations of the coming King? (Isaiah 1:10-17; 3:13-15; 5:7-13; 5:18-23; 10:1-4.)
2. What literary allusions and terms in these passages link these promises to what events in the New Testament?
3. Are there social overtones suggested in the texts in connection with the evangel of the coming of the Lord?
4. On the basis of these texts, what is the relation between the doing of justice by the coming King and his heralds and the salvation of the nations? How would you define evangelism on the basis of these texts?

2. The Coming of the Good News According to Luke
Main Texts:

Luke 1:19; 2:10-11; 3:15-18; 4:16-21; 4:42-44; 7:20-23; 8:1; 9:1-6; 16:16; 20:1; Acts 5:41-42; 8:4-13; 8:25,35,40; 10:34-41; 11:20; 13:32; 14:7-15; 14:21; 15:35; 16:10; 17:18.

The message of evangelism is the message of the Kingdom of God, of God's saving rule come in Christ (first coming) and still to be consummated in Christ (second coming). The bringer of the good news to the poor has appeared, the great moment of salvation and world change has begun. With the appearance of Jesus, the kingdom of God has drawn near. The gospel of the kingdom is the good news shared of the coming of God's transforming, saving presence in history. (1) It stands as a "new order of life: the new humanity and the new creation which have become possible through the death and resurrection of Jesus. This new order includes reconciliation with God, neighbour and nature and, therefore, participation in a new world. It involves freedom from the power of sin and death, and, consequently, the strength to live for God and humanity. It encompasses the hope of a more just and peaceful moral order, and thus it is a call to vital engagement in the historical struggles for peace and justice. (2) This transforming power is also disclosed as an eschatological reality. It is the beginning of the end. As such, it awaits the final consummation of history . . . (Orlando Costas, *The Integrity of Mission,* Harper and Row, 1979, p.6).

1. On the basis of the texts listed above, how would you evaluate the lengthy quotation of Orlando Costas in the preceding paragraph?
2. In what ways do these texts link together the coming of the Saviour, the preaching of the early church and the kingdom of God?
3. What signs of the kingdom are found in these texts that would indicate the liberating, healing power of the kingdom in the restoring of society and the creation of a "new order of life"?
4. Michael Green, speaking at the Lausanne International Congress on World Evangelization, argued our evangelism has tended to isolate what we call the gospel from what Jesus called the kingdom of God. Referring to the Congress, he asked: "How much have we heard here about the kingdom of God? Not much. It is not our language. But it was Jesus' prime concern. He came to show that God's kingly rule had broken into our world: it no longer lay entirely in the future, but was partly realized in him and those who followed him. The Good News of the kingdom was both preached by Jesus and embodied by him . . . So it must be with us" (*Let the Earth Hear His Voice,* World Wide Publications, 1975, p.176). Do you agree with this? In what way can it be said that we have stressed so much the otherness of the kingdom that we have forgotten its nearness?

3. Jesus as Saviour and Lord: The Kingdom in Word and Deed
Main Texts:

Matthew 4:23-25; Matthew 11:1-6; Acts 1:1-2.

We need to repossess the concept of the kingdom as the new reality that the gospel announces. We need to proclaim it in words and deeds — affirming it with our mouths and embodying it in our lives. Otherwise we drive a wedge between Jesus and the new age he inaugurated, between the gospel and the reality it proclaims, between the Word and its sign . . . Orlando Costas, *The Integrity of Mission,* Harper and Row, 1979, p.8.

1. In what way do the texts support the argument of Costas?
2. Which of the three texts makes a connection between the ministry of Jesus and the ministry of Jesus' people? What parallels exist in Romans 15:18-19?
3. A 27-year-old hair stylist was featured in a recent US magazine story. He won the New Jersey lottery and receives $1776 a week, or $92,352 a year for life. In the article he describes himself as a born again Christian. "The money has brought a lot of temptation. Without Christ, there is no inner peace." The article also describes other aspects of his life. His day is leisurely. He normally gets up before noon and the major decision facing him is whether to take a flying lesson, wheel around in his yellow Jaguar, or shoot pool. He lives with his girl friend, sips a Chivas Regal on the rocks in the mid-afternoon, and says, "I'm taking this year off to get my act together." — Ben Patterson, "Born Again '77: The Year of the Evangelical," *The Wittenburg Door,* No. 35 (1977), 2. If you were this young man's pastor, how would you advise him? What steps would you take to help him integrate more consistently his life and his profession in the kingdom?
4. Michael Cassidy has remarked: "For a long time, obedience to the Great Commission was seen simply in terms of evangelism and proclamation. But (we realize) that this is not enough. We are to go beyond proclaiming to winning and discipling — a disciple being one who follows (Mark 4:19) and obeys (Acts 5:29) and takes up his own cross (Mark 10:38) . . . We must not confuse means and ends. Preaching and teaching are not ends in themselves but means to making disciples. We must not settle for decisions or pew-warmers, but for disciples . . . Paradoxically, the Christian turns both from the world, and to the world. He turns from its life-style to its life-need . . . Justice, structural change,

compassionate caring and practical service now become new imperatives for us. Individual Christian salvation and Christian social ethics belong together." — "Disciples Not Decisions," *Africa Enterprise News*, August, 1975. Comment on these remarks in the light of how you see the relation between word and deed in the kingdom message of the gospel.

5. Must there be a commitment to Christ as Lord of one's life in order to be saved? C. C. Ryrie argues No to that question. "To teach that Christ must be Lord of life in order to be Saviour is to confuse certain aspects of discipleship . . . To make the conditions for the life of discipleship requirements for becoming a disciple is to confuse the gospel utterly by muddying the clear waters of grace of God with the works of man" (*Balancing the Christian Life*, Moody Press, 1969, p.178). John Stott says Yes. "I am suggesting, therefore, that it is as unbiblical as it is unrealistic to divorce the Lordship from the Saviourhood of Jesus Christ" ("Must Christ Be Lord to Be Saviour? — Yes," *Eternity Magazine*, September, 1959, p.37). What is your response to the debate? Do you see any relation between this discussion and the word/deed ministry of Jesus and his people in the kingdom?

4. The Poor, Promised Recipients of the Good News of the Gospel
Main Texts:

Psalms 10:12-18; 22:23-27; 35:10; 37:12-15; 40:17; 41:1-3; 70:4-5; 72:1-14; 74:19-21; 109:16-31; Prov. 22:22-23; Prov. 23:10-11.

The period of 400 years between the two Testaments was a time of social and political conflict and unrest. The despair and privation of the Jews produced an ethos of poverty. Some, like the Essenes of Qumran, accepted their poverty as a special mark of their righteous lives and referred to themselves as "the Poor". Members of the community surrendered all their goods to the community before being admitted. A "theology of the poor" was preserved in the apocryphal literature of that period. In the age to come, the literature argued, the poor would become rich, and the arrival of the new age would be preceded by a class struggle in which the poor would rise up and overthrow the rich who suppressed them. Poverty could be passively accepted in the confidence that divine deliverance would come.

1. In the light of the texts listed above, how would you evaluate this inter-testamental theology of poverty? What elements have been borrowed from the Old Testament? What distortions have entered?

2. In the texts cited above, what terms are used to describe "the poor"?

3. What do these texts tell us about God's redemptive purposes for the poor? Can one say, on the basis of these texts, that "God sides with the poor"?

4. Herman Ridderbos, in his book, *The Coming of the Kingdom* (1960), suggests that the designation, "the poor" (the meek) "represent the socially oppressed, those who suffer from the power of injustice and are harassed by those who only consider their own advantage and influence. They are, however, at the same time those who remain faithful to God and expect their salvation from his kingdom alone" (p.188). In contrast to those who have fastened their hope upon this world, they expect the salvation that God has held out to his people as "the consolation of Israel" (Luke 2:25, cf. Matt 5:4; Luke 6:24; 16:25). The term then in the Old Testament is a socio-religious designation, virtually a synonym of the "remnant" idea. How do you react to this argument?

5. By way of contrast, this position is opposed by Orlando Costas. For Costas, Ridderbos begs the question. "After all, whom do the Covenant People *represent*? What is the *meaning* of Israel in the world of nations? Are the true people of God a *paradigm* of the new society, or are they not? What is the meaning of the privileged place assigned to the poor in the Covenant?" (*The Integrity of Mission*, p.77-78). For Costas, the poor are important not just because of their faithfulness to God but because of his relationship with humanity. God's relationship with the poor reveals the redemptive quality of his justice, which restores the fallen and heals the bruised (cf. Ex.22:21; 23:9; Lev 19:33; Deut 27:19). By the same token, the poor, he continues, disclose the demands of the New Covenant: meekness, openness to God and trust in him alone (cf. Luke 18:18-25). How do you respond to Costas and to the debate between Ridderbos and Costas?

6. On the basis of the texts below, how would you begin to relate these Old Testament promises with the ministry of Christ? (Luke 1:51-55; 4:16-21; 6:20-28; 7:20-23.)

5. Jesus, the Inaugurator of the Jubilee Year of the Lord
Main Texts:

Lev. 25:8-28; Isaiah 11:1-10; 61:1-10.

Contemporary biblical scholars are arguing that the O.T. Jubilee year legislation is a major theme of the gospel of Luke. The Jubilee was intended to be the year of the great restoration (cf. Acts 1:6; 3:21). It called for a covenant lifestyle that would typify what God had promised to give. Jubilee was Exodus spelled out in terms of social salvation (Lev. 25:9). At the Jubilee year centre was the theocratic concept of rest. In the idea of "rest" the two themes of creation and redemption are joined together. Israel's occupying the promised land becomes an historical exemplification of the jubilee rest (Joshua 21:44-45). Possession, inheritance and rest function almost as synonymous ideas in Deuteronomy (1:8, 21, 35, 38; 3:20). The Jubilee legislation brings them all together. By obeying the Jubilee laws Israel would be a witness to the surrounding nations of God's just rule and her faith in that rule. "For what great nation is there that has a god so near to it as the Lord our God is to us, whenever we call upon him? And what great nation is there that has statutes and ordinances so righteous as all this law which I set before you this day?" (Deut. 4:7-8).

1. What are some of the themes of the Jubilee legislation? Do you see any connections through New Testament passages we have already noticed?
2. John Howard Yoder, in *The Politics of Jesus* (Eerdmans, 1972, pp.64ff), sees allusions to the four prescriptions of the Jubilee year in several of Jesus' sayings: (1) leaving the soil fallow (Lev. 25:20-21; Luke 12:29-31); (2) remission of debts, and (3) liberation of slaves (Matt. 6:16; Matt. 18:23-35; Luke 16:1ff); (4) the redistribution of capital (Luke 11:42; Luke 12:30-33). Comment and evaluate.
3. On the basis of the texts below, in what ways did Jesus as our substitute come to side with the poor and oppressed? (Luke 2:1-7; 2:22-24; Matt. 2:14-15; Matt. 2:19-23; Mark 2:23-28; Matt. 8:20; Matt. 10:9-14; Matt. 11:28-30; Matt. 17:24-27; Matt. 21:18-19; Matt. 27:35 with Ps. 22:18; Matt. 27:46 with Ps. 22:1; Matt. 27:57-60.)
4. How should the texts below be understood in terms of the relation between the poor and entrance into the kingdom that was the centre of Jesus' evangelistic message? (Matt. 19:20-24; 29-39; Luke 12: 13-21; 12:32-34; Luke 13:28-30; Luke 14:15-24; 14:33; Luke 16:19-31.)
5. Richard Batey argues that discipleship in the kingdom meant for Jesus a reversal of the existing social order. "One placed first the new righteousness that Jesus taught. Compassion for others, not greed, was to become the basis of the new economy. Those with riches were challenged to distribute to others as God's mercy and human needs dictated. In a world where avarice was the rule of the day, where even

many religious leaders were known to be lovers of money (Luke 16:14), where show of piety and eleemosynary acts were calculated to impress the observer (Matt. 6:1-4), Jesus called for deeds reflecting genuine justice and mercy . . . To be in the kingdom meant having faith in the sovereignty of a compassionate Father and reflecting his sovereignty within the unjust social order" (*Jesus and the Poor*, Harper and Row, 1972, pp.16-17). Does this comment do justice to the texts studied thus far?

6. Jesus' People, the Implementers of the Jubilee Year of the Lord
Main Texts:

Exodus 19:5-6; 1 Peter 2:9-12; Romans 8:23; James 1:18; 1 Cor. 12:12-27.

The new man and the new community called into being by the gospel of redemption anticipate the new creation as the climax toward which God is daily moving history, and the cosmos. Where the church is truly the church, she mirrors that coming new society of Kingdom of God in miniature. She reflects the joy of life of a Body whose Head is the exalted Lord himself and whose identity as future judge of all mankind has already been publicly published by his resurrection from the dead (Acts 17:31). — Carl J. H. Henry, *A Plea for Evangelical Demonstration*, Baker Book House, 1971, p.113.

1. Israel is to be a kingdom of priests by being a "holy nation unto God" (Ex. 19:6). On the basis of the texts below, what is the relation of holiness to justice and righteousness? (Ex. 22:21-23:3; Numbers 15:39-40; Deut. 7:6-11; 26:16-19; Psalms 47:7-9; 89:30-35; Romans 6:19.)
2. Israel's mission was to be "a kingdom of priests." At least three possible interpretations of this language have been suggested: (1) All Israelites individually will have the right of direct approach to the Lord; (2) Israel will be a state governed by a priesthood, a hierocracy (3) As a priest represents God before men, Israel is to represent the kingship of God in the world before the nations. Which of these three possibilities do you feel best fits the context (particularly the phrase, "all the earth is mine", Ex. 19:5) and the use of this passage in 1 Peter 2:9?
3. In terms of the church as the new Israel (1 Pet. 2:9), how would you define the mission of the church as the people of the kingdom come in Christ (Col. 1:13; 1 Thess. 2:12)?

4. It has been argued that "the church is the place where the eschatological kingship of God in Jesus Christ becomes visible." Do you find any support for this argument in the image used to describe the church in Romans 8:23 and James 1:18?

5. Hans Kung writes: "The reign of God, fulfilled, realized and personified in Christ, remains the horizon of the church, and the focal point of its own life and of its service. If the church wants to be a *credible* herald, witness, demonstrator and messenger in the service of the reign of God, then it must constantly repeat the message of Jesus, not primarily to the world, to others, but to itself; the church must accept in faith the message of the coming reign of God which has erupted into the present, and constantly accept anew and in obedience the reign of God which is already present, God's gracious and demanding salvific will" (*The Church*, Sheed and Ward, 1967, pp.96-97). In what way does the image of the church in 1 Cor. 12:12-27 implement this emphasis on the church's calling to serve the kingdom?

6. "The Church holds within itself the whole of Christ" (Lewis Smedes, *All Things Made New*, Eerdmans, 1970, p.229). In the light of Eph. 1:23 and 1 Cor. 12, what does this mean? In what sense, then, can we speak of the church as a "model" of the kingdom?

7. The Church and the Theopolitics of the Kingdom
Main Texts:

Matt. 5:13-16; 28:18-20; 1 Cor. 12:1-3; Gal. 6:9-10; 1 Tim. 2:1-2.

The church constitutes a new people, the people of the Messiah. It is a new community of those who have been delivered by God from the dominion of darkness and transferred to the Kingdom of his beloved Son, in whom they have redemption and the forgiveness of sins (Col. 1:13,14). "The church is unique among all the institutions and communities in this world. And the Gospel which has been entrusted to the church is equally unique. Every attempt, therefore, to erase the borderline between church and world by stressing the so-called 'secular meaning of the Gospel' must be resisted. At the same time, the church does not exist only for God and for itself. God Himself wants the church to be *related to the world* in a positive sense." In Abraham and his seed all the families of the earth will be blessed (Gen. 12:1-3). — *The Church and Its Social Calling* (Reformed Ecumenical Synod, 1979, p.36).

1. On the basis of the texts above, what specific tasks do you see given to the church with respect to its responsibility toward the world?
2. In a commentary on Matt. 5:13-16, John Stott sees the effects of salt and light as complementary. "The function of salt is largely negative: it prevents decay. The function of light is positive: it illuminates the darkness. So Jesus calls his disciples to exert a double influence on the secular community, a negative influence by arresting its decay and positive influence by bringing light into its darkness. For it is one thing to stop the spread of evil; it is another to promote the spread of truth, beauty and goodness. Putting the two metaphors together, it seems legitimate to discern in them the proper relation between evangelism and social action in the total mission of Christ in the world — a relation which perplexes many believers today." (*Christian Counter-culture*, Inter-Varsity Press, 1978, pp.64-65). May these comments be applied to the institutional church as it has its God-given place *in* this world and shows its concern *for* the world?
3. Is there any sense in which we may speak of the church as "an alternative society," a visible, beckoning, hope-giving, guiding sign of the shalom of the kingdom?
4. In what sense does the proclamation of Jesus as Lord have sociopolitical implications?
5. Every night as the trucks of the sanitation and police departments of Calcutta, India travel through the city they find, lying on the sidewalks and in doorways, people in the last extremity of life. Some are the victims of cholera which periodically sweeps through the city. Others are gasping final breaths in the grip of India's greatest killer, tuberculosis. Others, particularly little children and old people, are dying of starvation. To these, who have been described as the human garbage of the city, Mother Teresa came to dedicate her life. In a vast warehouse near a temple dedicated to Kali, the goddess of destruction, she established her reception home for the dying. Does her Christian service have social implications? In the light of her testimony, and others like her, would you agree that "true service is not just a matter of mercy in which the heart goes out to the suffering neighbour; it also calls for justice, so that there may be an end to the conditions which cause the suffering"?
6. What political overtones and implications are found in our call to pray for the authorities (1 Tim. 2:1-2)?
7. "Worship, which opens the door to a new week, is not a

retreat from reality, but a rallying-point, a launching-pad, a springboard which sends believers forth upon their way as 'living letters known and read of all men'. The preaching and teaching ministries of the church must shape and mould the Christian community to challenge the 'principalities and powers' of this world as it carries out its reconciling mission in society" (*The Church and Its Social Calling*, p.24). Comment and discuss in the light of the texts above.

8. In the light of the texts below, how did the early church demonstrate the new lifestyle shaped by the good news of the kingdom? (Mark 10:28-31; Mark 15:40-41; Luke 8:1-4; Acts 2:41-47; Acts 4:32-35; 1 Cor. 9:18; Phil. 4:12-13.)

8. Evangelism and the Obligations of the Kingdom: Love
Main Texts:

Lev. 19:13-18, 34; Deut. 10:12-19; Jeremiah 22:13-17; Micah 6:6-8; Mark 12:28-34; Matthew 25:31-46; Luke 10:25-37.

Is there a difference between the Christian and the humanitarian concepts of love and justice? The general humanist idea finds its central reference point not in God but in man. "It views justice as a natural demand. Furthermore, such justice is an achievement of human society. In this view nothing necessarily precedes man's doing of justice: no prior forgiveness of the offender, no infinite mercy of God, no law placed upon man from the outside, no empowering action by the Holy Spirit. While the humanistic view of love and justice has been an undeniable force for good in human history and often has responded to human need more quickly than have Christians, it is incomplete both in its motivation and in its purpose" (*And He Had Compassion on Them. The Christian and World Hunger*, Christian Reformed Board of Publications, 1978, p.52.)

1. Making use of the Old Testament texts above, how do you see the relation between love and justice? How is this perspective altered by the modern concept of "love" as primarily an inner emotion?
2. Drawing on the characteristics of love displayed in these texts, how would you contrast the Christian concept of love with that of humanitarianism described above?
3. What elements do you see that link together the Old Testament view of neighbour love with the New Testament passages cited above?
4. According to Matthew 25:31-46, how shall we understand the relationship between entrance into the kingdom and the way we have used our earthly gifts?

5. How would you compare the Old Testament and New Testament ideas of "neighbour"?

6. "One cannot codify all the possibilities of neighbourly behaviour. Instead, one must think in terms of being a neighbour, even as God is the great Benefactor of humanity" (Frederick Danker). Is this an acceptable summary of Luke 10:25-37? In what ways does the world church see "neighbour" more as an object that one defines rather than a relationship into which one enters in the kingdom?

9. Evangelism and the Obligations of the Kingdom: Compassion

Main Texts:

Gen. 21:22-23; Gen. 39:20-22; 2 Samuel 9:1-7; Isaiah 16:5; Psalms 25:8-10; Psalms 36:5-7; Jeremiah 9:23-24; Hosea 2:19-20; 6:6; 10:12-13; 12:6-7; Micah 6:8; Matthew 15:29-32; 20:29-34; Luke 7:11-15.

Compassion is more than maternal tenderness, more than Pharaoh's daughter seeing the baby Moses in his reed boat and hearing his cries. It is Pharaoh's daughter hearing the oppressed Hebrews' baby crying (Ex. 2:6). It is tenderness translated into action on behalf of the sinned against. "I have seen the misery of my people," Jehovah says to Moses at the burning bush. "I have given ear to their cries . . . I know their sufferings. I am resolved to deliver them" (Ex. 3:7ff, 16). Solomon understood this. At the dedication of the temple, he prays that God will show compassion for a sinning people. But he links compassion to their being sinned against. "Make them objects of compassion before those who have taken them captive" (1 Kings 8:50; cf. 2 Chronicles 30:9).

1. What indications are there in the texts cited above that would underline compassion's attention not so much to people as the subject of sin (sinners) but more to people as the objects of sin (the sinned against)?

2. What other terms are used in these texts paralleling the idea of compassion? In what sense do the terms complement and reinforce one another? What does this information say about evangelizing the publicans of our world cultures?

3. Do you see any continuations of these themes in the New Testament texts cited above dealing with the compassion of Jesus?

4. Raymond Fung, an industrial evangelist in Hong Kong, tells

of coming to know a textile worker in his early forties. At Fung's urging he came to church one Sunday at the cost of a day's wages. After the service they went to lunch. The worker said, "Well, the sermon hit me." It had been about sin. "You know, what the preacher said is true of me — laziness, a violent temper and addiction to cheap entertainment. I guess he was talking about me." Fung continues, "I held my breath, trying to keep down my excitement. Had the message of the gospel gotten through I wondered. 'But nothing was said about my boss,' he continued. 'Nothing about how he employs child labourers, how he doesn't give us legally-required holidays, how he puts on false labels, how he forces us to do overtime.' . . . My friend, the textile worker, agreed that he was a sinner. He heard that message — and sensed its validity. And yet he rejected the message of the very church that provided that diagnosis. He rejected the message because he sensed its incompleteness. It spoke to his sinfulness — but not to his sinned-againstness" (Raymond Fung, "The Forgotten Side of Evangelism," *The Other Side*, October, 1979, 17-18). Do you agree with Fung that "a gospel which ignores our sinned-againstness cannot possibly work among the overwhelming majority in Asia: the poor peasants and the workers"?

5. Lesslie Newbigin argues that at the heart of compassion is the idea of "suffering with" (Rom. 8:17), involvement in the pain of the Publican's sense of what is "not right" (*The Open Secret*, Eerdmans, 1978, pp.121-123). It invites the Publican inside. It does not keep him outside looking in. Do you agree? Comment.

6. What is the strategical significance and meaning of "identification" for the evangelist who seeks to exhibit compassion?

10. Evangelism and the Obligations of the Kingdom: Moderation

Main Texts:

Proverbs 30:15-16; Isaiah 56:10-11; Jeremiah 22:13-17; Ezekiel 18:7-17; Habakkuk 2:9-11; Matthew 6:24-33; 10:37-39; Phil. 4:5-6; 2 Cor.7:1-2; 1 Tim. 3:3.

With all the Old Testament says about wealth and prosperity, it sets them in clearly defined prespective. While not forbidding them, it hedges them about with restrictions and cautions. They are not to be accumulated just for the sake of getting more and more, they must not be gained by oppression and injustice, they can and do lead to covetousness. They do not belong to us but to God, who is the ultimate owner of all we have. Therefore, we are stewards, not proprietors, of our wealth. In our use of it, we are sinning if we do not reflect God's strong concern for the poor and hungry, the weak and the oppressed. *What we do with what we have must be in accord with the great command to love God with everything we are and have.* Frank E. Gabelein, "Challenging Christians to the Simple Lifestyle," *Christianity Today,* September 21, 1979, p.26.

1. John V. Taylor sums up the Old Testament perspective on wealth in the word *shalom*. It is "something much broader than 'peace': the harmony of a caring community informed at every point by its awareness of God . . . It speaks of a wholeness that is complete because every aspect and every corner of ordinary life is included . . . It meant a dancing kind of inter-relationship, seeking something more free than equality, more generous than equity, the ever-shifting equipoise of a life-system" (*Enough is Enough*, SCM Press, 1975, pp.41-42). Does this judgement express adequately to you the lifestyle described in the texts above?
2. According to the texts cited above, what is the relation between justice, greed and a moderate lifestyle?
3. Is "moderation" only a matter of our attitude toward material things? Or does having so many material things itself result in a wrong attitude?
4. Lenny Bruce, the sick comedian, is once reported to have said, "I know in my heart, by pure logic, that any man who claims to be a leader of the church is a hustler if he has two suits in a world in which most people have none." Respond to this in terms of the relationship between evangelization and the simple lifestyle.
5. How are we to understand the radical demands of Matthew 10:37-39 and related commands (e.g. Matt. 6:24; Luke 12:33) in relation to the good news of the kingdom? Do you agree with Herman Ridderbos when he says, "However paradoxical their form may sometimes be, and however indispensable the light of the whole law to interpret them is, they nevertheless give rules and not exceptions!" (*Coming of the Kingdom,* p.329)?
6. In the light of the texts above, how would you define "moderation" as the obligation of kingdom servants? Why is it

particularly a concern of Paul's as he evaluates his own ministry and that of the church's bishops?

7. Carl Henry writes: "To the whole community of mankind the church is called to proclaim the whole counsel of God and to seek by persuasion to evoke universal committal to his commands. Never is the church more effective in doing so than when she provides a living example in her own ranks of what new life in Christ implies, and never is she more impotent than when she imposes new standards on the world that she herself neglects. A social ethic is not some kind of bureaucratic imposition by the church upon the world, but a mirroring to the world of the joys and benefits of serving the living God" (*A Plea for Evangelical Demonstration*, p.67). Comment and discuss.

11. Evangelism and the Obligations of the Kingdom: Obedience
Main Texts:

Gen. 18:16-21; Ex. 19:5-6; Deut. 24:10-18; Ezek. 18:5-9; Ezek. 33:10-16; Matt. 5:38-48; Matt. 7:12-23; 1 John 3:16-18; James 1:27-2:6.

John Stott has stated that "the very word 'obedience' arouses hostility today. It smacks of a grovelling servility, a mindless conformity to inflexible laws, even a bondage which is destructive of the freedom and growth of responsible human beings" (*The Lord Christ*, Vol. 1 of *Obeying Christ in a Changing World*, Collins, 1979). But to Jesus it meant submission to the discipline of the kingdom, commitment to a lifestyle of righteousness, incorporation into a community of self-surrender and God-obsession. Without this dimension of obedience, the radical demands of the kingdom are reduced to a pocket God, cheap grace, a private version of the Bible, and a spiritualized church that is neither of the world nor in it.

1. In most of the Old Testament texts cited above, there is an intertwining of the concepts of obedience with those of "justice and righteousness." They are said by some scholars to have such associative force that sometimes they can be used interchangeably. How do you react to this suggestion? What insights does it provide regarding the nature of obedience?

2. What do the texts in Gen. 18 and Exodus 19 suggest regarding the doing of "justice and righteousness" in relation to the calling of Abram and the people of God toward the nations?

3. Gen. 18:20 speaks of the "outcry of Sodom and Gomorrah". The language may be an allusion to Gen. 4:10 and the crying out of the earth against interhuman injustice. In the light of Isaiah 1:10 and Ezekiel 16:49 (cf. Jer. 23:14), how shall we understand God's intervention in Sodom though there are only ten righteous?

4. In the light of the texts above, is it sufficient to describe "justice and righteousness" as largely repeated acts of moralistic virtue isolated from earthly justice? What cultural ideologies may have influenced our understanding of these terms?

5. Are there any suggestions from Jesus' Sermon on the Mount to indicate these relationships continue in the ethics of the kingdom?

6. "John Perkins, founder of the community of witness called Voice of Calvary in Mendenhall and Jackson, Mississippi, discovered early in his experience of evangelistic preaching in the black community that in order to give the message integrity and power, he had to flesh out the gospel in ministries of social and political activity. Poverty, injustice, and exploitation had to be dealt with in the name of the gospel. Such ministries involved him and his congregation with both church members and non-church members alike. The witness was corporate and identifiable as the church making disciples, but its activities and its strategy thrust it into the world without sharply defined 'churchly' and 'para-churchly' organization and functions!" (Norman Kraus, *The Authentic Witness,* Eerdmans, 1979, p.162). Do you see this model as a fleshing out of the testimony of 1 John 3 and James 1:27ff? Can you supply other models from your own experience?

12. Evangelism and the Obligations of the Kingdom: Prayer
Main Texts:

Isaiah 1:10-17; 59:1-4; 58:6-10; Micah 3:1-4; Luke 11:5-8; Luke 18:1-8.

It must be aserted that petitionary prayer only flourishes where there is a twofold belief: first, that God's name is hallowed too irregularly, his kingdom has come too little, and his will is done too infrequently: second, that God himself can change this situation. Petitionary prayer, therefore, is the expression of the hope that life as we meet it, on the one hand, *can* be otherwise and, on the other hand, that it *ought* to be otherwise. It is therefore impossible to seek to live in

God's world on his terms, doing his work in a way that is consistent with who he is, without engaging in regular prayer. — David F. Wells, "Prayer: Rebelling Against the Status Quo," *Christianity Today*, November 2, 1979, 34.

1. In the texts from the Old Testament cited above, God tells Israel he will hear her prayers no longer. What reasons does he give?
2. What links are suggested by these same texts that prophesy of the time of the coming kingdom as a time of answered prayer? What missionary dimension is added to these prophecies by such passages as Isaiah 56:6-7 and Malachi 1:11?
3. How does Luke's gospel point to the kingdom come in Christ as a fulfilment of these promises?
4. David Wells says that essentially petitionary prayer is rebellion. "It is, in this its negative aspect, the refusal of every agenda, every scheme, every interpretation that is at odds with the norm as originally established by God. As such, it is itself an expression of the unbridgeable chasm that separates Good from Evil, the declaration that Evil is not a variation on Good but its antithesis" ("Prayer: Rebelling Against the Status Quo," *Christianity Today*, 33). Comment in the light of Luke 11:5-8 and Luke 18:1-8.
5. Is there a relationship between our lack of prayer and the loss of our anger at the level of social witness? Is the basic problem over the practice of prayer or over its nature?
6. In what way will secularism as an attitude encourage resignation over the world as it is and cut the relationship between prayer and the theopolitics of the kingdom?

13. Evangelism and the Blessings of the Kingdom: Justification
Main Texts:

Gen. 15:3-6; Matt. 5:6; Luke 16:19-31; Luke 18:9-14; Romans 3:19-23; Romans 4:1-5; Galatians 5:3-6; James 2:14-24.

The good news of the kingdom is that the God of justice is also the God of justification. He who demands the right fulfills his own demands in Christ. The divine call for justice and righteousness, for doing the will of God on earth as it is done in heaven, cannot be met by an unjust and unrighteous world. So God himself comes in Christ to bear the shame and guilt of injustice and renew his call to a renewed people. The gift of righteousness demands the obligation of righteousness. Justification as a work of God alone requires justice and mercy for the naked and hungry. And in that exhibition, "a person is justified by what he does and not by faith alone" (James 2:24).

1. Jose Miranda comments on Gen. 15:6: Abram's hope (his faith) is "that the whole world would be transformed by Jahweh's intervention which makes men just and raises the dead. This is Abraham's faith which was considered as justice. Because it is justice. Because effectively to hunger and thirst for the realization of justice in the world is already justice" (*Marx and the Bible*, Orbis Books, 1974, p.227). Faith, then, on this understanding, is believing that there is hope for our world because God has promised to intervene in human history. Comment on this understanding (cf. Rom. 4:18, "against all hope he believed in hope").

2. G. Schrenk argues that the concept of "righteousness" always contains at least two elements. There is always the forensic, the legal aspect. That is, we are always talking about justice and right. Further, there is the idea of saving action. God's rule as King and Judge cannot be separated from it. And that ministry as Judge in the Old Testament is always saving rule. Judges are redeemers, dispensers of salvation. So the declaration of justness is a declaration of salvation (*Theological Dictionary of the New Testament*, Vol. II, Eerdmans, 1964, p.195). Do you see any reflection of these elements in Gen. 15:6, Rom. 3:19-23 and Rom. 4:1-5?

3. For Judaism in the first century the essence of justification lay in that it would take place in the future and in the heavenly judgment. The whole of life was regarded as a preparation for this. No one could obtain certainty of justification any earlier than in the great judgment itself. How does this compare with the New Testament emphasis?

4. In the light of the Old Testament understanding of "righteousness" as the exhibition of divine justice (Jer. 22:3, 15; 9:24), how shall we understand Matt. 5:6?

5. Do you see any tie-ins between the Pharisees' "self-righteousness", their love of money and their attitude to the poor? (cf. Luke 16:13-15). How then do you understand the core meaning of the parable of the rich man and Lazarus (Luke 16:19-31)?

6. In what way does this parable support what we have called the kingdom "theology of reversal"?

7. How, on the basis of these texts in Luke, would you define the meaning of "justification" in the gospels? Herman Ridderbos speaks of it as "that kingly justice which will be brought to light one day for the salvation of the oppressed and the outcasts, and which will be executed especially by the Messiah" (*Coming of the Kingdom,* p.190). Do you agree?

8. How do you harmonize this definition with the Pauline understanding of justification?
9. How can James 2:23 and Romans 4:2-3 use the same proof-text (Gen. 15:6) to support what looks on the surface like exactly opposite conclusions (compare Gal. 5:6)?
10. "The righteousness of Jesus Christ ever remains the exclusive ground of the believer's justification. But the personal godliness of the believer is also necessary for his justification in the judgment of the last day (Matt. 7:21-23; 25:31-46; Heb. 12:14)." Comment on this statement in terms of your harmonization of the emphasis of Paul and James, and the relation of justification to the pursuit of justice.

14. Evangelism and the Blessings of the Kingdom: Salvation
Main Texts:

Romans 8:18-23; Eph. 2:1-8; Titus 2:11-3:6; 1 Cor. 15:23-28; Col. 2:10-15; Phil. 2:9-11.

Salvation is in three tenses. It is the work of Christ "who has delivered . . . who does deliver . . . and in whom we trust that he will yet deliver" (2 Cor. 1:10). The implications of that for the understanding of a personal experience of God and His grace have long been de bated. "Once saved" or "always saved"? "Faith the result of the Spirit's work or its cause"? "Entire sanctification or indwelling sin"? But what of salvation's cosmic character? The God who created the world, who gave a land to his covenant people to live in, who gave them a task to fulfil in the midst of and toward the nations, and who judged them for their failures to perform that task, has sent Jesus as Lord. And he sends that Lord's servant people, born of the Spirit, into that world. We go seeking "not only to exhibit but also to spread (the kingdom's) righteousness in the midst of an unrighteous world. The salvation we claim should be transforming us in the totality of our personal and social relationships" (Lausanne Covenant, Paragraph 5).

1. Michael Green sees "in Paul a deep understanding of what Bultmann calls 'the Christian's betweenness'. We enjoy here and now an authentic first installment of salvation; but the best is yet to be" (*The Meaning of Salvation*, Westminster Press, 1965, p.154). What texts cited above stress the "already" of salvation accomplished? What texts point to the "not yet" of salvation still to be? How do you harmonize these facts? How do we understand our place in all this?
2. What is meant by our salvation from the old aeon (Eph. 1:21, 2:2, Gal. 1:4)?

3. In what sense may we speak of salvation as intended not merely for individuals but for the whole of creation?
4. How do we relate this to Oscar Cullmann's famous analogy of D-Day and V-Day? That is, the Allied invasion of Normandy in 1944 was the decisive battle in the war (D-Day). Victory (V-Day) is still to be achieved. And yet, in another sense, it is already in our grasp. The outcome was assured at D-Day. Paul Althaus puts it this way: "The parousia removes the hiddenness of the reality of Easter for history."
5. What relationship do you see between the saving Lordship of Jesus and his finished triumph over "the principalities and powers" (Col. 2:15)? How is this language to be understood?
6. In what ways can the church weaken or annul the eschatological fact that, by the coming of Christ and his death and resurrection, the "not yet" has broken into the present, although it has not yet been consummated?

15. Evangelism and the Blessings of the Kingdom: The New Creation
Main Texts:

Isaiah 43:14-19; 65:13-24; 2 Cor. 5:16-21; Eph. 4:17-30; Rev. 21:1-8.

A great change has occurred in human history and society with the death and resurrection of Christ. Paul calls it "a new creation". It is not meant merely in an individual sense ("a new creature"). "One is to think of the new world of the re-creation that God has made to dawn in Christ, and in which everyone who is in Christ is included . . . The 'old things' stand for the unredeemed world in its distress and sin, the 'new things' for the time of salvation and the re-creation that have dawned with Christ's resurrection. He who is in Christ, therefore, is new creation: he participates in, belongs to, this new world of God." (Herman Ridderbos, *Paul: An Outline of His Theology*, Eerdmans, 1975, pp.45-46.)

1. Which translation of 2 Cor. 5:17 ("new creature" or "new creation") do you think is more accurate and why?
2. Are there any allusions and references from the two passages in Isaiah cited above and quoted in 2 Cor. 5:17 that might reinforce the idea of "the new creation" as a new society or world called forth by God's omnipotence?
3. John Topel writes: "When Israel had arrived in the promised land, (it) had set up its government and legal structure,

it thought it had arrived. The kingdom *had* come, and there was nothing more to look forward to in the future. The thrust for achieving interhuman justice was blunted, and the country stagnated in patterns of gross social injustice. In spite of the thunderings of the prophets, it was only the Babylonian exile, where Israel's government and autonomous exercize of the law was destroyed, that brought about a renewed hope for a future of justice and peace" (*The Way to Peace*, Orbis Books, 1979. p. 90). How do you evaluate these judgments?

4. How was the New Testament a fulfilment of the expectations of the prophets? In what way can the Pauline understanding of the "new creation" help us avoid settling into the stagnation of an achieved state?

5. Moltmann points out that the emphasis on the "new" in the New Testament is in striking contrast to Greek philosophy's view of everything as past event recurring over and over again in history. In what areas do you agree? Do you see any relation between this and our calling to a "new" kingdom lifestyle?

6. What demands are placed upon us by the eschatological reality of "the new creation" already begun in us through Christ? What warnings should we draw from its eschatological promise yet to be fulfilled at the end of all things?

7. On the basis of these fifteen Bible studies, draw up ten propositions you can defend biblically on evangelization, justice and the simple lifestyle.

Notes

Notes

CHAPTER TWO (pages 42-53)

1. "Social responsibility and social structure in early Israel," *The Catholic Biblical Quarterly*, 32, 1970, p.186.
2. R. De Vaux, *Ancient Israel: Its Life and Institutions* 2nd Ed. (London: Darton, Longman and Todd, 1968), p.72f.
3. K. Nurnberger, ed., "The Message of the Old Testament Prophets During the Eighth Century B.C. Concerning Affluence and Poverty," *Affluence, Poverty and the Word of God* (Durban: Lutheran Publishing House, 1978), p.44.
4. A.Alt, cited by Wittenberg in Nurnberger, op. cit., p.144.
5. K. H. Henry, "Land Tenure in the Old Testament," *Palestine Exploration Society Quarterly,* 86, 1954, pp.5-15.
6. Ibid, p.6.
7. Nurnberger, op. cit., p.150.
8. Christopher Wright, *What Does the Lord Require?,* Shaftesbury Project, 1978, p.14.
9. See Francois Houtart, "Palestine in Jesus' Time," *Social Scientist,* Jan. 1976 (Trivandrum, Kerala, India) pp. 16-17.
10 John Howard Yoder, *The Politics of Jesus* (Grand Rapids, MI: Eerdmans Publishing Co., 1972).
   Robert Sloan, *The Favorable Year of the Lord* (Austin, TX: Scholar Press, 1977).

CHAPTER THREE (pages 54-66)

1. Cf. Martin Hengel, *Property and Riches in the Early Church* (London: SCM, 1974), pp.21ff.
2. Ibid., p.26.
3. *Good News to the Poor: The Challenge of the Poor in the History of the Church* (Maryknoll: Orbis Books, 1979).
4. Cf. Martin Hengel, op. cit., p.19.
5. Enrique Dussel, "The Kingdom of God and the Poor," *International Review of Mission* (CWME, 1980), p.124.

6. Robert Sloan, *The Favorable Year of the Lord: A Study of Jubilary Theology in the Gospel of Luke* (Austin, Texas: Scholar Press, 1977).
7. I. Howard Marshall, *The Gospel of Luke* (Exeter: Paternoster Press, 1979), ad. loc.
8. The interpretation of "the least of these my brethren" is basic to the interpretation of the whole passage. That the expression points to Jesus' solidarity with his own disciples is ratified by Matthew 10:40ff. (cf. Mk. 9:41), where the cup of cold water and the reward which are mentioned show also that the passage belongs to the same circle of ideas as Matthew 25:31-46.
9. Martin Hengel, op. cit., pp.32f.
10. Ibid., pp.54ff.
11. Quoted by Hengel, ibid., p.55.

CHAPTER FOUR (pages 67-83)

1. Hodder & Stoughton, p.185.
2. Preface to *The Young Church in Action*.
3. 2 Corinthians 2:17; 4:2; 6:3; 7:2.
4. Acts 20:18; 1 Thessalonians 1:5; 2:9.
5. 1 Corinthians 9:19-23.
6. *Enough is Enough*, SCM, p.62.
7. Dietrich Bonhoeffer, *The Cost of Discipleship*, SCM, pp.154-157.
8. Quoted in *Rich Christians in an Age of Hunger*, Hodder & Stoughton, p.87.
9. Bonhoeffer, op. cit., pp.158-159.
10. John White, *The Golden Cow*, Marshall, Morgan and Scott, p.39.
11. Op. cit., p.41-42.
12. Bonhoeffer, op. cit., pp.186f.
13. *Community of the King*, IVP, p.120.
14. Quoted in *Evangelical Missions Quarterly*, Vol. 15, No. 4, p.216.
15. *Thoughts about the Holy Spirit*, p.11.

CHAPTER FIVE (pages 84-128)

1. D. A. Hay, *A Christian Critique of Capitalism*, (Grove Booklet on Ethics No. 5, Bramcote, Nottingham, 1975).
2. C. J. H. Wright, *What does the Lord Require?* (Shaftesbury Project, 1978).
3. A. Richardson, *The Biblical Doctrine of Work* (SCM, 1963), pp.11-30.
4. J. V. Taylor, *Enough is Enough* (SCM, 1974).
5. But M. Hengel, *Property and Riches in the Early Church* (SCM, 1974) would disagree: see p.29.
6. *World Development Report 1978* (World Bank, OUP, 1978).
7. Quoted in A. I. MacBean, V. N. Balasubramanyam, *Meeting the Third World Challenge* (Macmillan, London and Basingstoke, 2nd edn., 1978), p.31.

8. See, for example, M. Crosswell, *Basic Human Needs,* (AID Discussion Paper 38, October 1978).
9. D. Jones, *Food and Interdependence* (ODI, London, 1976).
10. D. G. Jones "Malnutrition means People", *Interchange No. 20*, (1976) pp.223-234.
11. Op. cit. (6), Table 1.
12. K. Griffin, *International Inequality and National Poverty,* (Macmillan, London and Basingstoke, 1978).
13. Op. cit. (9).
14. Op. cit. (12), Chapter 1.
15. J. Bhagwati, W. Dellafar, *The Brain Drain and Income Taxation* (World Development, 1973), p.98, Table 1.
16. A. K. Sen, "Starvation and exchange entitlements" *Cambridge Journal of Economics* (1977, vol. 1), pp.33-35.
17. Op. cit. (9).
18. B. Balassa, "World Trade and the International Economy", *World Bank Staff Working Paper, 282* (May, 1978).
19. D. B. Keesing, *World Trade and Output of Manufactures* (World Bank paper, February 1978).
20. J. M. Finger "Effects of the Kennedy Road Tariff Concessions on the Exports of Developing Countries", *Economic Journal* (1976, vol. 86, pp.87-95).
21. See, for example, G. K. Helleiner, "Industry Characteristics and the Competitions of Manufactures from LDCs", *Weltwirtschaftliches Archiv,* (1976, Band 112, pp.507-524); F. Wolter, "Factor Properties, Technology and West Germany's International Trade Patterns", *Weltwirtshaftliches Archiv.* (1977, Band 113, pp.250-267).
22. Z. Iqbal, *The GSP and the Comparative Advantage of LDCs in Manufactures* (IMF Memorandum, 74/41, Washington DC, April 1974) p.18
23. I. Wolter, J. W. Chung, "The Pattern of Non-Tariff Obstacles to International Market Access", *Weltwirtschaftliches Archiv* (1972, Band 108, pp.122-136: Quotation on p.125).
24. *World Development Report 1978,* op. cit. (6), pp.14-16.
25. D. Jones, op. cit. (9).
26. I benefited much from unpublished work by J. P. Martin, *Measuring the Employment Effects of Changes in Trade Flows: A Survey of Recent Research* (OECD, Paris, February 1979), M. Wolf, *Adjustment Problems and Policies in Developed Countries* (World Bank and Nuffield College, Oxford, February 1979), A. O. Krueger, *Impact of LDC Exports on Employment in US Industry* (Trade Policy Research Centre, London, September 1978).
    See also, for UK only, Foreign and Commonweath Office, *The Newly Industrializing Countries and the Adjustment Problem,* (Government Economic Service Working Paper 18, 1979).
    For the US, C. R. Frank, *Foreign Trade and Domestic Aid* (Brodings, 1977).
27. H. F. Lydall, *Trade and Employment* (ILO, Geneva, 1975).
28. J. H. Dunning, ed., *The Multinational Enterprise* (Allen and Unwin,

London, 1971). P. J. Buckley, M. Casson, *The Future of the Multi-national Enterprises* (Macmillan, London and Basingstoke, 1976).
T. G. Parry, "The International Firm and National Economic Policy", *Economic Journal*, 1973, pp.1201-1221.

29. There is a stream of popular books on multinationals, e.g. R. J. Barnet and R. E. Muller, *Global Reach* (Jonathan Cape, London, 1975) and S. George, *How the Other Half Dies* (Penguin, Harmondsworth, UK, 1976). These contain a number of very striking examples of the harmful effects of the operations of MNCs. Suggestive though examples are, they cannot *establish* a case against MNCs in general, any more than a number of examples of corruption in a police force can be taken to demonstrate that the police are in general corrupt.

30. P. Streeten, S. Lall, *Foreign Investment, Transnationals and Developing Countries* (Macmillan, London, 1977).

31. R. Vernon, *Storm over the Multinationals: The Real Issues* (Macmillan, London, 1977).

32. M. D. Steuer et. al, *The Impact of Foreign Direct Investment in the UK* (Department of Trade and Industry, London, 1973).

33. Commonwealth Secretariat, *Towards a New International Economic Order* (London, 1975).

34. MacBean et al, op. cit. (7), pp.168-170.
K. Laursen, "The Integrated Programme for Commodities", *World Development* (Vol. 6, 1978), pp.423-435.

35. *World Development Report*, op. cit. (6), p. 20, Table 18.

36. Laursen, op. cit. (34), and references cited there.

37. J. Bhagwati, "Market Disruption, Export Market Disruption and GATT Reform" in Bhagwati ed., *The New International Economic Order: the North South Debate* (MII Press, Cambridge, Mass., 1977).

38. D. Jones, op. cit. (9).

39. K. Griffin, op. cit. (12), Chapter 3, MacBean et al, op. cit. (7), Chapter 8.

40. P. B. Kenen, *Debt Relief as Development Assistance* in Bhagwati ed., op. cit. (37).

41. J. Williamson, *The Link* in Bhagwati ed., op. cit. (37).

42. O. O'Donovan, *In Pursuit of a Christian View of War* (Grove Booklets on Ethics, No. 15, 1977).

43. MacBean et al, op. cit. (7).

44. MacBean et al, op. cit. (7), p.5.

CHAPTER SEVEN (pages 138-163)

1. J. Huizinga, *The Waning of the Middle Ages* (Anchor Books, Garden City, 1954), p.20.

2. A. Harnack, *The Mission and Expansion of Christianity in the First Three Centuries* (New York, 1962), Book 2, Chapter 2, esp. p.147.

3. M. Green, *Evangelism in the Early Church* (Grand Rapids, 1977), p.47.

4. Harnack, op. cit., Book 2, Chapter 3; E. Troeltsch, *The Social Teaching of the Christian Churches* (Harper Torchbook, New York, 1960), Vol 1, p.100f; Green, op. cit., pp.44ff.

5. A well-known theme of A. D. Nock, *Conversion* (London, 1933). Cf. Green, ibid., pp.144-165.
6. Troeltsch, op. cit., pp.39f, 61, 82-7; Green, ibid., p.148.
7. Harnack, op. cit., pp.149; Troeltsch, ibid., pp.62, 82; K. S. Latourette, *The First Five Centuries: (A History of the Expansion of Christianity*, vol. 1; Grand Rapids, 1970), pp.268-291.
8. Troeltsch, ibid., pp.116f, 133-8; Harnack, ibid., pp.149-198; Latourette, ibid., p.265f.
9. Latourette, ibid., p.116; cf. Green, op. cit. pp.173f, 203.
10. Troeltsch, op. cit., p.44.
11. Cf. Harnack, op. cit., p.154; Latourette, op. cit., p.120.
12. H. Lietzmann, *A History of the Early Church*, vol. 2: *The Founding of the Church Universal* (Meridian Books, 1961), p.148.
13. Cf. Green, op. cit., pp.248-255.
14. Nock, op. cit., p.250f; Troeltsch, op. cit., pp.113-5; Green, ibid., pp.246f, 271-5
15. Troeltsch, ibid., p.92.
16. Ibid., pp.113-8; Latourette, op. cit., pp.265, 291.
17. Both quotations are from H. Waddell's introduction to *The Desert Fathers* (London & Glasgow, 1962), p.33f.
18. Cf. Latourette, op. cit., pp.171-238, esp. p.237.
19. Troeltsch, op. cit., pp.138-142.
20. Ibid., p.136f; Latourette, op. cit., p.266f.
21. Cited in R. W. Southern, *The Making of the Middle Ages* (New Haven & London, 1967), p.110.
22. R. H. Bainton, *The Medieval Church* (An Anvil Original, Princeton, 1962), pp.15ff.
23. S. Neill, *A History of Christian Missions* (Pelican Book, Harmondsworth, 1964), p.62.
24. R. W. Southern, *Western Society and The Church in the Middle Ages* (Grand Rapids, 1970), pp.28, 33.
25. Troeltsch, op. cit., p.220.
26. Ibid., p.225f.
27. Ibid., pp.237-9.
28. Southern, *The Making of the Middle Ages*, p.161.
29. Ibid., p.158.
30. Cf. Latourette, *The Thousand Years of Uncertainty; 500 A.D. to 1500 A.D. (A History of the Expansion of Christianity*, vol. 2, Grand Rapids, 1970), pp.362-6.
31. Troeltsch, op. cit., p.253.
32. Huizinga, op. cit., pp.21f, 31f.
33. Troeltsch, op. cit., pp.331-349, the quotation is found in p.332.
34. J. Stacey, *John Wycliff and Reform* (Philadelphia, 1964), p.29f.
35. Cited in M. Spinka, *John Hus' Concept of the Church* (Princeton, 1966), p.384.
36. Troeltsch, op. cit., pp.337, 342.
37. *On the Pastoral Office* 1, 2 (*Advocates of Reform)* ed. by M. Spinka, LCC vol. 14; (Philadelphia, 1953), p.33).

38. Troeltsch, op. cit., p.365f.
39. Ibid., vol. 2, pp.477, 494ff, 511f.
40. *Selected Writings of Martin Luther* (Philadelphia, 1967), vol. 2, p.281f.
41. Ibid., pp.20, 32, 41.
42. Ibid., pp.23, 31.
43. *Table Talk,* 31:43 cited in P. S. Watson, *Let God be God* (Philadelphia, 1947), p.4.
44. *Augsburg Confession* art. vii (*The Book of Concord,* Philadelphia, 1959, p.32).
45. *Small Catechism* iii, 14 (*The Book of Concord)* p.347.
46. E.g. Troeltsch, op. cit., pp.518-520, 543.
47. *Selected Writings . . . ,* vol 3, p.329.
48. H. Bornkamm, *Luther's World of Thought* (St. Louis, 1958), pp.87, 266.
49. M. Walzer, *The Revolution of the Saints: A Study in the Origin of Radical Politics* (Cambridge, Mass., 1965), pp.3f, 11.
50. J. M. Tonkin, *The Church and the Secular Order in Reformation* (New York-London,1971), Chap. 3.
51. B. C. Milner, *Calvin's Doctrine of the Church* (Leiden, 1970), pp.46ff.
52. A Biéler, *La pensèe économique et sociale de Calvin* (Geneva, 1961), pp.295-301.
53. *Calvin's New Testament Commentaries: Romans* (Edinburgh, 1960), p.282.
54. R. H. Bainton, "The Left Wing of the Reformation," *Journal of Religion,* 21 (1941), pp.124-134; G. H. Williams, *The Radical Reformation* (Philadelphia, 1962).
55. F. H. Littell, *The Anabaptist View of the Church* (Boston, 1958), Chap. 2.
56. Ibid., chap. 3.
57. *Spiritual and Anabaptist Writers* (LCC vol. 25, Philadelphia, 1957), p.80, cf. R. Friedmann, *The Theology of Anabaptism* (Scottdale, 1973), pp.130ff.
58. E. Stauffer, "The Anabaptist Theology of Martyrdom," *MQR* 19 (1945), pp.179-214; H. S. Bender, "The Anabaptist Vision," *The Recovery of the Anabaptist Vision* (Scottdale, 1957), pp.29-54.
59. Williams, op. cit., p.859f.
60. J. D. Graber, "Anabaptism Expressed in Missions and Social Service," *The Recovery of the Anabaptist Vision,* p.152.
61. A. G. Gish, *The New Left and Christian Radicalism* (Grand Rapids, 1970), p.56f.
62. Cited in Bender, op. cit., p.45.
63. For example, D. W. Brown, *The Christian Revolutionary* (Grand Rapids, 1971); A. G. Gish, op. cit.
64. J. H. Nichols, *History of Christianity: 1650-1950* (New York, 1956), p.460.
65. D. W. Brown, *Understanding Pietism* (Grand Rapids, 1978), p.27.
66. S. E. Ahlstrom, *A Religious History of the American People* (New Haven & London, 1972), pp.230, 294, 314-329.
67. P. J. Spener, *Pia desideria* (Philadelphia, 1964), p.95.

68. A. C. McGiffert, *Protestant Thought before Kant* (New York, 1962), p.163; Ahlstrom, op. cit., p.301ff.
69. Neill, op. cit., p.227.
70. Ibid., p.239.
71. C. L. Becker, *The Heavenly City of the Eighteenth-Century Philosophers* (New Haven & London, 1959), pp.49, 129.
72. McGiffert, op. cit., pp.164, 169.
73. Brown, op. cit., p.28; Nichols, op. cit., p.87; Ahlstrom, op. cit., p.294.
74. Cited in Brown, ibid., p.134.
75. Nichols, op. cit., pp.135-150, 151-162; Neill, op. cit., p.251f; A. P. Johnston, *World Evangelism and the Word of God* (Minneapolis, 1974), pp.37-46.
76. Latourette, *The Great Century: Europe and the United States (A History of the Expansion of Christianity,* vol. 4, Grand Rapids, 1970), pp.1, 4.
77. Nichols, op. cit., p.320.
78. W. Rauschenbusch, *A Theology for the Social Gospel* (New York, 1917), p.167.
79. Neill, op. cit., p.452.
80. Nichols, op. cit., p.378.
81. J. W. Montgomery, *Ecumenicity, Evangelicals and Rome* (Grand Rapids, 1969), p.39f.
82. Latourette, *Advance through Storm (A History of the Expansion of Christianity,* vol. 7, Grand Rapids, 1970), p.3.
83. C. W. Williams, *The Church (The New Direction in Theology Today,* vol. 4, Philadelphia, 1968).
84. R. J. Sider, *Rich Christians in an Age of Hunger* (Grand Rapids, 1977), p.225. C.f. V. Eller, *The Simple Life: the Christian Stance toward Possessions* (Grand Rapids, 1973); J. V. Taylor, *Enough is Enough* (London, 1975).

Index